Perspectives from Social Economics

Series Editor
Mark D. White
City University of New York
College of Staten Island
Staten Island, USA

The Perspectives from Social Economics series incorporates an explicit ethical component into contemporary economic discussion of important policy and social issues, drawing on the approaches used by social economists around the world. It also allows social economists to develop their own frameworks and paradigms by exploring the philosophy and methodology of social economics in relation to orthodox and other heterodox approaches to economics. By furthering these goals, this series will expose a wider readership to the scholarship produced by social economists, and thereby promote the more inclusive viewpoints, especially as they concern ethical analyses of economic issues and methods.

More information about this series at
http://www.springer.com/series/14556

Ivan Boldyrev • Ekaterina Svetlova
Editors

Enacting Dismal Science

New Perspectives on the Performativity of Economics

Editors
Ivan Boldyrev　　　　　　　　　　Ekaterina Svetlova
Berlin, Germany　　　　　　　　　Leicester, UK

Perspectives from Social Economics
ISBN 978-1-137-49210-4 (hardcover)　　ISBN 978-1-137-48876-3　(eBook)
ISBN 978-1-349-95842-9 (softcover)
DOI 10.1057/978-1-137-48876-3

Library of Congress Control Number: 2016943198

© The Editor(s) (if applicable) and The Author(s) 2016, First softcover printing 2018
This work is subject to copyright. All rights are solely and exclusively licensed by the Publisher, whether the whole or part of the material is concerned, specifically the rights of translation, reprinting, reuse of illustrations, recitation, broadcasting, reproduction on microfilms or in any other physical way, and transmission or information storage and retrieval, electronic adaptation, computer software, or by similar or dissimilar methodology now known or hereafter developed.
The use of general descriptive names, registered names, trademarks, service marks, etc. in this publication does not imply, even in the absence of a specific statement, that such names are exempt from the relevant protective laws and regulations and therefore free for general use.
The publisher, the authors and the editors are safe to assume that the advice and information in this book are believed to be true and accurate at the date of publication. Neither the publisher nor the authors or the editors give a warranty, express or implied, with respect to the material contained herein or for any errors or omissions that may have been made.

Cover illustration: © INTERFOTO / Alamy Stock Photo

Printed on acid-free paper

This Palgrave Macmillan imprint is published by Springer Nature
The registered company is Nature America Inc. New York

Contents

1 After the Turn: How the Performativity of Economics Matters 1
Ivan Boldyrev and Ekaterina Svetlova

2 Performativity Rationalized 29
Francesco Guala

3 Performative Mechanisms 53
Carsten Herrmann-Pillath

4 'Doing' Laboratory Experiments: An Ethnomethodological Study of the Performative Practice in Behavioral Economic Research 87
Juliane Böhme

5 The Problem with Economics: Naturalism, Critique and Performativity 109
Fabian Muniesa

6 Performativity Matters: Economic Description as a Moral Problem 131
Philip Roscoe

7 The IS–LMization of the General Theory and the
  Construction of Hydraulic Governability in Postwar
  Keynesian Macroeconomics   151
  Hanno Pahl and Jan Sparsam

8 Performativity and Emergence of Institutions   183
  Ekaterina Svetlova

Index   201

List of Figures

Fig 2.1	The grazing game ('hawk-dove').	34
Fig 3.1	Triadic causation in semiosis	59
Fig 3.2	Incentives and social preferences (following Bowles and Polanía-Reyes 2012)	65
Fig 3.3	Bimodal causation in incentive systems	67
Fig 7.1	The IS-LM Model	159

CHAPTER 1

After the Turn: How the Performativity of Economics Matters

Ivan Boldyrev and Ekaterina Svetlova

1.1 EXPLAINING THE TURN

We bet notable macroeconomists, Alan Blinder and Charles Wyplosz, never heard of the 'performativity of economics' when they stated that 'the main purpose of central bank talk is to help markets "think like the central bank"' (2004, 7). It is, however, striking, that so many different aspects of what is commonly called 'performativity' are entangled in discussing central bank communication—a theme which is currently at the heart of macroeconomic debates. All our intuitive notions—to be explained below—are here: the context of economic governance, the inherent sociality of language, the role of explicitness, the importance of signification, and the enactment of ideas and theories. For successful performance of a central bank, successful communication is crucial. To govern, one has to use the resources of language, to create a community

---

I. Boldyrev (✉)
Higher School of Economics, Moscow, Russia

Witten Institute for Institutional Change, University of Witten/Herdecke, Witten, Germany

E. Svetlova
School of Management, University of Leicester, Leicester, UK

of those who comprehend one's message, to make explicit one's commitments, and, finally, in and through communication, to enact *the very economic theory* stating that central bank communication is essential for channeling economic agents' expectations and eventually for the proper functioning of this institution.

This is of course only one example of economics *not merely describing or explaining, but also actively shaping the economies*—this is how *performativity* is most commonly understood. The recent emphasis on *economics* in the performativity debate is not surprising: many studies document how a very—perhaps, the most—influential social science participates in building up social reality. The performative move thus refers to the venerable epistemological question of the *relation between 'reality' and 'theory,'* but goes beyond the traditional idea of economics describing more or less adequately some supposedly 'real' processes.

This performative turn took place at the beginning of the new millennium and culminated in books such as *An Engine, Not a Camera* (MacKenzie 2006) and *Do Economists Make Markets?* (MacKenzie et al. 2007). Afterwards, the performativity research proliferated. However, these new studies were not a replication of the essential work on performativity: We could clearly observe the drift toward a new understanding of the concept. In this new—'after-the-turn'—research, the focus has been shifted from the investigation of the one-way link 'theory→reality.' The search for a general proof that this link exists—in more or less strong form—was recognized by many as futile. Today, the performativity concept moved from the theoretical debate about the link between abstract theories and economic reality toward empirical studies of how this link works in various applied fields. There was a drift toward investigations of *performative practices.*

This shift had consequences. On the one hand, the proliferation of empirical studies diluted the term 'performativity' often reducing it just to a ubiquitous catch-all concept. One might deplore the limited theoretical advancement in the field. On the other hand, what we can state with certainty is that, in the last years, performativity became a part of the DNA in the social studies of economic phenomena. The performativity program delivered a framework for the discussion of what economic professionals do and, more generally, of what happens in economics.

In fact, it is now well established that economic theories of various kinds define standards of rationality and categories of risk, determine the rules undergirding investment decisions, influence macroeconomic expectations, and formulate microeconomic incentives. The performativity perspective also pertains to the phenomena of marketization, indoctrination, diffusion of theoretical knowledge via expertise, creation of new languages and ideologies. Economists formulate the norms for reconfiguring markets (Garcia-Parpet 2007; Holm and Nielsen 2007) and set criteria of efficiency (Breslau 2011, 2013); manage identities and produce subjectivities—be it through business education (Ghoshal and Moran 1996; Ghoshal 2005) or consumer testing (Muniesa 2014); they also specify policy agendas and generally play a crucial role in institutional design both by directly intervening and by providing a relevant 'cognitive infrastructure' (Ferraro et al. 2005; Friedman 2010; Hirschman and Popp Berman 2014). Choosing a pension plan in the US pension system with the mechanism of choice devised by experimental economists (Thaler and Sunstein 2008); taking part in the auctions following the rules formulated by the teams of game theorists and economic experimentalists (Guala 2001; Nik-Khah 2008; Boldyrev 2012, 2013); investing in index funds as embodiments of efficient market hypothesis in financial economics (MacKenzie 2006); establishing incentive systems inspired by microeconomic theory (Dix 2014; Herrmann-Pillath, this volume); confronting people with questions they never thought of before and thus constructing their preferences (Kahneman and Tversky 2000; Muniesa 2014); using a micro-credit scheme in Bangladesh or India on the terms proposed by experimental development economists (Banerjee and Duflo 2011; Favereau and Brisset 2013; Davis 2013)—all these actions suggest the ways economics helps in creating its own realities and attempts to make the agents, material infrastructures, and knowledge converge and mutually stabilize each other. Small wonder that in the postcrisis neoliberal era, the role of economists in facilitating (or neglecting) major economic instabilities sparks controversies (Krugman 2009; Hodgson 2009; Caballero 2010; Mirowski and Nik-Khah 2013).

The interest of performativity lies precisely in its radical stance: in blurring or at least questioning the boundaries between research and its object, in focusing on knowledge and its pragmatic realizations, we both challenge traditional epistemology and address the very texture of social life. That is why clarifying the meaning of performativity eventually matters for *understanding the social*. The studies on various 'performative practices' imply that the link between 'theories' and 'economic reality' cannot be understood in terms of a mechanical, one-way influence. It could be empirically demonstrated that clear distinction of this kind is often not possible. 'Realities,' while being theoretically assembled, also shape theories (via statistical data or observations).

This volume brings together sociologists, philosophers, and economists to investigate these recent developments in the performativity program. On the one hand, the volume's contributions continue theoretical work and discuss conceptual issues underlying the performativity of economics. On the other hand, some chapters follow more closely the empirical development in performativity studies. Overall, the texts scrutinize the concept's potential within the range of various disciplinary and empirical contexts. We hope that contributions in this book give an idea about what has happened in the performativity research in the last years.

Our task here is to introduce these contributions by providing some more context for them. In our overview (which remains necessarily selective!), we will name more explicitly the novelties recently brought about by the performativity program, the main critical arguments against performativity, and the perspectives opening up in this volume and beyond. Given the importance of the topic and the insightful debates over performativity so far, it is now high time to take stock.

1.2 Some Prehistory and Basic Ideas

There is no such thing as *the* performativity, for the idea of performativity travelled across various disciplines and theoretical discourses. While travelling, the concept changed its meaning. Performativity originated in the linguistic philosophy of John Austin (1962) who suggested a pragmatist account of language as something going beyond the mere description of the world 'out there' and, in fact, discovered the whole region of performative linguistic practices.[1] Subsequently, the idea of performativity was debated within the philosophy of language (Searle 1969; Derrida 1988) and was reappropriated in the political philosophy of gender (Butler 1990, 1997). Importantly, the discussion transcended the domain of linguistics, and the concept of performativity migrated into the sociology of scientific knowledge.

Many different lines of thought came together in this new movement. We can trace its inspiration back to Karl Marx (and, more recently, perhaps,

Pierre Bourdieu), claiming that social knowledge is historically situated and always already a weapon in social conflicts; we can think of Max Weber's and Karl Polanyi's theories of rationalization prefiguring modern ideas of economization, with the economic as both a social force and an epistemological resource in the overarching historical process of modernity; we might refer to pragmatist ideas of reality/action happening and being justified only in its practical consequences and not in its factors that precede actualization, the 'role' being real only in its performance, with no backstage behind, as Judith Butler would claim; we can recall the work of Michel Foucault who, in his studies of neoliberalism, reconstructed the idea of *governmentality* and demonstrated the decisive role played by economic knowledge in making society and subjectivity amenable to the rule of economic calculation and governance; and we should not forget many important constructivist accounts in the sociology of knowledge and science studies (Knorr-Cetina 1981; Barnes 1983; Pickering 1995; Bloor 1997) as an immediate precursor.

In fact, science and technology studies (STS), particularly in its specific tradition of the actor-network theory (ANT) (Latour 2005; Licoppe 2010 for an overview), formed the context for the major statements of performativity (Callon 1998a, 2007b; MacKenzie and Millo 2003; MacKenzie 2006). With its ideas of sociotechnical *agencements*—that is, arrangements endowed with agency—and *performation* (Callon 2007b), ANT reconfigured debates around the performativity of economics. For ANT scholars, economic knowledge does not merely 'construct' its own reality; it is not simply the production of the mind existing prior to its sociotechnical embodiment. Rather, many intermediaries and hybrids are at work in the process and the struggles of performation; it is a complex interaction of human and non-human technical entities that makes it possible for economists to act as social engineers and for economics to perform itself. Distinctive of this approach is thus its emphasis on material technologies—primarily in finance.

The turn to performativity involved some broader intellectual and institutional shifts. First of all, ANT scholars who had previously dealt primarily with (techno)science, focused on economics and finance as specific knowledge regimes and on the technologies created and sustained with the participation of economists and finance scholars (MacKenzie 2006). On the other hand, the performative program clearly set the agenda—at least in part—for the new economic sociology of markets (Pinch and Swedberg 2008; McFall and Ossandón 2014; Sparsam 2015).

The markets themselves were reconceptualized as 'calculative collective devices' (Callon and Muniesa 2005) and it was suggested that economic sociology refuse to treat economics as something utterly abstract. As Preda (2009, 119) formulates, 'the tables has been turned, in the sense that from being unrealistic, [economic] theoretical models have been characterized as being too realistic—not in the sense of an accurate representation, but in the sense of generating the phenomena they describe.' This also involved a shift from economic sociology to the sociology of economics (Fourcade 2006, 2009)—without, however, abandoning the sociological study of markets, but rather discovering its new, 'performative' dimension. A cross-fertilization of fields is clearly discernible here. Economic sociologists working on the construction of markets and ANT scholars discovered each other, the authors writing on economic matters learned more about STS and post-structuralist philosophy, while science studies authors saw how economics—and also marketing or accounting (see e.g., an overview in Vosselman 2014)—could provide fascinating material for them.[2]

As a consequence of this long transformative history of the performativity concept, researchers of various disciplinary lineages use or criticize the notion of performativity while picking out of the menu 'from Austin to MacKenzie.' This menu was recently 'fanned out' by Gond et al. (2015) who identified five central blocks of performativity studies: *doing things with words* (Austin); *searching for efficiency* (Lyotard); *constituting the self through citation* (Derrida, Butler); *bringing theory into being* (Callon, Latour, MacKenzie); and finally, *sociomateriality mattering* (Barad). Performativity concepts of various kinds were applied in organization and management studies to develop, for example, storytelling and critical discourse analysis in Austinian mode or to perform gender and identity analysis relying on Butler. These attempts, scattered and not always compatible with each other, suggest that there is hardly anything like a 'theory' of performativity—rather, this is a set of more or less shared intuitions and concerns.

However, from being a buzzword, performativity has become a guiding concept for the wealth of empirical work in the fields ranging from social studies of finance (MacKenzie and Millo 2003; De Goede 2005; Vollmer et al. 2009; Carruthers and Kim 2011; Zuckerman 2012; La Berge 2016) to statistics (McFall 2011; Sætnan et al. 2010) and from management and organization studies (D'Adderio and Pollock 2014; Gond et al. 2015) to social network analysis (Healy 2015). When it comes to the concrete applications, scholars use the notion of performativity that suits them more.

This inevitably leads to controversies and misunderstandings. Researchers often talk past one another enhancing the confusion.[3] By further engaging with performativity in this book, we demonstrate how this concept *works*—which, in a pragmatist mode, would contribute to understanding it.

It is not always helpful to strictly distinguish performativity 'as such' and performativity of economics, for many scholars regard them as synonymous, or at least make recourse to the heuristics behind various meanings of performativity. What we increasingly observe in the performativity debate is the effort to integrate the existing performativity concepts into one. This happens also in the debates on the performativity of economics. There is a generally shared understanding that economic ideas and models change, shape, and construct economic reality; they are both governing the behaviors of agents, and in many ways, conditioning the very existence of those behaviors, thus (co)constructing—or 'provoking' (Muniesa 2014) the 'agents,' phenomena, and institutions they deal with. In short, performativity always concerns *entanglement of knowledge, institutions, and practices*.

This generalized perspective on performativity might help avoid many dead ends and bitter unresolved disputes.[4] The understanding of performativity as *performative practice* (e.g., Cabantous and Gond 2011; Mason et al. 2015) and not merely as a theoretical construction of reality is one such way to reconcile positions. According to this understanding, theories are always a part of their application, while the business of applying them is in multiple ways embedded into theoretical work; moreover, important theoretical work is in part directly conducted by practitioners. Some recent examples will help illustrate this.

Performative practices figure prominently in the discussions of applied economic disciplines. Thus, Mason et al. (2015, 10) claim that the mobilization of performativity concept in marketing and market studies helps 'to unearth how marketing theories are shaped by market actors (academics and practitioners alike) who pick up theoretical tools and put them to work, and how such theories may come to influence market and marketing processes.' The performative analysis in marketing clearly questions the theory–practice dichotomy and invites us 'to treat the link between theory and practice as a practical, empirical matter, rather than a topic for discussions in principle' (Mason et al. 2015, 8; see also Jacobi et al. 2015).

Similar tendencies can be observed in the performativity studies of finance. Thus, Esposito (2013, 102) suggests extending this notion to the entire economy. Performativity, she argues, should be 'understood as the involvement of the observer in the objects and projects he/she describes.' Svetlova (2014) demonstrates, using examples of development and dissemination of various financial models, that theoretical knowledge in finance becomes a part of *hybrid contexts* in which science is entwined with policy, business, and other realms of society, while the boundaries between financial knowledge and its objects are being eroded. Financial models are created by academics and by practitioners (e.g., the so-called 'quants'); they travel from one modeling practice to the other and undergo substantial changes in their structures and functions. Particularly, the recent work by MacKenzie and Spears (2014a, b) on modeling in various 'epistemic communities' and 'evaluation cultures' of markets clearly develops Callon's (2007b) understanding of performativity 'as a "long sequence of trial and error, reconfigurations and reformulations" between a model or theory and the social context in which it is applied' (Spears 2014, 30).

The concept of performative practice was put forward by Cabantous and Gond (2011) in the analysis of rational decision-making. Their integrative concept of performativity reveals 'that what enables actors to express a theory in their routines, discourses, and behaviors [...] is the embeddedness of this theory's assumptions into procedures, devices and actors' beliefs' (578). They also unpack the interrelated mechanisms behind those sets of activities that allow to explain the persistence of rational decision-making in organizations classifying them as different rationalities—*conventionalizing* rationality (a concept should become a part of beliefs); *engineering* rationality (a concept should be embedded in tools); and *commodifying* rationality (increase of practitioner's influence on organizational decision-making, e.g., the increased importance of management consultants).

All those and many other developments have far-reaching consequences for the performativity debate 'at large.' At the risk of simplifying matters, we would still formulate some more general aspects of performativity that, explicitly or implicitly, frame any further discussions.

To begin with, the performativity perspective entails a new *ontology*—or at least leads us to rethink our ontological commitments. Revision of ontology takes a form of *epistemological scandal*, for many generations of scholars were and still are socialized with the idea of emancipated science for which a reference to an independent 'reality' at least does not complicate further inquiry and most often is not very problematic at all. The performativity perspective challenges these views and opens up the whole new ontological domain of 'economic things'[5]—the diversity of financial products as both descriptions and their references (Muniesa 2014); theoretical claims embodied in a rule or in a 'market device' (Callon 2007a, b); the staging of consumer qualities provoked by the marketing mechanisms (Araujo et al. 2010); and so on. This 'reality' populated by human and non-human 'actants' is complex, plural, malleable, and contingent; to explore it, non-conventional ways are needed—prompted, again, by these very ontological innovations.[6]

It would be wrong to assert that a unified ontology is being formulated. Rather, many different ideas are currently tried out, but all of them somehow inspire new general interpretations of what the (social) world is and how it works. In particular, the performativity perspective leads us to focus on agency distributed among 'individuals,' ideas, devices, and material practices—reinforced by many contemporary accounts of situated and distributed cognition (Hutchins 1995; Clark 2011; Herrmann-Pillath 2010, 2013).[7] This implies rethinking the way institutional reality is organized, and reconceptualizing the opposition between the natural and the artificial—for the reality we live in is always already an institutional one. Although one still could focus on rules and conventions as stuff of the everyday life (Searle 2005; Herrmann-Pillath 2012; Guala, this volume), performativity studies suggest abandoning or radically revising individualistic accounts of agency. For them, a convention is always already embodied in the world, and it is this unstable, heterogeneous, and contingent reality that lets individual agency or self-consciousness emerge. Institutional reality is not just 'socially constructed' or provoked from the outside—it is also self-provoking. The neorealist turn in philosophy (e.g., in Bryant et al. 2011), although not reducible to or fully reconcilable with the STS perspectives, is just another version of this general change of ontological sensitivity (Barad 2003; Law 2008).

Another overarching tendency consists in rethinking the place of *language* in social life. This is a huge theme in itself, but performativity perspective is quite naturally led in this direction due to the work of its progenitors, notably Wittgenstein and Austin. As this volume testifies, language reality remains an inherent part of the performativity accounts. How can our language—and, by analogy, our theories, our reflexive attempts—be intertwined with the sociality of our existence? In a narrower sense, new words, new terms and concepts, once introduced, may define their own realities (Ferraro et al. 2005). But all other kinds of mediatory phenomena, or 'mediating instruments' (Miller and O'Leary 2007)—rules, technologies, incentives—can be rephrased as signs and/or speech acts.[8] Economic things often come about after being written, as in the case of accounting (Vosselman 2014). Moreover, many economic entities, such as prices or organizations, can also be subject to this linguistic reinterpretation. The new understanding of 'reality' involves grasping it as a language phenomenon—without, however, indefinitely expanding the boundaries of language. The challenge is to properly invest our linguistic intuitions into broader frameworks.

Finally, there is a distinct *politics of performativity*. At their inception, performativity studies were concerned with the tendencies of economization, with economic theories imposing themselves onto the non-economic realms. At stake here are mutual autonomy, recognition, and tensions between the economic and the non-economic (or 'the social'). Now, a critical task is to reveal the genealogy of economization, to stop treating particular social structures as pre-given, to see them being constantly produced and reproduced, and sometimes to reveal a hypocrisy of certain practices—claiming to involve naturalistic or laissez-faire attitudes but actually doing otherwise (see also Muniesa, this volume). The concern is, of course, with the growing standardization and homogenization of the social, with *homo oeconomicus* and economic regimes asserting themselves, as it were; with quantification (Porter 1995, 2008), 'framing,' and 'disentanglement' penetrating into deeper structures of our communities (for critiques of this kind, see Marglin 2008). All kinds of more recent debates around 'libertarian paternalism' are also important for the political aspect of performativity (see e.g., White 2013).

Is performativity dangerous? Should we share concerns of the type expressed by Polanyi with his notion of a dis-embedded economy? Of course, but it is worth keeping in mind that these concerns are not only implicated by the critical attitudes of contemporary thought but also built in the picture of the social that the partisans of performativity (following similar ideas found in Polanyi as well) are trying to draw. A disentanglement is necessarily followed by a re-entanglement, a framing is not comprehensible without an 'overflow' disturbing it (Callon 1998a, b), this *dialectics* is at the heart of performativity approach. Economics can be different, and the worldviews it conveys can urge us, for example, to make money disregarding charity considerations—as famously stated by Milton Friedman (1970)—or develop serious concerns for inequality (Piketty 2014).[9] Both movements are compatible within the complex and contradictory reality we are trying to (speculatively) grasp. Both involve 'the struggles of performation,' a series of collective efforts to create and sustain certain realities based on one's vision—and often becoming struggles for devices, as demonstrated by Pahl and Sparsam in their chapter. If we do follow performativity theorists in their vigorous defense of *reality in the making*, we have to admit that no reflective theoretical undertaking, including their own, can remain without political consequences.

1.3 WHAT DOES THIS VOLUME DO: AN OVERVIEW OF INDIVIDUAL CONTRIBUTIONS

As briefly indicated above, this volume elaborates on the logic of performativity and puts it to test by invoking *various disciplinary contexts and concerns*: speech act theory and the theory of conventions (Guala), macroeconomics (Pahl and Sparsam), institutional theory (Svetlova), corporate governance (Herrmann-Pillath), experimental economics and ethnomethodology (Boehme), anthropology (Muniesa), and ethics (Roscoe).

The contributions of Guala, Muniesa, and Roscoe appraise the potential of performativity as it was advanced by Callon and MacKenzie and suggest ways of rethinking the original concepts. Other contributions focus more on specific analyses of economic knowledge, provide case studies that throw light on various forms of interaction between economic theories, ideologies, and social practices and thus enlarge the scope of empirical illustrations that are so vital for the performativity perspective on economics.

Guala deals primarily with the status of the performativity concept in current methodological debates on economics and with a critique of MacKenzie and Callon that has emerged from the philosophy of economics (Mäki 2013). Taking Austin's ideas as a point of departure, he seeks to expand the performative speech act theory by considering speech acts as coordinating devices (analogous to MacKenzie's analyses of financial models, see Millo and MacKenzie 2009; MacKenzie 2010). Drawing on game-theoretic accounts of institutions, Guala explores the rhetorical aspect of language (perlocution) in order to address the creation and formation of agents' beliefs as *conventions*.

Carsten Hermann-Pillath ponders the issue of how performativity works. He suggests an account of *performative mechanism* that explains the functioning of managerial incentive schemes—as the sites of entanglement of theoretical knowledge and practice. His contribution thus provides both a more general framework for performativity studies and an important empirical case—showing what ideas stood behind introducing those schemes and how they could subsequently form and transform the preferences of economic agents involved. But he demonstrates that it is precisely the performativity of incentive structures that does not allow us to formulate general rules and causal mechanisms for them. If economics participates in shaping its reality, it becomes, again, a historically situated epistemic enterprise, with no claims to universality, for there is no stable object ('reality') out there to which one has to adapt in a predictable way. Importantly, Herrmann-Pillath considers performative mechanisms to be a subset of general causal mechanisms that can help explain the emergence of novelty. He particularly emphasizes semiotic causation (treating incentives as signs) and observer-dependent interpretation (once introduced, the incentives transform the ways they are perceived) that enable the performativity of social mechanisms.

The chapter by Juliane Böhme discusses performativity from the ethnomethodological perspective. She shows in rich empirical detail how experimental economists and the participants of experiments challenge, test, and coproduce reality while *performing economic actors*. Economists make assumptions, define the rules and settings of the experiment, while participants react to those descriptions and sometimes disagree and break with them. Böhme shows how incentives work (or fail) in the experimental settings and how the participants themselves creatively react to the frames suggested by experimentalists *or impose the frames themselves*. This nicely illustrates Callon's dynamics of framings and overflows, while demonstrating the power of ethnomethodology in dealing with (self-)performance in microeconomic contexts.

Fabian Muniesa tests the reaction of various scholarly communities on performativity studies from the anthropological and even ethnographic point of view inspired by the work of Philippe Descola (2013). This engagement with anthropology leads us to rethink once more our ontological presuppositions. The focus of Muniesa's paper is to consider how far what he calls '*economic reason*' may be regarded as naturalistic— that is, roughly, non-constructivist—and what the challenge posed by the staunchly pragmatist orientation of performativity theory reveals about the possible coexistence of naturalistic rhetoric and the performative practice of economists.

Calling for the performativity concept that goes beyond the idea that economists (just) design markets, Philip Roscoe considers economic *description* as the primary task of economic theory and—following Austin, Butler, and Muniesa—suggests that economic descriptions possess a performative force. Thus, he highlights the illocutionary aspects of economic speech acts and shows how economic descriptions—facing the collapse of the fact/value dichotomy—transform social relations in various fields (e.g., online dating and organs donation). By doing so, he unearths the politics of economic descriptions taken as the blueprints for the society to come and the ideals (or real utopias) we would like to see actualized—demonstrating how we inadvertently help enact these visions by using this and not that description (cf. also Law and Urry 2004). Here, the moral dimension of economization comes to the fore.

The contribution of Hanno Pahl and Jan Sparsam focuses on modern *macroeconomics* and shows how new real economic phenomena emerged in parallel to new theoretical concepts (in this case—Keynesianism and its embodiment in the IS-LM model). The paper tries to find out whether in postwar West Germany a transformation of the economy into a manageable system occurred by means of economic theory. Pahl and Sparsam clearly demonstrate why the broader societal context should be taken into consideration while discussing the performativity of economics. Importantly, a part of this context is also the reverse effects of performative constitution, that is, the impact of the economy, society, and culture on economic science. In asking whether macroeconomic governance is possible, Pahl and Sparsam demonstrate that they only can find 'generic' performativity in their empirical case. As for stronger cases of performativity ('effective' or 'Barnesian' performativity as suggested by MacKenzie (2006)), the causation mechanism or model's verisimilitude with reality cannot be identified as so many factors play a role in the field of economic policy-making. This notwithstanding, the paper demonstrates the process of bundling and encapsulating things in a model—which is necessary for the model to operate. It shows how IS-LM became a *policy device* characterized by simplicity and plasticity and how ideas got incorporated into—and changed by—devices, how models could promote and reinforce certain empirical techniques and how the globalization of economic techniques (like national accounting) as a basis of decision-making went hand in hand with the globalization of the economics profession (see also Fourcade 2009).

Finally, the contribution of Ekaterina Svetlova explores some radical consequences of the performativity perspective, those based on perlocution as its important and so far neglected aspect. Svetlova claims that the performativity concept has the potential to address the issue of *novelty* in economics, namely to shed light on *the emergence of institutions*. Here, the perlocutionary aspects of speech acts and the theatrical nature of social interactions are at play. Performativity in this parlance is always about performance (theatricality of language). For Svetlova, at the heart of performativity is not the question of how economists form the economy but how economic phenomena come into being in the processes of joint staging of fictions and *making believe*.

1.4 WHAT NEXT? DEBATING PERFORMATIVITY AND LOOKING AHEAD

The contributions to this volume confirm that the performativity perspective is fiercely debated. Both fascination and aversion are involved, but there are also some essential difficulties. It is hardly possible to provide here the overview of all (or even the majority of) critical responses, rejoinders, and conceptual improvements undertaken by those who participate in these debates. Instead, we will try to single out what we think are the most challenging issues that the advocates of performativity will need to address. This discussion is, in fact, the way to assess the research program both in its current significance and in its future prospects.

First, the issue of *agency* is of interest. Most of the contributors to this book see the challenge in precisely articulating concrete mechanisms and regularities of 'performation.' There are a number of very helpful historical and empirical accounts of performativity—or thick descriptions—which, however, often do not help understand *how performativity works*.

Generally, the problem of agency persists in many discussions of performativity. Who performs what? Does economics perform itself or do economists promote their beliefs? What is at stake in the movement of performation—transformed beliefs ('agency') or artificial frameworks for action ('structure')? Is the social a *context* or a *result*, or both? Individuals, groups, ideas, practices, techniques, and so on can be endowed with agency, and we are clearly moving around the chicken-and-egg dilemma here—sometimes rephrased (as Roscoe does in this volume following Butler) as a hermeneutic problem: economics addresses the world it has already prefigured. Another version of the same claim implies that economics produces or provokes reality, but is also produced by this reality—both before and after performation.

Second, *there is an issue of novelty*. Performativity is about routine *reproduction* of social phenomena and *creation* of new social facts. Often, when performativity is discussed, shaping *and* creating are packed in one sentence. However, it is important to differentiate. The traditional interpretation of Austin suggests that illocutionary (performative) speech acts used in particular institutional settings reproduce the facts of everyday life (e.g., marriages). Derrida and Butler famously argued that this routine can be partly broken in the process of language application: while using utterances in different contexts, we change their meaning; still, they are not talking about radical novelty. Searle also explains the existence of social facts by the routine application of the rule 'X counts as Y in context C.' Here, we deal with interpretation of *performativity as convention*.[10]

However, most performativity scholars expect more from the concept. In this volume, Guala, Roscoe, and Svetlova explore this more radical connotation of performativity and suggest paying attention to perlocution as its most important and so far neglected aspect. The idea of perlocution was revived by Butler (2010) and was debated by the performativity scholars (Brisset 2014; Mason et al. 2015). Perlocution is not about speaking under given, already institutionalized conditions of felicity, but about the creation of those conditions through persuasion and 'making believe.' This renewed interest in perlocution again stresses the recent shift from constructionist to pragmatic understanding of performativity in speaking, interacting, and performing (also in the sense of acting and performance).

The third challenge concerns performativity as *critique*. Is the performativity perspective critical of economics and what kind of critical stance does it promote? Or is it, as some authors claim, excessively conformist to what (mainstream) economists do (Miller 2002; Mirowski and Nik-Khah 2007, 2008)?[11]

Indeed, there is an *overemphasis on knowledge* in performativity studies. This is understandable because the very idea was developed to a large extent in the sociology of knowledge and STS. Markets were discussed as a problem of knowledge: they mobilize knowledge in the form of judgment devices (Karpik 2010), models (MacKenzie 2006; Henriksen 2013a), routines (D'Adderio 2008), or 'minting work' (Carruthers and Stinchcombe 1999). And, in fact, there are many ways in which performativity can be instructive for the analysis of economics as an academic discipline. In particular, it might help understand the motivations of economists that contribute to the inherent normativity of economic discourses—ranging from market socialist rendering of general equilibrium theory and mechanism design (Myerson 2009; Boldyrev and Ushakov 2016) to experimental economics (Guala 2007). 'Building economic machines' (Guala 2001) and enacting rationality might be even seen as the last resort for unrealistic economic models to get implemented—or as a way to gain additional support. In any way, this perspective opens up an intriguing domain of attitudes and epistemic cultures of the economics profession—something that clearly needs to be explored if we want to understand how economic thinking used to operate (Giraudeau 2010) or how it is organized today (Fourcade et al. 2015).

However, Callon (2007a) already pointed out that while moving deeper into the realm of markets, we encounter not only academic researchers ('confined economists') but also 'economists in the wild.' The latter include professionals who develop and apply ideas and models in the 'wildness' of economies. Here, the importance of the theoretical knowledge becomes less pronounced, and the examples from marketing, finance, and organization studies (referred to above) support this point of view. In the fields of markets and economic policy-making, scientific models may be important, but they also fail (Esposito 2013) or become negligible due to institutional environment and bureaucratic constraints (Svetlova 2012; Henriksen 2013b; Brisset 2014) as well as due to the irreducible importance of marketing tools (McFall 2011) or political considerations (van Egmond and Zeiss 2010; Hirschman and Popp Berman 2014). In other words, theories and models are not always and automatically performative exactly because they are a part of the non-linear contexts of their application.

Moreover, models can be 'counter-performative' as MacKenzie and Spears (2014a) demonstrate: the practical use of a model helps create the opposite of what the model describes. Similar argument is put forward by Zuckerman (2012): the wide adoption of the efficient market theory undermines its validity. Thus, social 'conditions of felicity' are not given (as in the case of Austin) but cocreated while the model or theory is developing and traveling between 'evaluation cultures.' In other words, the importance of knowledge is always conditioned and limited in hybrid contexts.' Hence, when we discuss the performativity of economics, the larger societal context (Henriksen 2009), or Callon's '*economics at large*,' should be taken into consideration. However, if the focus moves away from scientific knowledge, the concept of performativity becomes inevitably vague.

But where does this vagueness really come from? A characteristic way to challenge the performativity thesis is to claim that the 'pure' cases of performativity in its most interesting, 'strong,' or 'Barnesian' form— when the reality, after being represented by economics, converges with its theoretical portrayal—are rather rare and it is thus not clear why the rest should interest us (Santos and Rodrigues 2009). For coming to grips with performativity, it is essential to recognize that these critics often reproduce the 'linear' view of innovation Callon (2007b, 312ff.) so fiercely rejects. This view implies that there is a separate entity called 'economics' (or a group called 'economists') that should have real 'effects' and exert 'influence.' However, the ANT perspective rejects this simple unilateral causation and treats economics as a Hegelian 'moment' in the complex heterogeneous world (or network, as Callon and Latour would say)—in the totality of devices, theoretical claims, policy briefs, university textbooks, experimental practices, statistical measures, ratings, rules, and so on.[12] What really matters for Callon and his followers is the back-and-forth, uncertain, and staggering movement of performation—for which nothing can be guaranteed. But it does not mean that the attempts to perform economic ideas do not exist. They all should be accounted for—within a more nuanced perspective on economics, markets, and society as their general frame or element. And it is this nuanced perspective that should both overcome Callon's alleged naïveté when treating 'economics' as 'economics at large' (Mirowski and Nik-Khah 2008), and provide nontrivial answers to the familiar question on why some forms of knowledge become performative while others do not.

All in all, recent performativity studies inscribe economics in the 'jungle' of the social and thus occupy an uneasy position between economists and their critics. Of course, there might still be economists who believe that they solely are entitled to reflect upon their discipline; and critics of economics who condemn the performativity perspective for its collusion with the foe. But we hope that both of these positions will prove untenable and eventually drop its radicalism, for it is not wise to see malicious criticism in any attempt to consider economics from outside, and it is even less so to ignore—or to uncompromisingly oppose—economics' and economists' entanglement in modern societies.

But in what sense is the performativity of economics, once it establishes economists' involvement, able to influence *economics?* To be sure, economists themselves, unlike management scholars, sociologists, anthropologists, political scientists, or cultural theorists, pay little attention to the idea of performativity. However, we suggest that, although economists rarely read and cite the literature from other social sciences, the general *cultural and social context* does matter both for their attitudes and their work. The general patterns of public opinion and intellectual trends (e.g., in poverty and inequality issues) do make a difference for them. Whenever public atmosphere and general cultural norms change, economists will also take account of the general performative consequences of their and others' work and eventually embark upon building a more reflexive—and, perhaps, more responsible—social science.

So, how does the performativity of economics matter? Perhaps the most immediate answer is that this perspective illuminates the role played by economic theories in our social life, in individual and collective sense-making, in struggles of visions becoming social struggles, and in the stabilization of collective practices. From vague 'conditions of felicity' for performative speech acts, we now move to the complex constitution of the social—with all the renewed significance of ontology, language, and politics we referred to above. After the turn, we cannot ignore anymore that economies are permeated and sustained by performative practices. Once this idea begins to inform both theoretical and metatheoretical accounts, once we add the performative dimension to our conceptual repertoire and abandon the traditional epistemological frameworks, some fascinating perspectives open up in addressing economies and/as economic knowledge. This volume, inspired by the developments in various disciplines, steps into this new terrain and invites the readers to follow.

Notes

1. For more on Austin, see Guala's contribution.
2. Importantly, adherents of performativity are not alone in claiming that (economic) knowledge matters. There are various literatures which deal with very similar issues—ranging from the ideational approach in political economy that explores the role of ideas in shaping economic policy (Blyth 2002; Béland and Cox 2011; Henriksen 2013a; Rodrik 2014; overview in Hirschman and Popp Berman 2014) to the authors who emphasize rhetorical shifts and intellectual change as key factors of modern economic development (Mokyr 2003; McCloskey 2010).
3. For example, Mäki (2013) reproaches MacKenzie for misinterpreting Austin's idea of performativity, while MacKenzie explicitly refers to Barnes (1983).
4. In 2009, there was a debate between Ferraro et al. (2005, 2009) and Felin and Foss (2009) about *ex ante* truthfulness of economic and social theories: While Ferraro et al. claimed that theories affect behavior and become self-fulfilling, Felin and Foss argued that this view implies significant arbitrariness and impossibility to differentiate between true and false theories.

5. In fact, as a subset of cultural, or 'epistemic things,' as Rheinberger (1997) would put it.
6. For an 'ontological turn' in STS, see specifically Woolgar and Lezaun (2013a, b) and a recent critique by Aspers (2015).
7. Callon's interpretation of institutions as 'socio-cognitive prostheses' is of particular relevance here.
8. Indeed, Law (2008) prefers to talk of ANT as 'material semiotics'—in some ways following Latour's earlier preoccupations.
9. See the recent study on the performativity of social network theory (Healy 2015) demonstrating how it promotes reciprocity and more communitarian attitudes.
10. This is an important issue behind understanding the perseverance of particular practices (e.g., rational decision-making in Cabantous and Gond (2011)).
11. Mirowski (2015) recently reiterated his critique claiming that performativity theorists 'retailed economists' own stories about their purported close coherence of theory and empiricism as if it were a 'radical' thesis, when in fact the target economic theory had rarely described how the constructed markets actually functioned 'in the wild' (108). This latter kind of response to performativity is sometimes plagued by internal inconsistency, for it 'has to claim, first, that economics does not matter ... and, second, that it needs to be criticized anyway. But why should we waste time criticizing something that does not matter?' (Muniesa 2014, 38). See more general political critiques of ANT in e.g., Fine (2003), Whittle and Spicer (2008) and Roberts (2012), and a response by Vosselman (2014).
12. That is why it is not enough to claim that, say, economy is 'expressed,' rather than performed (Didier 2007), for the economy itself should be conceived as depended of this 'expression,' and the stability of the 'expressed' should be questioned. For the Hegelian perspective on performativity, see Boldyrev and Herrmann-Pillath (2013); Herrmann-Pillath and Boldyrev (2014).

References

Araujo, Luis, John Finch, and Hans Kjellberg (eds.). 2010. *Reconnecting Marketing to Markets: Practice-Based Approaches.* Oxford: Oxford University Press.

Aspers, Patrik. 2015. Performing Ontology. *Social Studies of Science* 45(3): 449–453.

Austin, John. 1962. *How to Do Things with Words. The William James Lectures Delivered at Harvard University in 1955.* Oxford: Oxford University Press.

Banerjee, Abhijit and Esther Duflo. 2011. *Poor Economics: A Radical Rethinking of the Way to Fight Global Poverty.* New York: PublicAffairs.

Barad, Karen. 2003. Posthumanist Performativity: Toward an Understanding of How Matter Comes to Matter. *Signs: Journal of Women in Culture and Society* 28(3): 801–831.
Barnes, Barry. 1983. Social Life as Bootstrapped Induction. *Sociology* 17(4): 524–545.
Béland, Daniel and Robert Henry Cox (eds.). 2011. *Ideas and Politics in Social Science Research*. Oxford: Oxford University Press.
Blinder, Alan S., and Charles Wyplosz. 2004. Central Bank Talk: Committee Structure and Communication Policy. Paper prepared for ASSA meetings, Philadelphia, January 2005.
Bloor, David. 1997. *Wittgenstein, Rules and Institutions*. London: Routledge.
Blyth, Mark. 2002. *Great Transformations: Economic Ideas and Institutional Change in the Twentieth Century*. Cambridge: Cambridge University Press.
Boldyrev, Ivan. 2012. Philosophy of Science or Science and Technology Studies? Economic Methodology and Auction Theory. *International Studies in the Philosophy of Science* 26(3): 289–307.
Boldyrev, Ivan. 2013. Ökonomische Maschinen: Zur Performativität der Gleichgewichtstheorie. In *Wirtschaftswissenschaft als Oikodizee? Diskussionen im Anschluss an Joseph Vogls Gespenst des Kapitals*, edited by Hanno Pahl and Jan Sparsam, 77–90. Wiesbaden: Springer VS.
Boldyrev, Ivan, and Carsten Herrmann-Pillath. 2013. Hegel's Objective Spirit, Extended Mind, and the Institutional Nature of Economic Action. *Mind & Society* 12(2): 177–202.
Boldyrev, Ivan, and Alexey Ushakov. 2016. Adjusting the Model to Adjust the World: Constructive Mechanisms in Postwar General Equilibrium Theory. *Journal of Economic Methodology* 23(1): 38–56.
Breslau, Daniel. 2011. What Do Market Designers Do When They Design Markets? Economists as Consultants to the Redesign of Wholesale Electricity Markets in the U.S. In *Social Knowledge in the Making*, edited by Charles Camic, Neil Gross, and Michèle Lamont, 379–403. Chicago: University of Chicago Press.
Breslau, Daniel. 2013. Designing a Market-Like Entity: Economics in the Politics of Market Formation. *Social Studies of Science* 43(6): 829–851.
Brisset, Nicolas. 2014. Economics is Not Always Performative: Some Limits for Performativity. Accessed October 30, 2015. https://docs.google.com/file/d/0B5o02ki-WYWWbF8yLTdBR2ZnWVE/edit?pli=1
Bryant, Levi, Nick Srnicek, and Graham Harman (eds.). 2011. *The Speculative Turn: Continental Materialism and Realism*. Melbourne: re.press.
Butler, Judith. 1990. *Gender Trouble: Feminism and the Subversion of Identity*. New York: Routledge.
Butler, Judith. 1997. *Excitable Speech*. Abingdon: Routledge.
Butler, Judith. 2010. Performative Agency. *Journal of Cultural Economy* 3(2): 147–161.

Caballero, Ricardo J. 2010. Macroeconomics after the Crisis: Time to Deal with the Pretense-of-Knowledge Syndrome. *Journal of Economic Perspectives* 24(4): 85–102.
Cabantous, Laure, and Jean-Pascal Gond. 2011. Rational Decision Making as a 'Performative Praxis': Explaining Rationality's *Éternel Retour*. *Organization Science* 22(3): 573–586.
Callon, Michel. 1998a. The Embeddedness of Economic Markets in Economics. In *The Laws of the Markets*, edited by Michel Callon, 1–58. Oxford: Blackwell.
Callon, Michel. 1998b. An Essay on Framing and Overflowing: Economic Externalities Revisited by Sociology. In *The Laws of the Markets*, edited by Michel Callon, 244–269. Oxford: Blackwell.
Callon, Michel. 2007a. An Essay on the Growing Contribution of Economic Markets to the Proliferation of the Social. *Theory, Culture & Society* 24(7–8): 139–163.
Callon, Michel. 2007b. What Does It Mean to Say that Economics is Performative? In *Do Economists Make Markets? On the Performativity of Economics*, edited by Donald MacKenzie, Fabian Muniesa, and Lucia Siu, 311–357. Princeton, NJ: Princeton University Press.
Callon, Michel, and Fabian Muniesa. 2005. Economic Markets as Calculative Collective Devices. *Organization Studies* 26(8): 1229–1250.
Carruthers, Bruce, and Jeong-Chul Kim. 2011. The Sociology of Finance. *Annual Review of Sociology* 37: 239–259.
Carruthers, Bruce and Arthur L. Stinchcombe. 1999. The Social Structure of Liquidity: Flexibility, Markets, and States. *Theory and Society* 28(3): 353-382.
Clark, Andy. 2011. *Supersizing the Mind. Embodiment, Action, and Cognitive Extension*. Oxford: Oxford University Press.
D'Adderio, Luciana. 2008. The Performativity of Routines: Theorising the Influence of Artefacts and Distributed Agencies on Routines Dynamics. *Research Policy* 37(5): 769–789.
D'Adderio, Luciana, and Neil Pollock. 2014. Performing Modularity: Competing Rules, Performative Struggles and the Effect of Organizational Theories on the Organization. *Organization Studies* 35(12): 1813–1833.
Davis, John B. 2013. Economics Imperialism Under the Impact of Psychology: The Case of Behavioral Development Economics. *Oeconomia 3(1): 119–138.*
De Goede, Marieke. 2005. *Virtue, Fortune and Faith: A Genealogy of Finance*. Minneapolis, MN: University of Minnesota Press.
Derrida, Jacques. 1988. *Limited Inc*. Evanston, IL: Northwestern University Press.
Descola, Philippe. 2013. *Beyond Nature and Culture*. Chicago, IL: University of Chicago Press.
Didier, Emmanuel. 2007. Do Statistics Perform the Economy? In *Do Economists Make Markets? On the Performativity of Economics*, edited by Donald Mackenzie,

Fabian Muniesa, and Lucia Siu, 276–310. Princeton, NJ: Princeton University Press.

Dix, Guus. 2014. Governing By Carrot and Stick: A Genealogy of the Incentive. PhD dissertation, Amsterdam School for Cultural Analysis (ASCA) Amsterdam.

Egmond, Stance van, and Ragna Zeiss. 2010. Modeling for Policy: Science-based Models as Performative Boundary Objects for Dutch Policy Making. *Science Studies* 23(1): 58–78.

Esposito, Elena. 2013. The Structures of Uncertainty: Performativity and Unpredictability in Economic Operations. *Economy and Society* 42(1): 102–129.

Favereau, Judith, and Nicolas Brisset. 2013. How to Do Things with Randomization? Paper presented at the 17th annual conference of the European Society for the History of Economic Thought, Kingston University, Kingston upon Thames, UK, May 16–18.

Felin, Teppo, and Nicolai J. Foss. 2009. Performativity of Theory, Arbitrary Conventions, and Possible Worlds: A Reality Check. *Organization Science* 20(3): 676–678.

Ferraro, Fabrizio, Jeffrey Pfeffer, and Robert I. Sutton. 2005. Economics Language and Assumptions: How Theories Can Become Self-fulfilling. *Academy of Management Review* 30(1): 8–24.

Ferraro, Fabrizio, Jeffrey Pfeffer, and Robert I. Sutton. 2009. How and Why Theories Matter: A Comment on Felin and Foss (2009) Organization Science 20(3): 669–675.

Fine, Ben. 2003. Callonistics: A Disentanglement. *Economy and Society* 32(3): 478–484.

Fourcade, Marion. 2006. The Construction of a Global Profession: The Transnationalization of Economics. *American Journal of Sociology* 112(1): 145–195.

Fourcade, Marion. 2009. *Economists and Societies. Discipline and Profession in the United States, Britain, and France, 1890s to 1990s.* Princeton, NJ: Princeton University Press.

Fourcade, Marion, Etienne Ollion. and Yann Algan. 2015. The Superiority of Economists. *Journal of Economic Perspectives* 29(1): 89–114.

Friedman, Milton. 1970. The Social Responsibility of Business is to Increase Its Profits. *The New York Times Magazine*, September 13.

Friedman, Daniel. 2010. A New Mentality for a New Economy: Performing the Homo Economicus in Argentina. *Economy and Society* 39(2) 271–302.

Garcia-Parpet, Marie-France. 2007. The Social Construction of a Perfect Market: The Strawberry Auction at Fontaines-en-Sologne In *Do Economists Make Markets? On the Performativity of Economics*, edited by Donald MacKenzie, Fabian Muniesa, and Lucia Siu, 20–53. Princeton, NJ: Princeton University Press.

Ghoshal, Sumantra. 2005. Bad Management Theories are Destroying Good Management Practices. *Academy of Management Learning & Education* 4(1): 75–91.

Ghoshal, Sumantra, and Peter Moran. 1996. Bad for Practice: A Critique of the Transaction Cost Theory. *The Academy of Management Review* 21(1): 13–47.
Giraudeau, Martin. 2010. Performing Physiocracy. Pierre Samuel Du Pont de Nemours and the Limits of Political Engineering. *Journal of Cultural Economy* 3(2): 225–242.
Gond, Jean-Pascal, Laure Cabantous, Nancy Harding, and Mark Learmonth. 2015. What Do We Mean by Performativity in Organizational and Management Theory? The Uses and Abuses of Performativity. *International Journal of Management Reviews*, Published online July 7, 2015. http://onlinelibrary.wiley.com/doi/10.1111/ijmr.12074/full
Guala, Francesco. 2001. Building Economic Machines: The FCC Auctions. *Studies in History and Philosophy of Science, Part A* 32(3): 453–477.
Guala, Francesco. 2007. How to Do Things with Experimental Economics. In *Do Economists Make Markets? On the Performativity of Economics*, edited by Donald MacKenzie, Fabian Muniesa, and Lucia Siu, 128–162. Princeton, NJ: Princeton University Press.
Healy, Kieran. 2015. The Performativity of Networks. *European Journal of Sociology* 56(2): 175–205.
Henriksen, Lasse F. 2009. Are Financial Markets Embedded in Economics Rather than Society? A Critical Review of the Performativity Thesis. *Working Paper* 2009:10, Danish Institute for International Studies.
Henriksen, Lasse F. 2013a. Performativity and the Politics of Equipping for Calculation: Constructing a Global Market for Microfinance. *International Political Sociology* 7(4): 406–425.
Henriksen, Lasse F. 2013b. Economic Models as Devices of Policy Change: Policy Paradigms, Paradigm Shift, and Performativity. *Regulation & Governance* 7(4): 481–495.
Herrmann-Pillath, Carsten. 2010. A Neurolinguistic Approach to Performativity in Economics. *Journal of Economic Methodology* 17(3): 241–260.
Herrmann-Pillath, Carsten. 2012. Institutions, Distributed Cognition and Agency: Rule-Following as Performative Action. *Journal of Economic Methodology* 19(1): 21–42.
Herrmann-Pillath, Carsten. 2013. Performativity of Economic Systems: Approach and Implications for Taxonomy. *Journal of Economic Methodology* 20(2): 139–163.
Herrmann-Pillath, Carsten, and Ivan Boldyrev. 2014. *Hegel, Institutions, and Economics. Performing the Social*. London: Routledge.
Hirschman, Daniel, and Elisabeth Popp Berman. 2014. Do Economists Make Policies? On the Political Effects of Economics. *Socio-Economic Review* 12(4): 779–811.
Hodgson, Geoffrey. 2009. The Great Crash of 2008 and the Reform of Economics. *Cambridge Journal of Economics* 33(6): 1205–1221.

Holm, Petter, and Kåre Nolde Nielsen. 2007. Framing Fish, Making Markets: The Construction of Individual Transferable Quotas (ITQs). In *Market Devices*, edited by Michel Callon, Yuval Millo, and Fabian Muniesa, 173–195. Oxford: Blackwell Publishing.
Hutchins, E. 1995. *Cognition in the Wild*. Cambridge, MA: MIT Press.
Jacobi, Erik, James Freund, and Luis Araujo. 2015. Is There a Gap in the Market, and Is There a Market in the Gap? How Advertising Planning Performs Markets. *Journal of Marketing Management* 31(1–2): 37–61.
Kahneman, Daniel, and Amos Tversky (eds.) 2000. *Choices, Values, and Frames*. New York: Cambridge University Press.
Karpik, Lucien. 2010. *Valuing the Unique: The Economics of Singularities*. Princeton and Oxford: Princeton University Press.
Knorr Cetina, Karin. 1981. *The Manufacture of Knowledge. An Essay on the Constructivist and Contextual Nature of Science*, Oxford: Pergamon Press.
Krugman, Paul. 2009. How Did Economists Get It So Wrong? In *New York Times Magazine*, September 6, 2009.
La Berge, Leigh C. 2016. How to Make Money with Words: Finance, Performativity, Language. *Journal of Cultural Economy* 9(1): 43–62.
Latour, Bruno. 2005. *Reassembling the Social. An Introduction to Actor-Network-Theory*. Oxford: Oxford University Press.
Law, John. 2008. Actor-Network Theory and Material Semiotics. In *The New Blackwell Companion to Social Theory*, edited by Bryan S. Turner, 3rd ed., 141–158. Oxford: Blackwell.
Law, John, and John Urry. 2004. Enacting the Social. *Economy and Society* 33(3): 390–410.
Licoppe, Christian. 2010. The 'Performative Turn' in Science and Technology Studies. *Journal of Cultural Economy* 3(2): 181–188.
MacKenzie, Donald. 2006. *An Engine, Not a Camera: How Financial Models Shape Markets*. Cambridge, MA: MIT Press.
MacKenzie, Donald. 2010. Models as Coordination Devices. In *Débordements*, edited by Madeleine Akrich, Yannick Barthe, and Fabian Muniesa, 299–302. Paris: Presses de Mines.
MacKenzie, Donald, and Yuval Millo. 2003. Constructing a Market, Performing Theory: The Historical Sociology of a Financial Derivatives Exchange. *American Journal of Sociology* 109(1): 107–145.
MacKenzie, Donald, Fabian Muniesa, and Lucia Siu (eds.). 2007. *Do Economists Make Markets? On the Performativity of Economics*. Princeton, NJ: Princeton University Press.
MacKenzie, Donald, and Taylor Spears. 2014a. 'The Formula that Killed Wall Street': The Gaussian Copula and Modelling Practices in Investment Banking. *Social Studies of Science* 44(3): 393–417.

MacKenzie, Donald, and Taylor Spears. 2014b. 'A Device for Being Able to Book P&L': The Organizational Embedding of the Gaussian Copula. *Social Studies of Science* 44(3): 418–440.
Mäki, Uskali. 2013. Performativity: Saving Austin from MacKenzie. In *Perspectives and Foundational Problems in Philosophy of Science, The European Philosophy of Science Association Proceedings*, edited by Vassilios Karakostas and Dennis Dieks, 443–453. Berlin: Springer.
Marglin, Stephen. 2008. *The Dismal Science: How Thinking Like an Economist Undermines Community*. Cambridge, MA: Harvard University Press.
Mason, Katy, Hans Kjellberg, and Johan Hagberg. 2015.Exploring the Performativity of Marketing: Theories, Practices and Devices. *Journal of Marketing Management*. 31(1–2):1–15.
McCloskey, Deirdre N. 2010. *Bourgeois Dignity: Why Economics Can't Explain the Modern World*. Chicago: University of Chicago Press.
McFall, Liz. 2011. A 'Good, Average Man': Calculation and the Limits of Statistics in Enrolling Insurance Customers. *Sociological Review* 59(4): 662–684.
McFall, Liz, and Jose Ossandón. 2014. What's New in the 'New, New Economic Sociology' and Should Organisation Studies Care? In *Oxford Handbook of Sociology, Social Theory and Organization Studies: Contemporary Currents*, edited by Paul S. Adler, Paul du Gay, Glenn Morgan, and Michael Reed, 510–533. Oxford: Oxford University Press.
Miller, Daniel. 2002. Turning Callon the Right Way Up. *Economy and Society* 31(2): 218–233.
Miller, Peter, and Ted O'Leary. 2007. Mediating Instruments and Making Markets: Capital Budgeting, Science and the Economy. *Accounting, Organizations and Society* 34(5): 638–653.
Millo, Yuval, and Donald MacKenzie. 2009. The Usefulness of Inaccurate Models: Towards an Understanding of the Emergence of Financial Risk Management. *Accounting, Organizations and Society* 32(7–8): 701–734.
Mirowski, Philip and Edward Nik-Khan. 2013. Private Intellectuals and Public Perplexity: The Economics Profession and the Economic Crisis. *History of Political Economy* 45 (Annual Supplement): 279-311.
Mirowski, Philip. 2015. Review of *The Economics of Economists: Institutional Setting, Individual Incentives, and Future Prospects, Edited by Alessandro Lanteri and Jack Vromen. Erasmus Journal for Philosophy and Economics* 8(1): 105–109.
Mirowski, Philip, and Edward Nik-Khah. 2007. Markets Made Flesh: Performativity, and a Problem in Science Studies, Augmented with Consideration of the FCC Auctions. In *Do Economists Make Markets? On the Performativity of Economics*, edited by Donald MacKenzie, Fabian Muniesa, and Lucia Siu, 190–224. Princeton, NJ: Princeton University Press.

Mirowski, Philip, and Edward Nik-Khah. 2008. Command Performance: Exploring What STS Thinks It Takes to Build a Market. In *Living in a Material World: Economic Sociology Meets Science and Technology Studies*, edited by Trevor Pinch and Richard Swedberg, 89–128. Cambridge, MA: MIT Press.

Mokyr, Joel. 2003. *The Gifts of Athena: Historical Origins of the Knowledge Economy*. Princeton, NJ: Princeton University Press.

Muniesa, Fabian. 2014. *The Provoked Economy: Economic Reality and the Performative Turn*. Abingdon: Routledge.

Myerson, Roger B. 2009. Fundamental Theory of Institutions: A Lecture in Honor of Leo Hurwicz. *Review of Economic Design* 13(1): 59–75.

Nik-Khah, Edward. 2008. A Tale of Two Auctions. *Journal of Institutional Economics* 4(1): 73–97.

Pickering, Andrew. 1995. *The Mangle of Practice: Time, Agency and Science*. Chicago, IL: University of Chicago Press.

Piketty, Thomas. 2014. *Capital in the Twenty-First Century*. Cambridge, MA: Harvard University Press.

Pinch, Trevor, and Richard Swedberg (eds.). 2008. *Living in a Material World, Economic Sociology Meets Science and Technology Studies*. Cambridge, MA: MIT Press.

Porter, Theodore M. 1995. *Trust in Numbers: The Pursuit of Objectivity in Science and Public Life*. Princeton, NJ: Princeton University Press.

Porter, Theodore M. 2008. Locating the Domain of Calculation. *Journal of Cultural Economy* 1(1): 39–50.

Preda, Alex. 2009. *Information, Knowledge, and Economic Life: An Introduction to the Sociology of Markets*. Oxford: Oxford University Press.

Rheinberger, Hans-Jörg. 1997. *Toward a History of Epistemic Things: Synthesizing Proteins in the Test Tube*. Stanford, CA: Stanford University Press.

Roberts, John M. 2012. Poststructuralism Against Poststructuralism: Actor-Network Theory, Organizations and Economic Markets. *European Journal of Social Theory* 15(1): 35–53.

Rodrik, Dani. 2014. When Ideas Trump Interests: Preferences, Worldviews, and Policy Innovations. *Journal of Economic Perspectives* 28(1): 189–208.

Sætnan, Ann Rudinow, Heidi Mork Lomell, and Svein Hammer (eds.). 2010. *The Mutual Construction of Statistics and Society*. London: Routledge.

Santos, Ana C., and João Rodrigues. 2009. Economics as Social Engineering? Questioning the Performativity Thesis. *Cambridge Journal of Economics* 33(5): 985–1000.

Searle, John R. 1969. *Speech Acts: An Essay in the Philosophy of Language*. New York: Cambridge University Press.

Searle, John R. 2005. What is an Institution? *Journal of Institutional Economics* 1(1): 1–22.

Sparsam, Jan. 2015. Die zwei Soziologien des Marktes. Konstitutionstheoretische Defizite der neueren Wirtschaftssoziologie. *Zeitschrift für kritische Sozialtheorie und Philosophie* 2(2): 255–284.
Spears, Taylor C. 2014. Engineering Value, Engineering Risk: What Derivatives Quants Know and What Their Models Do. PhD dissertation, University of Edinburgh. Edinburgh.
Svetlova, Ekaterina. 2012. On the Performative Power of Financial Models. *Economy and Society* 41(3): 418–434.
Svetlova, Ekaterina. 2014. Modeling Beyond Application: Epistemic and Non-epistemic Values in Modern Science. *International Studies in the Philosophy of Science* 28(1): 79–98.
Thaler, Richard H., and Cass R. Sunstein. 2008. *Nudge. Improving Decisions About Health, Wealth, and Happiness.* New Haven, CT: Yale University Press.
Vollmer, Hendrik, Andrea Mennicken, and Alex Preda. 2009. Tracking the Numbers: Across Accounting and Finance, Organizations and Markets. *Accounting, Organizations and Society* 34(5): 619–637.
Vosselman, Ed. 2014. The 'Performativity Thesis' and Its Critics: Towards a Relational Ontology of Management Accounting. *Accounting and Business Research* 44(2): 181–203.
White, Mark D. 2013. *The Manipulation of Choice: Ethics and Libertarian Paternalism.* New York: Palgrave Macmillan.
Whittle, Andrea, and André Spicer. 2008. Is Actor Network Theory Critique? *Organization Studies* 29(4): 611–629.
Woolgar, Steve, and Javier Lezaun. 2013. The Wrong Bin Bag: A Turn to Ontology in Science and Technology Studies? *Social Studies of Science* 43(3): 321–340.
Woolgar, Steve, and Javier Lezaun (eds.). 2013. Special Issue: A Turn to Ontology in Science and Technology Studies? *Social Studies of Science* 43(3): 321–462.
Zuckerman, Ezra W. 2012. Market Efficiency: A Sociological Perspective. In *Oxford Handbook of the Sociology of Finance*, edited by Karin Knorr-Cetina and Alex Preda, 223–249. Oxford: Oxford University Press.

CHAPTER 2

Performativity Rationalized

Francesco Guala

2.1 INTRODUCTION

The concept of performativity originates from the philosophy of language of the 1950s, and in particular, from John Austin's speech act theory. Since then, however, it has attracted a motley crew of supporters, ranging from Jacques Derrida to Pierre Bourdieu, Judith Butler, and John Searle. More recently, performativity has become a key term in the 'new economic sociology' of Donald MacKenzie and Michel Callon, inspiring a number of projects and case studies aimed at showing how economic science may 'perform' economic markets.[1]

When technical terms enjoy wide circulation in different disciplines, they seldom retain a sharp connotation. Uskali Mäki (2013) has denounced

---

A preliminary version of this chapter was presented at a workshop organized at Medialab Prado in Madrid by UNED (Universidad Nacional de Educación a Distancia) and the Urrutia Elejalde Foundation. I am grateful to the members of the audience and especially to Don MacKenzie, David Teira, Nicolas Brisset, Ivan Boldyrev, and Ekaterina Svetlova for their feedback. My research was supported by grant FFI2011-28835 of the Spanish Ministry of Science.

F. Guala
Department of Economics, Management and Quantitative Methods,
University of Milan, Milan, Italy

this drift: the concept of performativity in his view has been stretched too far in the economic sociology literature. He sees two main problems: (i) attaching different meanings to the same term creates confusion; (ii) none of these meanings, he claims, is faithful to the original Austinian notion. So economic sociologists should better dispense with performativity.

Mäki's first critique is, I believe, justified. The time is ripe to regiment our language and seek a precise definition of the concepts used in the new economic sociology programme. However, I disagree with Mäki on the second point: economic sociologists, in my view, should retain the concept of performativity. The linguistic mechanisms identified by Austin shed light on some interesting phenomena studied by sociologists of financial markets. So keeping performativity in current sociological discourse is not incompatible with seeking more conceptual and linguistic precision.

To support this claim will require some argumentation, however. Part of the problem is that 'performativity' is not a well-defined object. Different scholars have interpreted Austin's theory in different ways, and have developed his approach in different directions. The question of economic sociologists' fidelity cannot be settled by purely exegetical means, and quite inevitably we will have to make some theoretical decisions as we proceed. My approach will be scientific rather than interpretive: I will move from the assumption that Austin identified an important linguistic phenomenon, that he provided invaluable insights and tools to understand its functioning but that he left a lot of work to do for his followers. The distinction between 'illocutionary' and 'perlocutionary' aspects of speech acts, upon which Mäki's critique is based, has been a major topic of discussion, for example. I will endorse a deflationary interpretation, according to which illocutionary effects do not have any major ontological implications. This interpretation in turn is based on a specific account of constitutive rules and the role they play in the definition of institutional terms. While neither of these accounts can be found in Austin's writings, they fill important holes in his theory and they provide a plausible picture of the mechanics of performativity.

My strategy will develop as follows: in Sect. 2.2, I will briefly illustrate Austin's theory and complement it with Searle's account of constitutive rules to define the felicity conditions of speech acts. Constitutive rules hold by agreement or convention, so Sect. 2.3 outlines the standard (Lewis-Schelling) theory of conventions as equilibria of coordination games. In the same section, I will argue that a performative speech act in Austin's sense is essentially a correlation device. Having introduced the fundamental tools, in Sect. 2.4, I will illustrate how economic theories may work as correlation devices in coordination games, focusing on MacKenzie's study of the Black–Scholes model of option pricing. The goal is to show that Austin's speech acts and the models of economic theory may perform similar functions in certain conditions. So economics may be performative in Austin's sense. In Sect. 2.5, I will discuss Michel Callon's claim that the success of economic models depends on factors that have nothing to do with people's beliefs about the theory itself. Section 2.6 defends the account of performatives as correlation devices from Mäki's charge of ignoring the distinction between constitution and causation. Section 2.7 concludes with a summary of the argument.

2.2 Austin on Performativity

In his masterpiece, *How to Do Things with Words* (1962), John Austin showed that many linguistic utterances have primarily pragmatic functions. Such utterances are aimed not at describing the world but at *acting* in a social environment (warning, insulting, admonishing, joking, etc.). Austin's pragmatism was a reaction to the narrow concern for the truth value of propositions displayed by his contemporaries. Against the logical positivist tradition, Austin argued that many utterances are not to be evaluated according to their truth or falsity but according to their *felicity*. Felicity is a pragmatic notion of success: an utterance is successful ('felicitous') if it satisfies certain pragmatic criteria, or if it is appropriate in the given circumstances. For example: a warning is felicitous if the speaker believes that there is danger, if she intends to alert her audience, if the signal is appropriate to the source and gravity of the threat, and so on. Truth matters, but the main purpose of the utterance is not to convey information about a state of affairs: shouting 'there is a lion!' may be appropriate even if the utterance is false (if, say, the lion turns out to be a tiger) provided it satisfies the conditions of felicity. And the opposite may be the case: 'there is a beetle!' may be a totally infelicitous warning, even if it is true.

A surprising feature of performative speech acts, noticed by Austin and his followers, is their fecundity: in some occasions, we can create something simply by saying it. Consider the following classic examples:

> I promise to give you ten dollars.
>
> You are now man and wife.

In uttering the first statement, one is making a promise, or creating an obligation that did not exist before. In the second case, by uttering the formula, an official creates a marriage—she brings into existence a husband, a wife, a set of reciprocal rights and duties that did not exist before. Speech acts, however, cannot create social objects out of the blue. Performative statements presuppose the existence of social conventions 'in the background', so to speak. In *How to Do Things with Words*, Austin lists some background conditions for the functioning of performatives. The first one is:

(A1) There must exist an *accepted conventional procedure* having a certain conventional effect, that procedure to include the uttering of certain words by certain persons in certain circumstances. (Austin 1962, 14; added italics)

If condition (A1) does not hold, a performative speech act 'misfires'. When my daughter performs a 'wedding ceremony' with her dolls, for example, she is not creating a marriage: the utterance misfires.[2] Austin adds that when a speech act misfires, 'it is presumably persons other than the speaker who do not accept it' (1962, 27). So performativity presupposes sociality—'a *whole* code of procedure', in his own words.

What is the relation between performative statements and 'accepted conventional procedures' exactly? Austin does not say much. His examples, however, contain insights that can be turned into a full theory. In the case of marriage, the procedures are expressed by rules such as 'the bride and groom must speak in front of witnesses', 'the ceremony must be administered by an official appointed by the Church or State', and the like. These rules are conventional in two intuitive senses at least: (i) they are partly arbitrary (why should there be two witnesses rather than three or four? Why a priest rather than a doctor or a lawyer?), and (ii) they hold by agreement among the members of the community.[3]

John Searle (1969, 1995) has developed this aspect of Austin's theory by introducing the concept of *constitutive rule*. A 'constitutive rule' is a statement of the form '*X* counts as *Y* in *C*'. For example:

Saying 'I do' in front of witnesses and a public official in the appropriate place (etc.) counts as getting married.

An individual who is born in the USA, is at least 35 years old, has won the majority of delegates in a national election (etc.) counts as the President of the United States.

In Searle's abstract formula, X stands for a pre-existing entity (an individual, or a linguistic act, in the above examples); Y is a *status function*, a set of roles, duties, rights that are assigned conventionally; C stands for the context in which the assignment takes place. An institutional fact thus requires that X is the case, that C is the case, and that there is general agreement in a population that X counts as Y in C—or in other words, that the members of a social group accept the constitutive rule.

An important point made by Searle concerns the nature of status functions (Y, in the formula above). A crucial difference between institutional entities on the one hand, and natural entities and artefacts on the other, is that in the former case, the relation between the function (Y) and its substratum (X) is purely conventional. This is not true in the case of natural functions: the heart is able to pump blood in virtue of its physical features and of the structure of the human body. In the case of artefacts, a function (e.g. the function of a chair) is attributed to an object (a piece of wood) in virtue of its physical characteristics (it can be used to sit on). Social entities are different because the conditions that ought to be satisfied are often conventional. Status functions can usually be attributed independently of the physical characteristics of the status-bearing object (X). A classic example is money: pieces of metal, paper, shells, fur can all be used as currency. What really matters is that there is general agreement that X (say, shells) count as Y (money) in C (the Solomon Islands). There is no difference between being money and being accepted as money, once the conditions of acceptance have been satisfied.

2.3 Coordination and Convention

To say that speech acts require conventional constitutive rules is not very illuminating, unless we can explain what a convention is. Luckily, social scientists and philosophers have a well-worked-out theory, built on the seminal contributions of Thomas Schelling and David Lewis. The theory is based on game-theoretic concepts—in particular the notion of coordination game—and helps clarify the connection between conventions and performativity.[4]

A *coordination game* is a strategic situation with multiple Nash equilibria. A Nash equilibrium is a steady state where each player's action is an optimal response to the actions of the other players. Since social scientists typically aim at explaining robust patterns of behaviour, and out-of-equilibrium actions are unlikely to be repeated over time, the concept of Nash equilibrium is attractive both for explanatory and for predictive purposes. Coordination problems, however, have long been a puzzle for game theorists, because the standard theory lacks the resources to identify which, among the many possible patterns, will be chosen by rational individuals. Schelling (1960) and Lewis (1969) argued that, in the case of social conventions, arbitrary elements of the environment and the history of play often create focal points that people exploit to coordinate successfully.

Lewis' analysis is mostly devoted to games with symmetric payoffs, such as the 'driving game' that we unwittingly play every time we drive our cars (should we keep right or left? It does not matter, provided we all follow the same convention). The theory, however, can be easily extended to games with asymmetric payoffs. Consider the following scenario: two tribes settle in a new valley with their cattle. When they spot a patch of green land, they must decide whether to graze or not. If they both graze, they are likely to clash and fight; if they both abstain, they will forego an opportunity to feed their cattle. The best solution is that one tribe grazes and the other one does not: but who should give way?

The problem can be represented by means of a game matrix known as 'hawk-dove' in biology and 'chicken' in economics (Fig. 2.1). G, NG (Graze, Not Graze) and NG, G (Not Graze, Graze) are both Nash equilibria of this game. The problem is to identify an equilibrium selection device that will help avoid the two inefficient outcomes (G, G and NG, NG). Lewis and others pointed out that history may be such a device: whoever arrives first acquires the right to use a piece of land.[5] For every future interaction, precedence can work as a conventional signal that regulates coordination in the grazing game.

	G	NG
G	0, 0	2, 1
NG	1, 2	1, 1

Fig. 2.1 The grazing game ('hawk-dove').

The key idea is that the players can achieve a superior equilibrium if they use a *correlation device*.[6] They may, for example, adopt a profile of conditional strategies like the following:

If you occupied the land first, then graze it; if you arrived second, then do not graze it (if F then G; if S then NG)

A pair of strategies like this guarantees each tribe an average payoff of 1.5 in repeated play, if we assume that roughly 50 % of the time one tribe occupies first and 50 % of the time the other does it. It also guarantees that no resource is wasted, since the two tribes will never end up in (G, G) or (NG, NG). Finally, the strategy is analogous to a rule that assigns a primitive property right (the right to use). Notice that it is not important that the tribes have a special term or concept for the institution of private property. Perhaps they are only following a custom or a rule of thumb, and we—as external observers—see in these behavioural regularities a primitive institution of property. Be that as it may, a conventional coordination device can bring about a state of affairs (an institution of property) that did not exist before.[7]

Speech acts so far do not play a role in the story. But language as we know is a powerful coordination device. It is easy to concoct an alternative story of the grazing game where the problem of coordination is solved by means of a speech act: suppose that when they first entered the valley, both tribes met in the middle of the plain. To resolve their dispute, they called a shaman who, after some smoking and chanting, declared in public: 'All the land that lies north of this point is your territory; all the land that lies south is their territory; and this is the border that separates the two territories.'

Nothing much has changed from the earlier story, except that now a speech act works as coordination device. The speech act seems to create by magic a state of affairs (with territories, borders, and grazing patterns) that previously did not exist. But so did the coordination device (precedence) in the old story. So there does not seem to be anything special with speech acts, except that they are extremely handy and flexible tools to achieve coordination.

Notice that performative speech acts involve conventions at two different levels: (i) a speech act may create a focal point that solves a coordination problem with multiple equilibria. The solution is conventional in the sense that it is one among several possible coordination equilibria. (ii)

The speech act is just one among several possible coordination devices that could have achieved the same outcome. Another speech act, or even a non-linguistic device (a river, a pointing gesture) could have played the role of correlation device.

The same applies to other paradigmatic performative speech acts, like wedding ceremonies or appointments. A marriage between two individuals (Ann and Bob) is conventional in the sense that it is one among several possible arrangements: Ann in principle could have married Dave, and Bob could have married Carol. But the coordination device—the wedding ceremony—is also conventional, because the same result could have been achieved in several alternative ways. Ann and Bob could have tattooed each other's name on their shoulders, or could have performed a ceremonial dance, or any other ritual that is publicly associated with the rules of marriage.[8] Saying 'I do' in front of a priest is one among many ways to signal that two individuals will adopt a certain set of rules (the rules of marriage) to regulate their behaviour.

An advantage of speech acts over other ceremonial acts is that they are particularly transparent devices to achieve coordination. If I say 'I'll see you in my office at noon', there is little doubt that I am setting a meeting. Similarly, when the priest says 'you are now man and wife', everyone understands what outcome (coordination equilibrium) he is trying to implement. But it is worth emphasising that speech acts can help coordination only if they change beliefs in the appropriate manner. And this is true of performative utterances in general. When I say 'I promise to give you ten euro next week', I am trying to change your beliefs, to convince you that I will return the money if you lend it to me.[9]

This point is often made by distinguishing between the 'illocutionary' and the 'perlocutionary' aspects of a speech act (both terms were introduced by Austin). The *illocutionary* aspect pertains to the conventional meaning of the speech act, for example, to the fact that saying 'I do' in certain circumstances counts as getting married, or that saying 'I promise' counts as making a promise. The *perlocutionary* aspect instead pertains to the 'consequential effects upon the feelings, thoughts or actions of the audience, or of the speaker, or of other persons' (Austin 1962, 101). Although the distinction has been widely debated, it is customary to interpret the illocutionary aspect of an act as being essentially communicative, and the perlocutionary one as causal or pragmatic.[10] Mäki criticizes MacKenzie for mixing illocutionary and perlocutionary acts, so I will have to return to this distinction later. For the time being, let me state a claim that will play a crucial role in my argument: performative speech acts 'create' things (institutions, promises, etc.) by manipulating beliefs, and in particular, the systems of mutual beliefs that are crucial for coordination and cooperation in complex societies.

2.4 Economic Models as Coordination Devices: The Case of Option Pricing

Let us suppose that performatives facilitate coordination, by changing the beliefs of individuals involved in complex strategic interactions. In this section, I will show that scientific theories can play the same role, in the appropriate circumstances. Economics, in particular, can 'perform' economic reality by changing the beliefs—and hence the behaviour—of the agents in the economy. To drive this point home, I will rely on a paradigmatic study in the new economic sociology literature: the case of option pricing analysed by MacKenzie in several articles and in an influential monograph (MacKenzie 2006). Since the theoretical and historical details are complex, I will stick to a general level of description. Interested readers are invited to read the full account in MacKenzie's book.

Let us begin with some basic theory of pricing. Prices solve coordination problems: imagine two individuals, Ann and Bob, who would like to trade a commodity (say, a book). Ann is willing to buy the book for no more than $100; Bob is willing to sell the book for no less than $80. Any price between $100 and $80 constitutes a possible contract: Ann of course would prefer to trade at a price close to $80, and Bob would prefer a price close to $100, but for both of them, agreeing on any price within that range is better than not trading at all.

The classic theory of market exchange predicts that in a perfectly competitive market commodities will be traded at the clearing price, that is, the price that makes the quantity demanded equal to the quantity supplied. This holds—*ceteris paribus*—for mundane goods like books and groceries, as well as for financial products like shares and bonds. Economists however have struggled to extend the theory to peculiar products like stock options or derivatives. Stock options give the opportunity to buy ('call') or sell ('put') a certain commodity at a given price in the future. They can be used to manage risk, protecting investments from unforeseen fluctuations in the price of stock or commodities. But suppose you want to buy an option: who is going to sell it to you, and how much will it cost?

Valuing options has been for centuries a major headache for economic theorists and practitioners. The lack of a sound theory of pricing in fact was one of the factors that delayed the development of markets for derivatives. The staggering diffusion of these products in the last three decades can be partly attributed to the introduction of a satisfactory pricing formula by Fischer Black, Myron Scholes, Robert Merton, and other financial economists in the 1970s.[11] Although the model is relatively complex, the basic idea of the Black–Scholes approach can be explained by means of a simple analogy. Suppose you want to know the weight of an item—an apple, for example—but you cannot measure it directly because it is never found separately from other commodities. As an alternative solution, you can try to determine its weight indirectly by measuring the weight of a basket that includes some apples and, say, some bananas, if you already know the weight of the bananas. Out of metaphor, in the case of option theory, the weight of an apple stands for the price of an option, and the basket of fruit for a 'riskless portfolio'. A riskless portfolio is a set of financial products the value of which is equal to the riskless rate of interest (the return of 'safe' government bonds). So if the portfolio is riskless, its price must be equal to that of government bonds (we know the weight of the basket, so to speak). And if the portfolio includes items of known value, by mere subtraction, we can derive the price of an option (see Box 2.1). The Black–Scholes formula generalizes this approach, whereby the price of an option is a function of the current price of the stock, the exercise price, the time it can be exercised, the interest rate, and the variance of the probability distribution of future prices.

MacKenzie stresses that the Black–Scholes model was important not just from a scientific point of view but also because of its practical applications. Black initially made money by selling spreadsheets with the estimated price of options in the Chicago derivatives market. This may seem a strange move: in principle, it would have seemed a good idea to keep the formula secret and to exploit the difference between the true price of options (which nobody else knew) and their market price. This technique, known as 'arbitrage', is widely used in the stock market, and is a crucial mechanism to keep prices close to their efficient value. Once Black and Scholes had decided to make the formula public for academic reasons, however, it made sense to circulate it among practitioners in a format that could be applied easily in the trading pit. Surprisingly, this move played an important role in the subsequent success of their model.[12]

It may be argued that without the formula, the market for derivatives would have not existed. Before the development of modern finance theory, option markets were underdeveloped because of the difficulty to determine the true value of derivatives. Another way to put it is that before the formula was made public, there were too many possible pricing equilibria. Two dealers could agree in principle to exchange options at several different prices, some of which however might have turned out later to be excessively high or low. The Black–Scholes model thus provided a way to identify one price as the *right* price. But for traders to act on such information, they had to believe the theory to be correct. The publication of the Black and Scholes model changed traders' beliefs about the value of options, and simultaneously it changed higher-order beliefs about other traders' beliefs: if I buy an option today for a price that I consider correct, I must be confident that I will be able to sell it tomorrow for a price that will not diverge too much from what I will consider to be the real value of the option. But I will be able to do this only if the other traders agree, that is, if they endorse the same theory that I use to determine the value of the option. The theory can work as a coordination device only if it is common knowledge among traders.

MacKenzie claims that the theory did play such a coordinating role. The Black–Scholes model, to begin with, 'inherited the general cognitive authority of financial economics' (2007, 70). In other words, it was seen by traders as *scientific* and as such provided a credible focal point for pricing in the derivatives market. Second, the model was *simple*: in spite of the underlying mathematical complexity, it was based on a small set of parameters and concepts that could be easily understood and discussed even by non-economists. This was crucial because traders had to use the formula in their everyday work, an activity that was facilitated by the spreadsheets prepared by Black. Finally, as already mentioned, the model was *publicly available*, because its inventors had decided to circulate it and to sell calculating tools (like Black's spreadsheets) that could be used by practitioners. Other models were not made available and thus never influenced traders' behaviour in the same way as the Black–Scholes equations did.

It is clear that the Black–Scholes model has the typical features of a successful coordination device, in the Schelling–Lewis sense. The first feature (epistemic authority) is analogous to the shaman's authority in the story of the previous section: even though nobody understands the fine details, the shaman is recognized to have a skill that no one else has, and his speech acts are taken on faith by other individuals. This is sufficient, in a situation of indeterminacy, to trigger convergence of beliefs and hence coordination. The second feature (simplicity) is also an important property of focal points: a salient strategy must be immediately identifiable by everyone, so as to short-cut complex chains of reasoning, and must lead straight to action. The third key feature is the uniqueness of the focal point—in this case, no other model could compete because no other model was commonly used by traders. Making the model public unwittingly ensured that it would act as an equilibrium selection device.

The Schelling–Lewis theory of coordination offers only a general account of the mechanics of coordination. The three features mentioned above are typical but by no means jointly necessary or sufficient to ensure coordination. Each one of them, moreover, is dependent on the instantiation of a number of psychological and social mechanisms that are context-specific and of which we only have a partial understanding. So the claim is not that publication sufficed to guarantee the success of the Black–Scholes theory but merely that its public circulation was an important element of the story. And the story probably involves a loop from theory to behaviour and from behaviour to theory again.

Box 2.1
The following example is borrowed from MacKenzie (2006, 285–288). Imagine a binomial world, that is, a situation that can only develop in one of two ways: in Future1, one unit of stock that today is worth $100 will be worth only $50 in, say, one year's time. In Future2, it will double its price and be worth $200. Now, what is the value (today) of a call option to buy a unit of that stock in one year at $150? If somebody asked you to sell such an option, how much should you request in exchange? To answer this question, we start from a riskless portfolio consisting of one stock plus the sale of three call options at $150. The crucial point is that the value of the portfolio in a year's time is $50 whatever happens. The proof is simple:

- If the price of stock goes down to $50 (Future1), the options will go unexercised, so the portfolio will be worth the value of one unit of stock ($50).
- If the price goes up to $200, you lose $3 \times (200 - 150) = \$150$ when the options are exercised, so the portfolio is worth one unit of stock ($200) − $150 = $50.

Moving from this simple idea, we can determine the price of the options. From the future nominal value of the riskless portfolio, we ought to subtract the rate of interest to obtain its discounted value. With a 5 % interest rate, for example, we would obtain $50 \times (1/1.05) = 47.62. Since the unit of stock is worth $100 today, the difference ($100 - 47.62 = 52.38) must be due to the three options; therefore, each option is worth $52.38/3 = 17.46. Notice that because prices change constantly, a riskless portfolio must be continuously adjusted. This is basically the technique used by hedge funds to manage risk, or to put 'ceilings' and 'floors' to potential gains and losses. Moving beyond a simple binomial world adds considerable complications, like the use of a log-normal distribution, but fortunately none of this is relevant for our purposes.

2.5 Performativity, Arbitrariness, and Failure

Before we proceed, let us examine a couple of objections that could be raised against this account. First, one might say that the Black–Scholes model could not work as a coordination device because the choice of the model was not conventional: no other theory could satisfy the scientific requirements of finance theory. Arguably, an option *must* have a Black–Scholes price, for example, because any other price would be vulnerable to arbitrage.

Notice however that vulnerability to arbitrage is an empirical hypothesis. Far from being a logically irrefutable statement, the Black–Scholes theory was based on a number of assumptions that could (and did, at some point) turn out to be wrong. Black–Scholes prices are correct only if certain conditions hold—if the market is perfectly efficient, for example—and we know that this is not necessarily the case. So the choice of the model was not forced by purely logical reasons. Its acceptance and its use required coordination among various players, as well as the setting up of institutional mechanisms that facilitated the functioning of the model and its use by traders in the derivatives market.

Second, one might say that the Black–Scholes model could not be a convention because its success did not depend solely on its acceptance: it is not true that any other formula proposed by a 'shaman' with epistemic authority would have worked equally well. The model had special features that made it fit a particular social and technological environment, and which explain its acceptance in a community that had previously rejected other pricing models.

Michel Callon (2007) has noticed that theories like the Black–Scholes model do not just depend on the beliefs of market participants. Callon claims that the Black–Scholes model could work correctly as a predictive device only in an adequate environment—a 'sociotechnical *agencement*', in his jargon. Callon defines an *agencement* as 'a combination of heterogeneous elements that have been carefully adjusted to one another [...] endowed with the capacity of acting in different ways depending on their configuration' (2007, 319–320). The emphasis on the materiality of *agencement* is meant to refute the account of performativity as a self-fulfilling prophecy:

> Whereas the notion of a self-fulfilling prophecy explains success or failure in terms of beliefs only, that of performativity goes beyond human minds and deploys all the materialities comprising the sociotechnical *agencements* that constitute the world in which these agents are plunged: performativity leaves open the possibility of events that might refute, or even happen independently of, what humans believe or think. (Callon 2007, 323)

Callon disagrees with the idea that the formulation of an economic theory (like a declaration or a speech act) is *sufficient* to bring about effects that are consistent with the theory itself. He points out that the background conditions may occasionally constitute obstacles to the fulfilment of a prophecy, preventing the theory from creating its own confirmatory effects. The Black–Scholes model in fact failed empirically, and failed for reasons that are independent of the beliefs of the economic agents.[13]

Callon's point about the fallibility of economic models is correct, although his distinction between performatives and self-fulfilling prophecies is questionable. Performative statements and self-fulfilling prophecies are two aspects of the same phenomenon. But most self-fulfilling prophecies, including performative speech acts, are dependent on the instantiation of background conditions that have little to do with agents' beliefs. Suppose that I say 'I'll meet you here at noon', for example. Suppose that with this sentence I am trying to influence your beliefs in such a way as to facilitate coordination. Successful coordination cannot depend exclusively on my speech act, surely, and its effect does not merely depend on your beliefs; a number of other background conditions must be in place, even if the belief mechanism works well. Perhaps you really intend to be here at noon, but one of your tires breaks along the way and as a consequence you do not show up. The prophecy has failed, for reasons that have little to do with your beliefs or mine. So the success of self-fulfilling prophecies does not depend on beliefs only. The self-fulfilling character of a speech act merely requires that it contributes to create expectations that—together with other background conditions—causally contribute to make the theory true (it is part of its perlocutionary aspect, in Austin's terminology). But it is always possible that some background conditions fail. Similarly, in the Black–Scholes case, traders' faith in the theory was an element that contributed to fulfil the prophecy, but other conditions were required for its successful performance.[14]

2.6 Constitution and Causation

MacKenzie's account of the Black–Scholes theory illustrates how an economic model may work as a coordination device. I will now argue that this is the same role played by paradigmatic performative speech acts like ceremonial formulae, promises, and appointments. If correct, this would legitimize the use of Austin's performativity in the new economic sociology programme.

In spite of the similarities, there may be non-trivial differences between the phenomena studied by economic sociologists and Austin's performative acts. An important difference, according to Mäki, concerns the relation between speech acts and institutional acts (or facts):

> The connection between speaking words and doing things is one of *constitution* rather than causation. Saying 'I apologize' constitutes the act of apologizing. Saying 'I agree' constitutes the act of agreeing. Those utterings do not *cause* those acts, rather they are constituted by those utterings. To utter those sentences is to take those actions. (Mäki 2013, 447)

Mäki goes on to say that the 'performative' theories studied by economic sociologists do not play the constitutive role that characterizes Austin's performative utterances: by stating a theorem or proposing a model, an economist may well change the beliefs and behaviour of market participants (a case of causal efficacy) without creating or constituting anything new. No 'Black–Scholes institution' comes into being when the formula is stated, as opposed to the way in which a promise, a president, a meeting, or a marriage comes into being when the relevant speech act is uttered. Another way to put it is that while performative statements are both illocutionary and perlocutionary acts, the 'utterance' (publication) of an economic theory can only be a perlocutionary act (see Mäki 2013, 449–450).

Mäki's critique is challenging, partly because the notion of constitution is notoriously difficult. The cases that philosophers have studied, moreover—like part–whole relations—are usually of little help to address the problems that we are concerned about.[15] To say that Michelangelo's statue of David is constituted by a certain piece of marble is to say that whenever the statue is there, the piece of marble is also necessarily there. Necessity here may be interpreted in a conceptual or in a more robust ontological fashion, but definitely not in a causal sense. The piece of marble does not cause or bring about Michelangelo's David: in an intuitive sense, it *is* Michelangelo's David, or at least a crucial aspect of the entity that we call 'David'. But the relation of constitution that applies to statues, however, does not necessarily apply to performative statements. Some philosophers in fact are convinced that invoking constitution in the case of speech acts is misleading, because the analysis of performatives does not require any esoteric metaphysical relation of this sort.

Ruth Millikan, for example, has argued that constitution is always either a semantic or a causal relation, and that the 'robust' ontological interpretation results from unnecessarily conflating the two. As she puts it in the abstract of a recent paper:

> Intentions and conventions can 'make a thing be what it is' in two different ways. Taken separately, neither has any magic in it at all. Neither produces objects of a kind that is in any way remarkable or that requires any special mode of understanding. Only by running these two ways together in our minds do we imagine 'socially constructed' or 'socially constituted' objects to be other than wholly mundane. (Millikan 2014, 27)

Many philosophers agree with Millikan on this point. Roughly speaking, the idea is that there is a semantic relation that corresponds to the illocutionary aspect of speech acts; and there is a causal relation that corresponds to the perlocutionary one. This way of framing the issue has some striking consequences: it helps seeing, in particular, that the essential aspect of performative statements is the perlocutionary or causal one, while the illocutionary (semantic) aspect is secondary and even dispensable.

The first step is to ask what, if anything, could be constituted by a performative speech act. In Searle's formula of constitutive rules, this amounts to ask what the Y-term stands for. Unfortunately, the 'X counts as Y' formula is elliptic, because the content of the Y-term is left undefined. To say that:

saying 'I do' in front of a priest counts as a getting married,

or that

being voted by the majority of delegates in a national election counts as being the President of the United States,

is vacuous unless we specify the meaning of the institutional Y-terms that appear in these formulae. What is 'to get married', and what is 'the President of the United States'? Joseph Ransdell (1971), Amedeo Conte (1988), and Frank Hindriks (2009) have pointed out that in order to make the meaning of constitutive rules explicit, it is necessary to expand the formula by adding another term that specifies the import of the institutional term. And in most cases, the import of the Y-term is a set of rules or actions that indicate what various individuals can or must do in various circumstances.

For example, in the case of marriage, the Y-term is associated with a series of rights and duties that regulate the behaviour of married couples. Husband and wife must support each other economically, are responsible for the welfare of their kids, have a right of sexual monopoly, and so on and so forth. Similarly, the rules of conduct of the President of the USA— what she can or must do—are specified in the constitution, in the legislation, and in the unwritten customs of US politics. Analogous accounts can be provided for other paradigmatic cases of performative speech acts, like promises, decrees, christenings, and so on.

In order to unpack the meaning of the Y-term, it is useful to modify the structure of constitutive rules by adding a Z-term that refers to the rules associated with the Y-term. The formula now becomes:

in C, X counts as Y and Y implies Z.

Even though this analysis seems innocuous, it has non-trivial consequences. The constitutive rule formula now gives the full definition of the meaning of the Y-term: X defines its denotation (the entities that are conventionally called Y) and Z its connotation (the normative consequences of being called Y, according to local conventions). This helps seeing how performatives can simultaneously describe and prescribe behaviour: they are, in the terminology of Millikan (1995), 'pushmi-pullyu representations'. But the XYZ formulation also shows that the Y-terms of constitutive rules are dispensable. If their meaning is captured by the X- and

Z-terms, then constitutive rules can be translated into simpler formulae where the Y-terms do not appear.

> When I say that the game-term [the Y-term] is eliminable, I mean that it has no *logical* function in the game that cannot be handled by its replacement with an expression of its import: aside from its (replaceable) function of linking connotation with import, the function of the term in the game is merely mnemonic and practical. (Ransdell 1971, 390)

There is no difference between, on the one hand,

> saying 'I promise to do A' counts as promising to do A, and promising to do A implies that you ought to do A (X counts as Y, and Y implies Z),

and, on the other,

> saying 'I promise to do A' implies that you ought to do A (X implies Z).

Now, the fact that Y-terms are eliminable does not mean that the social entities they refer to do not exist. Marriages, borders, promises, and presidents are very real things that we must retain in our ontology. The XYZ analysis of constitutive rules rather helps us appreciate what sort of things these institutional entities are. And once we see it more clearly, the idea that the illocutionary aspect of performative statements is primary becomes rather dubious. When Y is eliminated, the illocutionary aspect of the performative disappears, leaving only the perlocutionary one. This is the second striking consequence of the XYZ analysis, and the one that matters most for the purposes of this chapter.

So, to return to Mäki's argument, the idea that the relation between performative speech acts and institutional facts is one of constitution is probably a grammatical illusion. Even though it appears plausible when institutional entities and phenomena are described in XY terms, it becomes odd as soon as the full meaning of constitutive rules is unpacked using the XYZ formula. Take promising again: the content of 'you ought to do A' may be analysed in detail, specifying a set of things that the promisee is entitled to do if A is not done. The promisee can blame, criticize, get compensation from the promisor, for example. And these entitlements in turn may be specified by listing other actions that other parties (the police, the judiciary, the community members) are expected to implement (fining, expropriating, jailing, or just gossiping) in case the promisor does not fulfil her obligation. At bottom, an institutional term refers to a complex set of normative expectations.[16]

Similarly, to say that this garden is John's property means that Ann and Bob must not use it without his permission. That if they try to use it, and John applies reasonable force to keep them out, he believes that he will not be fined or jailed. That if John calls the police, he expects that they will help him, and so on and so forth. These beliefs and expectations constitute the institution of private property: in a very obvious sense, there are no genuine property rights in a society where people do not expect each other to enforce the actions implied by the Y-term.

Now, recall that according to Mäki (2013) institutions like promises, weddings, and so on are constituted by performative speech acts. But the idea of a constitutive relation linking speech acts with institutional facts loses much of its appeal once we realize that the Y-terms are eliminable. Take the following cases:

(1) Saying 'I promise to return the money' constitutes promising.

(1') Saying 'I promise to return the money' constitutes the expectation that people will form a bad opinion of you if you do not return it.

(2) Saying 'I do' constitutes getting married.

(2') Saying 'I do' constitutes the expectation that a judge will make you pay alimony if you betray me.

Although (1) and (2) sound grammatically correct; (1') and (2') are odd. But if the XYZ account of constitutive rules is right—as argued by Ransdell, Conte, and Hindriks—then we should take our intuitions regarding (1') and (2') seriously, because (1) and (2) are elliptic statements that include unanalysed institutional terms.

Clearly, the right way to adjust (1') and (2') is to recognize that the speech acts in question have *causal* force with respect to the expectations. Saying 'I do' *brings about* a set of beliefs concerning the actions of your spouse and of third parties. Uttering 'I promise to do A' *triggers* a set of expectations concerning your own actions and the actions that others will perform if you do not do it. But bringing about and triggering are causal relations, rather than relations of conceptual or ontological dependence. Once the meaning of the Y-term has been made explicit, it becomes apparent that the causal, perlocutionary aspect of performative speech acts is primary, while the illocutionary aspect is accessory.

If this is the case, then there is a close analogy between the effect of these performative speech acts and the causal effects of a theory like the

Black–Scholes model. 'Uttering' the Black–Scholes model creates shared beliefs about the correct way of pricing options, and sets in motion expectations concerning the behaviour of traders in the market. Mäki is right that stating an economic theory does not constitute a new institutional act, but this simply means that we do not use an institutional term to refer to its effects. It does not make it ontologically different from promising or marrying. The idea that there is a separate institutional act that is constitutively dependent on a speech act is as misguided as the idea that there is a thing that travels from Jill to Jack when she gives him a kiss. It is an illusion of grammatical form that is easily dispelled by reformulating the statement in an equivalent but ontologically less mysterious form.

Institutional facts are nothing but sets of actions and expectations about actions. Whether or not we use a special name to refer to the latter is irrelevant. Many familiar institutions are not associated with a Y-term: driving on the right-hand side of the road, for example, lacks a name. But Y-terms are eliminable and unnecessary, as we have seen, so driving on the right is a genuine institution like getting married or making promises: it stands for a set of actions (which can be described in Z-terms) that people must perform when driving, the shared expectation that most drivers will perform those actions, and that those who will not do it will be punished by the relevant authorities.

2.7 Concluding Remarks

My goal in this chapter has been to argue that economic sociologists have not illicitly appropriated the concept of performativity. In order to do so, I have outlined a theory of performativity that builds on the insights of Austin and his followers, with a little help from the theory of conventions of Schelling and Lewis. The latter helps to lay out the analogy between the coordinating role played by speech acts in ordinary institutional contexts, and the coordinating role that economic models may play vis-à-vis market behaviour. Since the effect of correlation devices on behaviour is primarily causal, I have defended this account from Mäki's charge of ignoring the fundamental constitutive role of performative speech acts. This required revisiting the illocutionary–perlocutionary distinction and analysing the deep structure of constitutive rules. Once institutional acts (and facts) are demystified, the analogy between Austin's performative speech acts and the coordinating role of theories like the Black–Scholes model becomes even more apparent. And with this step, my defence of the way in which performativity has been used in the economic sociology literature is complete.

It is important to stress that I have not offered an exegesis of what Austin or Searle meant when they originally articulated the notion of performative statement. The argument is based on a *theory* of performativity, which is partly independent of Austin's and Searle's texts because it addresses issues that they did not clarify, and ventures in areas that they did not explore. The claim that institutional facts are not constituted but caused by performative statements depends crucially on a specific interpretation of the content of Y-terms—namely the idea that they refer to sets of behavioural rules, and that the latter entail (normative) expectations. This idea is not widely accepted, to be sure. Some philosophers think that the notion of constitution is ontologically thicker, and disagree with the attempts made by Millikan and others to reduce it to more basic relations. As long as the concept of performativity is used as an explanatory tool in the context of a scientific research programme, however, I find the interpretation of performatives as coordination devices entirely natural and plausible. Whether there is more to them than this, is something that philosophers will continue to discuss for a long time, but that is unlikely to have much influence on the practice of social science.

Notes

1. See e.g. Callon (1998), MacKenzie (2006, 2009), Callon et al. (2007), MacKenzie et al. (2007).
2. In the sense that it is not creating any institutional fact; it is not misfiring as a piece of gameplay, of course.
3. The agreement may or may not be sanctioned by legislation; the important point in any case is that the rules do not hold by natural necessity.
4. Many philosophers consider the linguistic approach to social ontology based on constitutive rules incompatible with the scientific approach of game theory. This is not true, however, as Guala and Hindriks (2015), Hindriks and Guala (2015), and Hédoin (2015) try to explain.
5. See also Sugden (1986), for example.
6. The interpretation of Lewis' conventions as correlated equilibria is due to Vanderschraaf (1998). Correlated equilibria were introduced in the game-theoretic literature by Aumann (1974).
7. Something similar may have happened with promises: perhaps they began as rules that allowed Jill to punish Jack if Jack did not do what he said he would. In *The Genealogy of Morals*, Nietzsche (1887) outlines an intriguing story about the emergence of sociality based on this simple mechanism.

8. On the importance of public rituals for coordination, see Chwe (2001). Chwe emphasizes that the coordination device (or ceremony) must be common knowledge, so that the right system of mutual beliefs is in place. For a sceptical view on common knowledge requirements, see e.g. Binmore (2010).
9. Austin and Searle have stressed that a promise is not just a prediction (I'm not just saying 'I believe that I will give you ten euro next week'). The key point is that it creates an *obligation* that did not exist before. The obligation implies that if I will not give you ten euro next week, then you will be entitled to punish my behaviour—either informally (e.g. by reproach or ostracism) or formally (calling the police, or taking me to court). So the promise, if successful, changes a wide set of beliefs, for example, the expectation that other parties will help you get the money back if I do not return it.
10. See, for example Schiffer (1972) and Bach and Harnish (1979).
11. Since it is commonly known as the Black–Scholes theory or model, I shall use for simplicity that expression from now on. Scholes and Merton received the Nobel Prize in 1997 (Black had died two years earlier). The key publications are Black and Scholes (1973) and Merton (1973).
12. From now on, I will take the publication of a scientific model to be analogous to the performance of a speech act. This is potentially contentious, especially for those philosophers who take models to be non-linguistic entities. These philosophers agree, however, that models are routinely used to construct or derive linguistic statements (predictions, hypotheses), and that these statements in turn guide the behaviour of scientists and practitioners. For our purposes, we only need to claim that models provide signals and that these signals can be used for coordination.
13. At some point during the 1987 financial crisis, the theory seemed to work as a self-*defeating* prophecy—in the sense that it invited traders to take actions that increased the spread between predicted and actual market prices (MacKenzie calls it 'counterperformativity').
14. On this point, see also Brisset (2014).
15. For two notable exceptions, see Thomasson (1999) and Epstein (2015).
16. The idea is originally in Lewis (1969) but has been further articulated by Sugden (1986, 1998), Bicchieri (2006), and others.

References

Aumann, Robert. 1974. Subjectivity and Correlation in Randomized Strategies. *Journal of Mathematical Economics* 1(1): 67–96.

Austin, John. 1962. *How to Do Things with Words. The William James Lectures Delivered at Harvard University in 1955*. Oxford: Oxford University Press.

Bach, Kent, and Robert M. Harnish. 1979. *Linguistic Communication and Speech Acts.* Cambridge, MA: MIT Press.
Bicchieri, Cristina. 2006. *The Grammar of Society.* New York: Cambridge University Press.
Binmore, Ken. 2010. Do Conventions Need to Be Common Knowledge? *Topoi* 27(1–2): 17–27.
Black, Fisher, and Myron Scholes. 1973. The Pricing of Options and Corporate Liabilities. *Journal of Political Economy* 81(3): 637–654.
Brisset, Nicolas. 2014. Performativité des énoncés de la théorie économique: Une approche conventionnaliste. PhD dissertation, Université de Lausanne and Université Paris 1 Panthéon Sorbonne.
Callon, Michel. 1998. The Embeddedness of Economic Markets in Economics. In *The Laws of the Markets*, edited by Michel Callon, 1–58. Oxford: Blackwell.
Callon, Michel. 2007. What Does It Mean to Say that Economics is Performative? In *Do Economists Make Markets? On the Performativity of Economics*, edited by Donald MacKenzie, Fabian Muniesa, and Lucia Siu, 311–357. Princeton, NJ: Princeton University Press.
Callon, Michel, Yuval Millo, and Fabian Muniesa (eds.). 2007. *Market Devices.* Oxford: Blackwell.
Chwe, Michael Suk-Yong. 2001. *Rational Ritual: Culture, Coordination, and Common Knowledge.* Princeton, NJ: Princeton University Press.
Conte, Amedeo G. 1988. Semiotics of Constitutive Rules. In *Semiotic Theory and Practice: Proceedings of the Third International Congress of the IASS*, edited by Michael Herzfeldand and Lucio Melazzo, Vol. 1, 141–150. Berlin: DeGruyter.
Epstein, Brian. 2015. *The Ant Trap: Rebuilding the Foundations of Social Science.* Oxford: Oxford University Press.
Guala, Francesco, and Frank Hindriks. 2015. A Unified Social Ontology. *Philosophical Quarterly* 65(259): 177–201.
Hédoin, Cyril. 2015. Accounting for Constitutive Rules in Game Theory. *Journal of Economic Methodology* 22(4): 439–461.
Hindriks, Frank. 2009. Constitutive Rules, Language, and Ontology. *Erkenntnis* 71(2): 253–275.
Hindriks, Frank, and Francesco Guala. 2015. Institutions, Rules, and Equilibria: A Unified Theory. *Journal of Institutional Economics* 11(3): 459–480.
Lewis, David. 1969. *Convention: A Philosophical Study.* Cambridge, MA: Harvard University Press.
MacKenzie, Donald. 2006. *An Engine, Not a Camera: How Financial Models Shape Markets.* Cambridge, MA: MIT Press.
MacKenzie, D. 2007. Is Economics Performative? Option Theory and the Construction of Derivatives Markets. In *Do Economists Make Markets? On the Performativity of Economics*, edited by Donald MacKenzie, Fabian Muniesa, and Lucia Siu, 54–86. Princeton, NJ: Princeton University Press.

MacKenzie, Donald. 2009. *Material Markets: How Economic Agents are Constructed*. Oxford: Oxford University Press.
MacKenzie, Donald, Fabian Muniesa, and Lucia Siu (eds.). 2007. *Do Economists Make Markets? On the Performativity of Economics*. Princeton, NJ: Princeton University Press.
Mäki, Uskali. 2013. Performativity: Saving Austin from MacKenzie. In *Perspectives and Foundational Problems in Philosophy of Science, The European Philosophy of Science Association Proceedings*, edited by Vassilios Karakostas and Dennis Dieks, 443–453. Berlin: Springer.
Merton, Robert. 1973. Theory of Rational Option Pricing. *Bell Journal of Economics and Management Science* 4(1): 141–183.
Millikan, Ruth G. 1995. Pushmi-Pullyu Representations. *Philosophical Perspectives* 9: 185–200.
Millikan, Ruth G. 2014. Deflating Socially Constructed Objects: What Thoughts Do to the World. In *Perspectives on Social Ontology and Social Cognition*, edited by Mattia Gallotti and John Michael, 27–39. Dordrecht: Springer.
Nietzsche, Friedrich. 1887. *On the Genealogy of Morality*. Cambridge: Cambridge University Press, 1994 edition.
Ransdell, Joseph. 1971. Constitutive Rules and Speech-Act Analysis. *Journal of Philosophy* 68(13): 385–400.
Schelling, Thomas C. 1960. *The Strategy of Conflict*. Cambridge, MA: Harvard University Press.
Schiffer, Stephen R. 1972. *Meaning*. New York: Oxford University Press.
Searle, John R. 1969. *Speech Acts: An Essay in the Philosophy of Language*. New York: Cambridge University Press.
Searle, John R. 1995. *The Construction of Social Reality*. London: Penguin.
Sugden, Robert. 1986. *The Economics of Rights, Co-operation and Welfare*. Oxford: Blackwell.
Sugden, Robert. 1998. Normative Expectations: The Simultaneous Evolution of Institutions and Norms. In *Economics, Values, and Organization*, edited by Avner Ben-Ner and Louis Putterman, 73–100. New York: Cambridge University Press
Thomasson, Amie. 1999. *Fiction and Metaphysics*. New York: Cambridge University Press.
Vanderschraaf, Peter. 1998. Knowledge, Equilibrium and Convention. *Erkenntnis* 49(3): 337–369.

CHAPTER 3

Performative Mechanisms

Carsten Herrmann-Pillath

3.1 Towards Constitutive Explanations in Economics

This paper advances the idea that the current literature on performativity can be put on a stronger methodological footing if it is combined with the literature on mechanisms in the social sciences. I think that what authors such as Donald MacKenzie or Michel Callon actually did in their seminal contributions is presenting thick descriptions of *performative mechanisms*. Yet, what is missing is a general conceptual framework that allows to extend these thick descriptions into analytical approaches to causal explanations of the observed phenomena. This framework is provided by the methodology of constitutive explanations. In this paper, I merely sketch a few bare bones of this. The core task is to relate the notion of performativity to established bodies of research in economics. I think that the pivotal notion is that of incentives working on a given set of preferences in order to generate a certain behaviour, which underlies the different kinds of mechanisms about which economists propose generalizations that aspire to assuming the form of universal laws. Against this idea, I present the view that incentives and preferences are embedded into performative

C. Herrmann-Pillath
Witten/Herdecke University, Witten, Germany

mechanisms that generate behaviour, which implies that universal laws cannot be formulated, as performative mechanisms are local and contextualized in essence. In particular, performative mechanisms endogenize the causal loops between incentives and preferences, thus suspending the analytical independence between the two, which is the core condition for the possibility of generalizations about the causal link to behaviour.

Most economists maintain the implicit methodological stance of the 'covering law' benchmark for scientific explanations. This mostly means that given certain *ceteris paribus* conditions, economics can identify regularities in economic phenomena that are universal. As a consequence, economists also believe that there are certain causal mechanisms with most general scope that can be implemented in policy interventions to achieve a certain goal. For example, if economists can show that private property rights have certain universal efficiency features, they would recommend privatization as a standard policy under most circumstances. In practical applications, this might require to make the *ceteris paribus* conditions explicit, which would result in a much more detailed analysis of conditions of application, but without affecting the theoretical and methodological core.[1]

Consider as one example that I will further detail in Sect. 3.6 of this chapter, the 'legal origin' theories of corporate governance which claim that common law institutions are more efficient than civil law institutions in arranging for external finance. This claim is based on a conception of causality that underlies the design of pertinent econometric testing, suggesting recommendations for interventions that were rapidly picked up by organizations such as the World Bank. By this reasoning, a universal regularity was stated, and its application would follow the universal claim while judging certain conditions of application (such as the state of the court system). However, when this research was later scrutinized in more detail, it turned out that the causal parameters could not be defined in a de-contextualized way. For example, considering certain elements of corporate governance schemes, functional equivalences between apparently different elements in social practices were not identified, or the impact of extra-legal embedding determinants was overlooked. Once researchers try to catch these aspects in a more exact way, a principle of indeterminacy seems to hold: The causal relations in the econometrics vanish, and no universal regularity can be established anymore, resulting in an apparent trade-off between exactness and universality. The fundamental methodological issue that comes to the fore here is that of contextuality: Against the background of the standard econometric approaches, the different parameters and variables are mutually and externally contextualized, so that in the end, one can certainly maintain the idea that there is a causal interdependence between them, but has to acknowledge that this causality cannot be covered by generalizations that hold for a larger number of cases.

There are different possible reactions to problems like this one, which easily crop up in many specific areas of economic research. One is to maintain the covering law stance (and mostly refer to protective arguments such as the *ceteris paribus* clause), another is to search for alternative methodological frameworks. In this paper, I argue that this framework is the notion of constitutive explanations, or the analysis of 'mechanisms'. The notion of mechanisms has made a rapid career in the social sciences recently, but has rarely been received in economics so far.[2] For sure, there is the notion of 'mechanism design', but this differs fundamentally from the approach of constitutive explanations. 'Mechanisms' in mechanism design are mathematical structures that identify certain rules of games that relate individual strategic choices with a social value function defined by the designer, aiming at achieving the social optimum while incentivizing all agents to reveal truthful information. These are equilibrium solutions that do not identify causal mechanisms in the real world. If these mathematical models are applied to design real-world institutions, they actually refer to what is a causal mechanism, yet without identifying this directly. In other words, the 'mechanism' is a mathematical structure that is projected on real-world mechanisms, but without firstly trying to identify those causal mechanisms by means of theory-driven empirical research.[3]

In comparison, the notion of mechanism in the social sciences has been received from the sciences, in particular, the neurosciences. Here, mechanisms are conceived as multi-level complex causal structures, with different levels being approached by different disciplines or disciplinary subfields. The covering law criterion has been questioned by many philosophers of science over the recent decades, not only for principled reasons but also for the empirical observation that beyond physics, most sciences do not meet this benchmark, at least in current practice. In our context, this is certainly true not only for the social sciences in general but also for another field that focuses on the explanation of human behaviour, the neurosciences.[4] Both areas have got into close touch recently via the emergence of a new field in economics, namely neuroeconomics. This is part of a broader movement to introduce science-based methods into economics, behavioural and experimental economics. The question arises whether in such cross-disciplinary interactions, unification of methodological principles is necessary in order to achieve conceptual and empirical integration. Against this backdrop, the recent convergence of views about mechanisms in both the neurosciences and the social sciences is highly significant.

In this paper, beyond elaborating on the mechanism methodology in economics, I advance the additional thesis that in a general taxonomy of mechanisms, the specificity of the social sciences is that certain core mechanisms are 'performative'. I distinguish between two categories of mechanisms, causal mechanisms in general and performative mechanisms as a subset. The general notion of mechanism already includes the defining feature that mechanisms are productive: This means, the coming together of parts and levels in a composite structure generates effects that are novel in the sense of new combinations of causes and effects. Therefore, the notion of mechanism also plays an important role in evolutionary theories which aim at understanding the emergence of novelties: A neuronal structure is a mechanism that produces novel phenomena in the physical world. Mechanisms in the social sciences are a special case because the productive function has the additional property of performativity. A most important class of social mechanisms are institutions in the broadest sense, and, following Searle, we can approach these as being observer-relative facts.[5] A mechanism in the general sense is an observer-independent fact (neurons fire independently from observers watching them), whereas a social mechanism is an observer-relative fact in the sense that causes and effects are necessarily mediated by the cognitive or, more general, neuronal systems of the individuals whose interactions are part of the mechanism.

Stated in this way, it is important avoiding the conceptual short-cut that a performative mechanism is simply a more complex chain of causes and effects that includes physical phenomena of neuronal systems. This would define a reductionist position; constitutive explanations, however, are non-reductionist.[6] Neuronal systems enable symbolic behaviour, and so mediation means semiotic causation: An observer-relative fact is a fact that comes into existence because the productive mechanism incorporates signs that are produced by neuronal systems and that establish channels for information transmission between neuronal systems that are themselves physically mediated not by neuronal mechanisms but by signs (such as body movements, utterances, and artefacts). Semiotic causation enables performativity of social mechanisms. The crucial phenomenon in establishing semiotic causation is interpretation: The effect is constituted by the interpretation of the receiver of the sign, and hence in principle independent from the original intention of the sender. This theoretical framework, I argue, allows to provide the analytical foundation for the phenomenon of contextuality that I introduce in the example of 'legal origin' theories.[7]

Subsequently, I continue with outlining the basic conceptual framework for analysing performativity in terms of semiotic causality. I show that this is reflected in the cross-disciplinary literature on the relationship between incentives and preferences, thus violating the standard assumption in economics that preferences and incentives are perfectly separable. I demonstrate that an incentive structure is performative, implying that there are no universal regularities that allow transplanting certain general models of incentive structures into different contexts while keeping the chain between causes and effects stable and uniform. Finally, I draw conclusions for the analysis of corporate governance mechanisms and the related incentive structures.

3.2 A BASIC CONCEPTUAL FRAME FOR MODELLING PERFORMATIVE MECHANISMS

In this section, I add more detail to the basic framework for analysing performative mechanisms. I start out from further clarifying the two elementary terms: 'mechanism' and 'performativity'.

- A mechanism-based explanation is a *constitutive* one in the sense that explanations are based on the analytical and empirical identification of causal processes that are specific to time and space, hence do not result in universal regularities ('covering laws'). Mechanisms operate under the constraint of universal laws, but for the explanation of the observed regularities, the universal laws are not sufficient: Under conditions of scientific and disciplinary specialization, therefore, particular disciplines such as the neurosciences focus on the identification of mechanisms as the primary epistemic goal. Mechanisms are complex as they include different levels of aggregation, and mostly are part of larger structures in relation to which the mechanisms are separated via boundaries; across these, further causal interactions occur which involve the inputs and the outputs of the mechanisms. The most important aspect of disciplinary methodological standards is how they delineate the criteria of acceptable mechanistic explanations and

for causal relevance. Generally, this defines a naturalistic ontology, structured according to the criterion which entities are seen as having causal powers.[8]
- In the social sciences, some mechanisms have the special property that human cognitive systems are involved which enable intentional actions towards other individuals that are based on cognitive states through which interpretations of those actions are mediated. As a result, mechanisms include those cognitive states, and a full explanation requires the reconstruction of the specific ways how a mechanism emerges from cognitively mediated interactions between individuals. I call this 'performativity', and the causal process involved is semiotic or is 'semiosis'. Hence, whereas in the sciences mechanisms are givens (such as the physical structure of neurons), in the social sciences mechanisms are part and parcel of a social ontology of observer-relative facts that is continuously being created and reproduced by the individuals involved in interactions. In a nutshell, chains between external causes as inputs and behaviour as outputs are always mediated via cognitive states, which are distributed across many individuals, and are thus also determinants of the external causes.[9]

As a consequence, a social mechanism always manifests what I call a 'triadic' pattern of causation, involving both physical interactions between individuals and semiotically mediated interactions which can be embodied in the same physical phenomenon, but need not be. For example, if an individual hands over a banknote to another individual, this is the cause of a behavioural effect, but the effect cannot be explained by the mere physical fact of moving the banknote in space by means of bodily movements. The banknote is a sign, and semiotic causation necessarily involves the physical movement; both causal modes are indispensable for producing the effect, namely, a particular action of the receiver of the banknote. At first glance, that would suggest that semiotic causation supervenes on the physical movement. But a brief reflection shows that this is not the case, unless one adopts a naive sender–receiver perspective on the relationship. In this case, one would assume that the sender has the intention to use the banknote as a sign, and that this meaning is transferred to the receiver together with the physical item. However, as economists well recognize for the case of money, this does not match with the way how banknotes actually adopt the role of a sign, as this is only constituted on the level of the collective of individuals who mutually recognize this sign. Hence, we cannot apply the simple framework of efficient causality here that underlies the explanation of the physical movement of the banknote, although that might appear to be reasonable as long as we look at the interaction in isolation.[10]

Social mechanisms have a triadic structure that can be conceptualized as in Fig. 3.1, which depicts a semiotically mediated performative mechanism$_s$ in which a physical mechanism is a constituent part.[11] We consider a physical object O that is a cause in the mechanism that produces an effect. This is mediated via the physical structure of the mechanism$_p$ M. In our example, this is the physical transfer of the banknote. I emphasize that in analysing social mechanisms, the explicit treatment of physical aspects is indispensable, such as arrangements of individuals in space, temporal sequences of actions, the shape and properties of artefacts, or technologies of interaction.[12] However, the ultimate effect of the mechanism$_p$ is determined by the semiotic causation mediated via the sign S (mechanism$_p$ is a necessary but not a sufficient cause of the effect). This effect is relative to the interpretant I which refers to the sign S. Thus, between O and I, a relationship is established that is conventionally called 'meaning'. However, this is dependent on the embedding of the performative mechanism into a larger context, the social system, in which the effect in terms of the subsequent action has a function. Thus, semiotic causation establishes a conjunction of meaning and function. This is enabled by the role of the sign in categorizing the physical mechanism M. For example, the banknote has a particular value, and depending on the value,

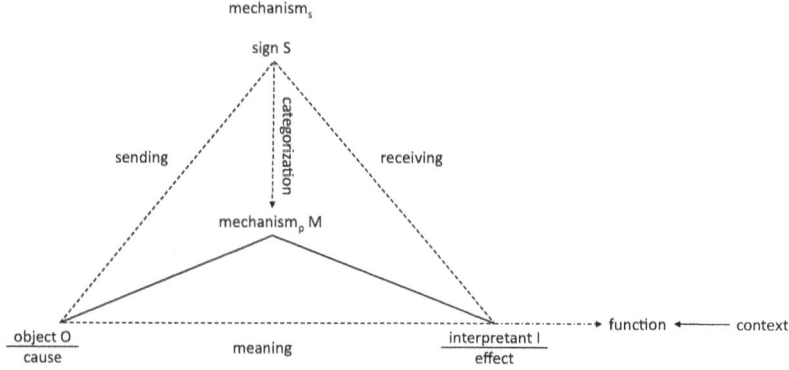

Fig. 3.1 Triadic causation in semiosis

a physically similar movement will lead to different effects in terms of subsequent actions of the interpretant *I*. The assignment of value is context-dependent, more specifically established by the usages of the sign in a population of interacting individuals.

I call the causal relationship between *O* and *I* 'bimodal', both physically and semiotically mediated. This turns *O* into an observer-relative fact, and is therefore, constitutive of the performativity of social mechanisms. It is important to emphasize that this does not depend on the individual intentionality of sign usages in social relationships: For example, the colour of the skin is a sign that operates independently from intentionally sending the sign. Further, the general category of 'sign' subdivides into different kinds, with different physical manifestations of the relationship between sign and object.[13]

I argue that performative mechanisms build on semiotic causation. Semiotic causation establishes performativity, which more specifically roots in the collective assignment of meaning to signs that trigger certain actions in a community of sign users. In this process, collectives of agents establish observer-relative facts, that is, social entities, and thereby, enrich the social ontology by creative acts. If we refer this view with the mechanism approach, we notice central elements, in particular, the identification of different levels (individual vs. collective) and objects (artefacts, embodied actions, individuals) and particular causal pathways that embed a mechanism into a larger unit (such as the embeddedness of the single action in a network of recurrent actions involving a collective). The triadic framework is just a most general conceptual structure guiding the more detailed analysis of performative mechanisms.[14]

3.3 Performing the Ultimatum Game: Which Way is the 'Right' One?

Analysing performative mechanisms as being based on semiosis has far-reaching methodological implications for understanding the relationship between external causes of actions and the actions that result from the causal impact. A covering law approach to incentives would assume that all human individuals are following the same principles of decision-making, so that a particular incentive structure would produce regular outcomes under *ceteris paribus* conditions. This is also the assumption that underlies the practical uses of 'mechanism design' theory: Then, results of game theory would be interpreted as stating universal laws across different actualizations of human behaviour. Interestingly, in practical applications of mechanism design theory, many additional activities are necessary that fine-tune the contexts and even the behavioural stances of actors in order to make sure that they 'perform' the mechanism in an appropriate way. This is what we have to expect against the background of the triadic model.[15]

In the triadic model, semiotic causation makes the role of the context explicit, thus rendering arguments obsolete that would refer such necessary adaptations of models to the real world as taking place in the *ceteris paribus* domain or during the necessary tinkering in turning theory practical. Some well-known examples are the simple experiments such as the ultimatum game: In approaching models in terms of the covering-law methodology, human individuals would be expected to manifest similar behaviour, independent from their actual contexts in everyday life, allowing for random variations. If this cannot be proven, explanations would have to consider the *ceteris paribus* conditions. These conditions include states of knowledge in the experiment, such as the beliefs of the individuals (hence cognitive states). However, these beliefs can differ from the conceptualization of the experiment by the researcher, resulting in different interpretations. A common phenomenon is that the individuals subsume the experimental situation under familiar types of interactions outside the experimental setting. This can explain systematic variations across different groups of individuals which share certain social contexts that result in these beliefs. Hence, the experiment cannot be fully controlled by the experimenter, in the sense that she would be the conductor who fully determines the way how the experiment is performed. The individuals perform the experiment autonomously, and consequently, we cannot identify universal regularities over different applications of a standard experimental setting. This performance is mediated via the semiotic causation that is driven by the interpretive acts of the test persons: The incentive structure causes their behaviour, but incentives are simultaneously signs.[16]

The game-theoretic structure underlying the experiment describes only one part of the real-world causal mechanism that links the incentives (pay-offs) with the results. The game-theoretic description of the performative mechanism is incomplete. Contrary to the expectations of the experimenter, the cognitive states are not fully described by the information that the participants obtain from the description of the game provided by the experimenter. The question is how far we can say that their state of knowledge is simply 'false beliefs': This may become evident if games are played recurrently, and individuals learn, so that they might finally converge to the 'rational' solution, hence perform the game according to the expectations of the experimenter. Yet, if this means de-contextualization in an artificial environment, we are not allowed to draw any conclusions about behaviour in a recontextualized real-life environment. Individuals simply perform the experiment differently. In the triadic framework, the experimenter achieves to impose another function on the interpretant *I*, which is to play the game properly; but this also changes the meaning of the sign, namely, the pay-offs.[17]

In the social sciences debate about mechanisms, this interdependence between cognitive states and outcomes of interactions is mostly referred to as 'self-fulfilling prophecy' in the sense of Merton's.[18] However, I argue that this is misleading, as the notion of self-fulfilling prophecy means that there is a belief that is initially false, but leads towards actions that changes the beliefs of others, resulting in further actions that ultimately confirm the original beliefs, thus rendering them truthful (like in the example of the bank-run triggered by wrong assessments of the financial status of the bank). If we call a mechanism 'performative', this is a much stronger proposition in the sense that the reference for the truth value of a belief is endogenous to the process even to the degree that it does not exist independently from the process under scrutiny. This reflects the creation of observer–relative facts via semiosis. The standard example for this is money, which does not exist before being performed collectively (to the opposite, the financial status of a bank in the bank-run does exist already).

Consider the case of the ultimatum game, again. Can we really say that playing the game 'correctly' turns originally false beliefs into true beliefs? This question touches upon a foundational issue in behavioural and experimental economics, namely the existence of social preferences in human individuals. Do subjects 'unlearn' false preferences in correct treatments of the experiment? Are these therefore 'errors'? Are we justified in judging the learned preferences as the 'true' ones? I argue that these questions do not grasp the real meaning of the ultimatum experiment, which in all the realizations actually involves the working of performative mechanisms.

3.4 Incentives Performing Preferences

Interestingly, the issue of human sociality is raised in many different disciplinary contexts, under different labels. What is 'social preferences' in behavioural economics is 'collectivism' or 'allocentrism' in psychology, or 'empathy' in the neurosciences. In the neurosciences, interest is directed at the question whether there are universal human (neuro)biological features that condition certain kinds of social behaviour. If that could be proven, this certainly would have implications for the other disciplines. In psychology, the issue is partly seen as an aspect of individual psychological properties, but in the context of collectivism, mainly as a cultural feature. This differs from the neuroscience question about universal human properties in hypothesizing that there are cultural properties shared by individuals belonging to the same social group which are stable in the long run; some groups might manifest higher degrees of collectivism than others. At first sight, both the neurosciences and the psychological approach would suggest that there is a set of fixed properties that would also be reflected in certain 'true beliefs' about the degree of other-mindedness among a group of human individuals. However, this expectation has not materialized.

In the neurosciences, research on empathy has resulted in a complex mechanism-based explanation that combines bottom-up and top-down processes, hence multi-level causal feedback loops. In a nutshell, there are certain species-specific neuronal mechanisms that enable other-oriented cognitive states and respective behaviours, but at the same time, these are only triggered under certain conditions which depend on higher-level states of knowledge mediated by symbolic systems, hence semiotically caused, in my parlance. In particular, this refers to cognitive categorizations of other individuals into in-group and out-group members, with no 'natural' delineation of the group in question. Although this behavioural tendency towards 'groupishness' is presumably a universal feature of humans, this fact alone cannot explain group boundaries under specific circumstances. Hence, one cannot identify universal regularities of human social behaviour rooted in shared biological properties but only complex mechanisms of empathy that involve different ontological levels and kinds. This result can be easily put into the triadic framework: The mechanism$_p$ is the neurophysiological structure that is triggered by certain sensory inputs and generates certain bodily reactions, but these reactions can only be fully explained via the mechanism$_s$, that is, the semiotic categorizations. Emphatic behaviour has a function in the larger context of social systems, and there is no universal mechanism, as these functions are specific to particular social systems located in space and time. In other words, empathy is a performative mechanism that includes neuronal structures as mediating physical entities, but does not simply supervene on these structures, being embodied in mechanisms that reach far beyond the brain, including social systems and the signs used therein.[19]

In psychology, suffice to mention one line of thought dubbed the 'ecological approach to culture'. This rejects the idea that people carry along certain inherent cultural characteristics such as 'values' that define their degree of 'collectivism', but posits that in social interactions, individuals take actions that create a certain environment unintendedly which incentivizes their behaviour in a way such that a stable pattern of interaction is achieved reflecting certain regularities which are context-specific (the 'niche'). This results in a conjunction between those incentives and cognitive states, that is only broken when fundamental parameters of the interaction are changed, especially involving the symbolic representations through which the interactions are mediated. As a result, what appears to be an internal 'value' explaining behaviour in terms of efficient causality (the value causes an action pattern), turns out to be a context-dependent regularity that is triggered by certain semiotic mechanisms. Once the experimenter achieves de-contextualization, the 'value' disappears.[20]

Both strands of research on human sociality therefore result in a general hypothesis about performative mechanisms that underlie social behaviour: Incentives, cognitive states, and symbolic media work together in generating performative actions that establish degrees of sociality specific to time and place. Therefore we cannot state a universal regularity about the degree of 'other-mindedness' of individuals. The 'mechanism' that is stated in the game-theoretic structure of the ultimatum game cannot be extended to a 'covering law' that is empirically meaningful. This also implies that we certainly can de-contextualize the behaviour of individuals by appropriate experimental settings, thus apparently producing evidence on the validity of 'rationality' as a universal human characteristic. However, this is only another instance of performativity, imposed by the experimenter.

Fortunately, a related view has been also articulated in economics recently, mostly under the heading of 'framing'. There is a large and growing literature showing that individuals do not have a fixed endowment with preferences that manifest a certain degree of 'sociality', but that 'social preferences' are endogenous to the context of a certain situation of choice, and in particular how choice is framed. In their comprehensive review of this literature, Bowles and Polanía-Reyes (2012) employ a general structure which directly matches with my model of triadic semiotic causation (Fig. 3.2). They argue that the standard economic view

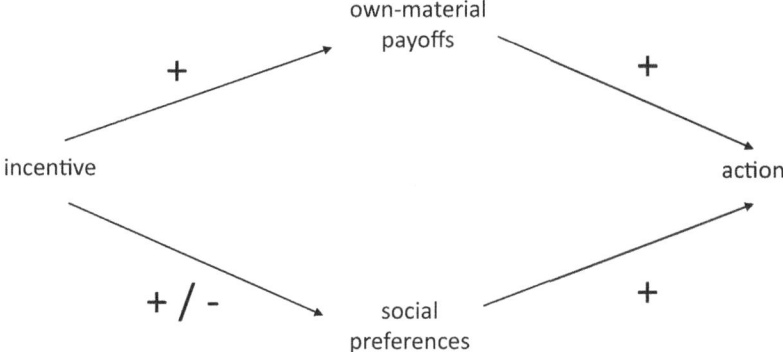

Fig. 3.2 Incentives and social preferences (following Bowles and Polanía-Reyes 2012)

posits the 'separability' thesis: Incentives work independently from the given level of social preferences in generating behavioural outcomes. To the contrary, there is ample evidence that incentives also change the level of social preferences, so that there can be both crowding in and crowding out in terms of the resulting behaviour. This results in a two-channel or, in my parlance, 'bimodal' model of causation that connects incentives and actions.

Bowles and Polanía-Reyes categorize the precise effects into four groups, always considering the introduction or the strengthening of a material incentive to perform a certain action.[21]

- The incentive changes the framing of an action such that self-interested motivation becomes salient and is seen as legitimate. This even applies for behaviour that does not involve social preferences at all: For example, introducing a fine on a certain behaviour can increase its frequency because the fine is interpreted as a price that is paid for allowing deviance.
- The incentive is interpreted as an information about the relatively low share of individuals with social preferences in a population, and increases uncertainty about the motivation of observed cooperative behaviours, that is, whether this behaviour is signalling social preferences. Therefore, the incentive decreases individual motivation to act socially.

- The incentive signals information of the designer about her assessment of the distribution of types in a population, and also gives information about how she perceives the nature of the action to be performed.
- The incentive reduces the sense of individual autonomy and therefore triggers resistance.

Resulting from these four constellations, there is no universal regularity between certain incentive structures and observed behaviour. We notice that economic research concurs with the aforementioned research in other disciplines, and suggest the interpretation that there is no fixed pattern of sociality in human individuals, but that sociality is based on performative mechanisms that result from the interaction between the environment of choice and distributed cognitive states in the group of interacting individuals, mediated by semiotic causation. Thus, incentives are always being interpreted, and interpretation is always contextualized. Scientific analysis, however, has to move beyond this general statement and needs to make the performative mechanisms explicit that result in particular causal chains between incentives and actions.

3.5 Semiotic Causation and Performativity of Incentive Systems

The economic problem of sociality raises an intricate question about the nature of incentives as signs. This is straightforward to grasp in the triadic model: The incentive as object O is at the same time the material embodiment of the sign S. Hence, there is a direct function of the incentive in creating the performative mechanism that produces the 'performance' of the incentivized individual. Bimodal causality works embodied in one single physical form. This is not a necessary feature of incentive systems but the most interesting case for our discussion.[22]

In terms of the economic conceptualization of preferences and choices, bimodal causality means that the incentive exerts causal effects via two channels. One channel is the direct effect on choice mediated by the given structure of preferences. The other channel works via the circumstance that this structure of preferences is also shaped by the effects of the incentive on cognitive states. This implies that preferences are not independent from the incentives. The following action is caused bimodally, ending

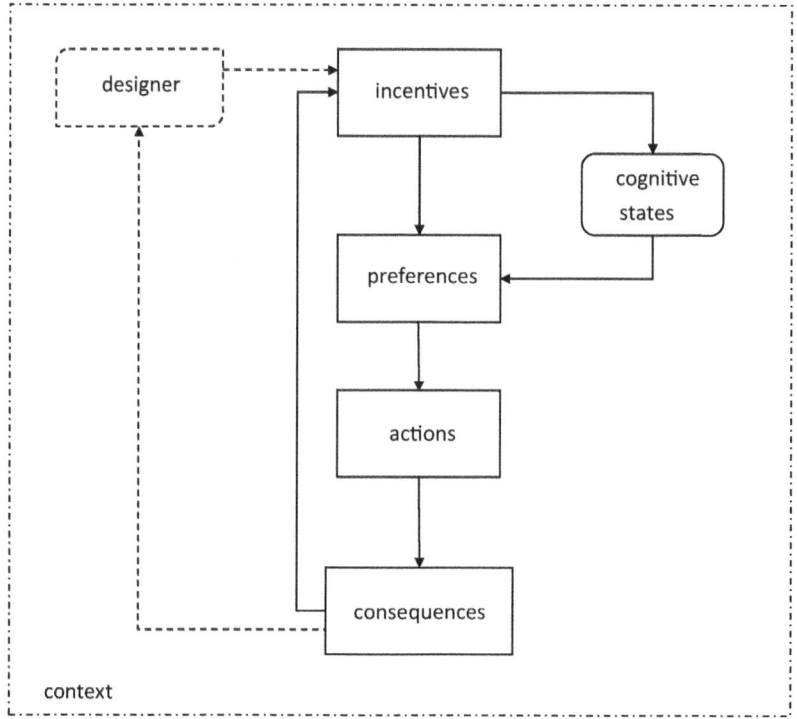

Fig. 3.3 Bimodal causation in incentive systems

up with certain consequences (pay-offs). These consequences work as incentives, in turn, thus resulting in feedback mechanisms. We end up with a recursive structure as pictured in Fig. 3.3. Here, I add the role of the designer of the system, because the interpretation of incentives certainly is changed fundamentally when interpretation also involves reference to the supposed intentions of the designer to create the system. Yet, this remains a simplified picture because I do not include the obvious mediating role of the designer's cognitive states in the perception of consequences and in her response.

How do the incentives influence the structure of preferences? Building on the previous summary of Bowles and Polanía-Reyes, I add some detail and emphasize the following.

- Under conditions of incomplete and imperfect information, all individuals are aware of the fact that their action consequences will depend on the behaviour of others; therefore, they need to construct beliefs about the preferences of others and their cognitive states. Then, the incentive system provides information about the composition of types of individuals in a population. This can directly involve reference to the designer of the system, because individuals may reasonably conclude that the designer of the system has designed it according to her information about that distribution. For example, as an employer, she may have even selected individuals according to those criteria. If the incentive system is geared towards individualistic behaviours, individuals may adapt their preferences to this information.[23]
- The qualitative nature of incentives influences the way how situations of choice are perceived, especially in terms of interactions with others. In particular, it is not warranted that monetary values are just approximations to underlying preferences. Monetary incentives change frames of valuations and even induce shifts across categories of valuations. For example, monetary expressions of value induce behaviour that is more individualistic, and they shift the reference frame towards an exchange context focusing on notions of reciprocity, in comparison with the direct benefits of action consequences.[24]
- Most generally, any kind of incentive system shifts the balance between intrinsic and extrinsic motivation. This effect is the more pronounced if the incentive system is cast in quantitative terms and can be anticipated in terms of the action consequences. If we consider the previous point, the effects of monetary incentives are actually twofold: one is the effect of the quantification and targeting of the incentive, the other is its explicit casting into monetary terms.[25]

The result of this analysis is unequivocal. Incentive systems are social mechanisms, and therefore, are performative. As performative mechanisms, they involve distinct elements, such as the roles of designer and actor, the physical entities that represent the incentive system (such as operating procedures), or the entities in which the incentives are embedded and embodied (such as numbers in bank accounts). These elements are causally connected in a bimodal way, mediated via semiosis, that is, interpretations on part of the actors. Finally, these mechanisms are embedded into the context of the social system, such as the organization that implements the system. There is no way to predict the effects of certain incentives based on a universal regularity of causation. Causation is always semiotically mediated, and the same incentives can lead to very different behavioural responses, depending on the way how they are interpreted.

Incentive systems are important elements in the real-world design of economic institutions and organizations. The upshot of my analysis is that one cannot directly transfer results of generic economic models of incentive systems into particular social contexts. A real-world incentive system is a performative mechanism that extends beyond the part of the social system that is subject to the direct intervention of the designer of the system. In practice, this means that the designer would have to contextualize the incentive system. Naturally, this raises the question how to identify the relevant contexts. A case in point is the aforementioned issue of corporate governance institutions.

3.6 Implications for the Analysis and the Design of Corporate Governance Mechanisms

The case of corporate governance is of interest here, because it involves different forms of performativity. In the recent decades, corporate governance schemes have diffused across the globe that build on modern economic theory, such as principal-agent theory, transaction cost economics, and incomplete contract modelling. The problem driving these developments is the division between ownership and management in the modern public corporation: How can managerial behaviour be aligned with shareholders', that is, owners' goals? The theoretically grounded corporate governance schemes are themselves complex mechanisms, involving institutional regulations of the interaction between different groups and bodies of the corporation, and including a range of high-powered incentive systems for top-level management. These schemes originated in the Anglo-Saxon world, and are being promoted as best practices grounded in theory until today, with prominent cases as the ongoing reforms of corporate governance in Japan. One conspicuous feature of this diffusion is that on the one hand, the corporate governance schemes are seen as particular mechanisms that can be copied in other societal, cultural, and political contexts, and that on the other hand, these contexts are often blamed for dysfunctional performances of corporate governance. At the same time, however, there is no general agreement about the idea that the corporate governance schemes being promoted are factually the most efficacious ones. One issue highlighted in the 'post-Piketty' world is the possible impact on rising inequality and a disconnection between managerial compensation and actual performance.[26]

Compared to the real-world use of mechanisms derived from generic reasoning in economics, according to the results of the previous sections, a mechanism in the domain of the economy would be conceptualized as a causal structure that involves a complex social ontology, namely constituent units and levels of the underlying performative mechanisms. For example, one would consider individuals, groups, or institutions as parts of the mechanism of corporate governance, as well as different specific mechanisms that establish their interactions, in particular focusing on semiotic causation. We would no longer approach a corporate governance mechanism based on de-contextualized economic models. Instead, we would reconstruct empirically the social ontologies that embed these mechanisms and show how they result in a certain pattern of 'performing performances', in the sense of performatively producing certain outcomes of actions.

In the first section, I have already referred to the 'legal origin' theories of corporate governance which are of special interest here as they start out from empirical research about determinants of external finance, and ground the interpretation of the results on economic theory.[27] This research posits a causal linkage between a set of variables that affect performance in terms of making external finance available at lowest costs and largest scope. At the same time, the argument operates on a higher level of aggregation in claiming that entire legal systems historically determined the emergence of these differences in performance, such as civil law versus common law. This is a multi-level analysis which was then tested statistically without making the underlying mechanisms explicit. When this research was put under closer scrutiny, serious empirical flaws became apparent. These flaws can be interpreted in terms of inaccurate and biased conceptualization, identification, and measurement of social mechanisms, in particular[28]:

- The list of potentially relevant elements of corporate governance mechanisms was incomplete;
- Functional equivalences of included elements were not properly identified; vice versa, different functions of similar elements were not recognized;
- Measurement criteria were implicitly referring to US conditions as benchmark;

- The boundaries of the mechanisms were not properly identified and the role of extra-legal factors in determining performance was not recognized.

If researchers improve the empirical approach, they reach the conclusion that, on the one hand, it is possible to explain improvements of corporate governance and their effects for single countries through historical times, but that at the same time, statistical regularities across countries are difficult to establish. This clearly indicates that the research factually resulted in the identification of mechanisms that are specific to time and place, but cannot achieve generalizations over time and place.

I take this result as an indication that corporate governance schemes are performative: The 'legal origins' theory failed to take account of the contextualization of elements of corporate governance. This compares with the development of mainstream theory of corporate governance that converged on a shareholder-value paradigm in the recent decades. Against the background of the aforementioned problem structure resulting from the separation of ownership and management in the public corporation, the proposed mechanism mainly focuses on directly activating the investor's valuations of companies on the capital markets in incentivizing the executive managers' behaviour via specific compensation schemes. This transition was part and parcel of a broader trend of 'financialization' of capitalist economies.[29]

This process has met a lot of criticism, both scholarly and public. As in the case of the 'legal origins' theories, which are closely connected to it, the idea is that one single mechanism is the most efficient one, and that the entire institutional set-up has to be geared towards this goal. However, if corporate governance mechanisms are performative, this assumption is not warranted. This point can be made in two different, though closely related ways. The first is to consider the interaction between corporate governance institutions and the economic system in general, the other is to scrutinize specific incentive systems which are parts of the corporate governance arrangements.

Without referring to performativity explicitly, Aoki's model of the cognitive division of labour is actually presenting corporate governance as a performative social mechanism.[30] Aoki argues that there are different ways how the knowledge is distributed in a company that determines its competitive success. In my framework, competitive success is a function, and the governance mechanism is designed to mediate between certain incentives, behaviours, and this function. Aoki uses the term 'cognitive assets' and adopts the perspective of distributed cognition theorists: Cognitive assets are not strictly individualized but are distributed across individuals and technological artefacts.[31] This has implications for the distribution of decision rights. For example, if cognitive assets are mostly individualized on part of the managers, workers' participation would introduce inefficiencies in incentivization, and vice versa, if workers' cognitive assets are highly complementary to managers' cognitive assets, a participatory corporate governance mechanism would be more efficient.

However, these interdependencies cannot be simply cast into a universal regularity in turn, because they are performative. Performativity emerges on different levels, thus revealing a complex structure of performative mechanisms. First, within the company, the distribution of cognitive assets is endogenous to the corporate governance scheme. For example, if workers are excluded from decision-making procedures in the company, they are lacking incentives for adopting skills and knowledge that are highly complementary to managers' cognitive assets, and vice versa. Second, the distribution of cognitive assets is partly determined by other institutions in the economy, such as education and training and the labour market structures in general. The more portable skills are across companies, the lower are the incentives for forming company-specific or complementary skills. As a result of these and similar effects, similar levels of corporate performance can be achieved by different mechanisms of corporate governance. However, this is not simply a self-fulfilling mechanism, because performativity depends on certain determinants that remain givens, in particular technology. Even though technology can also be performative, the question is how far the temporal and spatial contiguities play together in enabling performativity. For example, the Silicon Valley Hi-Tech model typically even enables the outsourcing of the entire production process, because there are very low complementarities of cognitive assets between workers and high-skilled managers and engineers.[32]

Evidently, it is not possible to define a 'one size fits all' corporate governance scheme only taking theoretical analyses of the generic problems of principal–agent relations, asymmetric information, and so on into consideration. On the systemic level, corporate governance schemes become performative via the endogenous adaptation of the 'cognitive division of labour' in the economic system, thus changing the perception of the incentives that emanate from a certain corporate governance structure.

The other aspect to be discussed here is the incentive systems in the narrow sense, such as the stock option schemes. Here, we can directly apply the results of the previous section. Interestingly, it has been argued that the transition to those systems was also bolstered by management education, thus also establishing a possible case for the performativity of economic theory in conjunction with incentive structures. This argument runs in the following way. If education of managers is based on the mainstream theories about corporate governance and incentive schemes, as explicitly done in textbooks of managerial economics, students actually learn about the distribution of types at least in the environment of companies. So they will adopt the respective patterns of individualistic preferences. This confirms the expectations of the theorists and the designers of incentive systems, and therefore even empirically vindicates the underlying theories. This mechanism can be also supported by separating equilibria in sorting individuals with different levels of social preferences into different environments.[33]

Further, we can apply the entire range of particular hypotheses about the performativity of incentive systems here, such as regarding the trade-off between intrinsic and extrinsic motivation when extrinsic incentives are quantified and announced in advance, or on the priming effects of money on behaviour. In the light of these hypotheses, one can argue that the introduction of high-powered incentive systems that directly aim at individual behaviour will also change the regularities that are assumed to hold for this behaviour. Indeed, one would expect that the behavioural patterns become more similar to the assumptions of opportunism and individualist rationality.

If we take together these two perspectives on corporate governance schemes, the institutional and the incentive structure, we realize that such schemes are in fact complex performative mechanisms with a high degree of contextualization. One important consequence is that similar incentive systems can operate in a different way at different times and places. This applies also on different levels of analysis: A corporate governance scheme can operate under the contextualization of single companies, working for one case and failing in another, or can be contextualized on higher levels, such as referring to national-level institutions and culture. For example, the Japanese system was working well after World War II into the 1980s. Since then, strong pressures emerged reforming the system, theoretically conceived as convergence to the Anglo-Saxon model. However, the process is slow and protracted, thus reflecting the complexity of the causal determinants. New mechanisms will also show idiosyncratic features, though of a different kind.

3.7 Conclusion

In this paper, I propose that the literature on performativity should be combined with the literature on social mechanisms in order to create a powerful approach to understanding and explaining the variance of human behaviour across different institutional contexts. This requires a fundamental shift in the methodological conceptualization of the economist's work, namely from a 'covering law' view to a 'constitutive explanations' view.

In more detailed work, constitutive explanations require the precise identification of levels of social ontology, kinds of particular mechanisms and types of social entities that are involved in a constitutive explanation. I have provided a few hints with the example of corporate governance schemes. One important consequence of this is that for the analysis of mechanisms in the economy, economics as it stands is not sufficient. There is a huge explanatory gap between economic theories and the derived models and the mechanisms that work in the real world. As in the reference case for constitutive explanations, the neurosciences, the analysis of economic mechanisms is multi-disciplinary, involving the entire range of the social sciences, and also disciplines such as psychology or biology. Therefore, the mechanism approach is also providing a framework of disciplinary integration. However, it is important to get the direction of the underlying theoretical effort right here: The theoretical achievement in terms of providing explanations of real-world phenomena is the identification and substantiation of a mechanism. It is the mechanism that defines the patterns of cross-disciplinary integration, and hence these patterns can differ across different mechanisms. We cannot achieve cross-disciplinary integration in directly linking theoretical premises and results of the different disciplines.

This is especially important when we consider the phenomenon of performativity. As has been amply demonstrated by experimental economics, human behaviour can be shaped by the proper establishment of mechanisms that trigger certain performances. As such, the experiments do not test given theoretical hypotheses, but are actually implicit instructions how to design real-world institutions in order to generate similar behavioural results. If we create incentive systems based on the assumption of rational opportunism, we also create the agents that behave according to these predictions. By implication, the patterns of cross-disciplinary linkages are also endogenous to the application of the theories in the real world, again making any vision of a particular pattern of cross-disciplinary integration obsolete.

In other words, theorizing about human behaviour and social systems means to work on inventories of performative mechanisms, possibly resulting in taxonomies, historical and evolutionary trajectories. This is the true sense in which the economist becomes a naturalist. The first task of the economist-as-naturalist is to grasp the complexity and diversity of human behaviour in institutionalized contexts, and only then to work out regularities that apply across them. These regularities may in turn be rooted in universal laws, which apply for certain aspects and elements of the mechanisms that define the social ontology of the economy. In spite of being universal, however, they can only offer partial explanations of the causal processes that are mediated by complex performative mechanisms.

Notes

1. On the central role of *ceteris paribus* assumptions in the covering law approach to economic hypotheses, see Hausman (1992: 131ff, 2013: 14ff). Hausman argues that these clauses enable economics to maintain 'inexact laws'. Of course, the precondition is that there is a precise and reliable method to distinguish between acceptable and unacceptable c.p. clauses (on the complex questions here, see Reutlinger et al. (2015)).
2. For a comprehensive survey of this literature, see Hedström and Ylikoski (2010) or the volume edited by Demeulenaere (2011). This is mostly pursued under the heading of 'analytical sociology', but contributing strands of thought are broader in scope, including seminal works such as Elster (1989). Philosophically, an important pacesetter was Bhaskar (1989), although this example also shows how the reception in economics was ending in a heterodox cul-de-sac that left no impact on mainstream economics (so-called 'realism' à la Tony Lawson). For a rare reception of the mechanism methodology in economics, see Vromen's (2011) analysis of routines as multi-level mechanisms.
3. For example, an auction is a 'mechanism' in mechanism design theory with certain optimality features. In the real world, auctions often do not work as designers imagine. For example (see The Economist, August 29, 2015: 60), on the eBay website, the share of auctions has been declining continuously, partly because of the 'hassle costs' of auctions. One cause of these costs is

'sniping', when users wait until the last minute in order to submit a winning bid, thus disappointing other bidders. The experience of sniping drives many users away from auctions. Systematic research on empirical issues of mechanism design models include, for example, the experimental testing of the solutions of the hold-up theorem provided in the theory of incomplete contracts (Maskin and Tirole 1999; Maskin 2002), which were widely regarded to resolve this problem; Hart (2009) therefore declared it as obsolete for theories about contracting and the firm. Yet, this strong conclusion was only tested recently by experimentalists (e.g. Fehr et al. 2014; Erlei and Roß 2014). Erlei and Roß, for example, show that the sheer complexity of the theoretical mechanisms may give a role to bounded rationality in determining the experimental subjects' choices, which systematically and strongly diverge from the theoretical predictions.
4. Neuroscience research has been the most important object of studying mechanistic explanations in philosophy of science, with path-breaking contributions such as Craver (2007).
5. Searle (1995) distinguishes between observer-independent and observer-relative facts, thus assigning the ontological status of existence to both. For example, a tree is an observer-independent fact, a holy tree is an observer-relative fact. The property of 'holiness' can cause a change of state on part of the observer (such as fear), and thus exists in terms of having causal powers.
6. Craver (2007: 107ff, 233ff) distinguishes between the reductionist and the systems tradition in neuroscience, showing that in spite of the fact that many neuroscientists pursue a reductionist agenda, the field advances in developing multi-level integrative theories about complex mechanisms that produce a certain phenomenon in question.
7. Typically, reference to interpretation appears to entail hermeneutic approaches. However, even purely naturalistic theories of communication such as Aunger's (2002: 255ff) argue that communication in populations of agents communicating via signals cannot be viewed in the sender–receiver paradigm, but as a population-level phenomenon in which the effects of communication events on the receivers determine the meaning, and not the intentions of the senders. In fact, this amounts to the naturalization of Wittgenstein's approach to meaning. In my definition of a 'social' mechanism, I actually stay in line with Max Weber's definition of a 'social action' as being a type of action which intrinsically relates to actions of others.
8. This understanding of 'naturalism' follows Bhaskar (1989) and should not be misunderstood as 'physicalism', although the general assumption of physical closure of the world would hold (Papineau 2009). In Bhaskar's view, assigning causal powers to entities is constitutive for defining the ontology that underlies the design and testing of theories. So, in the social sciences constructing mechanisms is tantamount to creating a social ontology.

9. The current literature on performativity includes a range of different uses of the term, which my most general definition covers. One important strand is to investigate into the performativity of economic theories, following seminal contributions such as MacKenzie (2006). I treat a 'theory' simply as an instance of a cognitive state which is mediated via the artefacts that embody the theory (such as books and experimental devices). Callon (2007) extends this approach by including all ideas, practices, and devices that enable economic action, such as accounting practices. I have further expanded this approach to include materially mediated cognitive states in general (Herrmann-Pillath 2010, 2012a). This notion is also more general in not only referring to strong 'Barnesian' performativity in the sense of MacKenzie (2007) but also including all phenomena that relate to the emergence of collective intentionality via human interaction, in the sense of Searle (2010) or Tuomela (2007). This use is grounded in the original meaning of performativity in speech act theory.
10. In fact, this analysis is standard lore in the philosophy of language, referring to the overcoming of referential theories of meaning to rule-based theories which relate meaning to conventions and practices in communities of language users, for a survey, see e.g. Lycan (1999). Searle's theory of institutions transfers this fundamental shift of perspective to the analysis of institutions.
11. This diagram is a modification of standard graphic representations of Peirce's semiotics in biosemiotics, see, for example, El-Hani et al. (2006) or Salthe (2009). For a more detailed exposition, see Herrmann-Pillath (2012b). Peirce laid the ground for the analytical distinction between two modes of causality that are involved in social interactions, efficient and final; for a comprehensive discussion of Peirce's views on causality, see Short (2007).
12. This point corresponds to the revival of 'materiality' in sociology, see the seminal volume edited by Pinch and Swedberg (2008), which also plays an important role in performativity theory, partly reflecting the intellectual impact of actor-network theory that emphasizes the emergence of agency in networks of human individuals and artefacts (Latour 2005). This goes back to the origins in science and technology studies, where the physical location and structure of the laboratory is a central concern. In economic sociology, this has centred interest on the role of 'market devices' in enabling economic interactions (see the contributions in Callon et al. 2007).
13. Peirce's major contribution in creating the discipline of semiotics was to elaborate on a complex taxonomy of signs that starts out from studying the nature of the underlying mechanisms. For example, a sign can be embodied information, such as a facial expression signalling an emotion, or purely

conventional, such as a linguistic expression. For a survey of the Peircian taxonomy, see Short (2007).
14. It is straightforward to relate the semiotic model to sketches of mechanistic explanations such as Schmid (2011). Schmid distinguishes four steps in analysing social mechanisms: The explanation of the individual action, the analysis of the interaction patterns, the aggregation process, and the feedbacks between the aggregate level and individual action.
15. See Muniesa and Callon (2007) who give many examples of how theoretical models of game theory need to be supported by transformational measures aiming at the particular group of actors that are intended to perform the models in a particular context. This can refer to design of locations, design of forms of interactions, and also the training of participants. For example, in real-world spectrum auctions even the economists themselves who designed the mechanisms would be hired by participating companies to perform the mechanism properly.
16. This exposition summarizes the famous experiments in testing the ultimatum game predictions across a number of 'small scale' societies (Henrich et al. 2005). Deviations from the predictions of the model are a standard result which is mostly interpreted in a twofold way. One is to argue that humans are more altruistic than assumed by standard theory. This would be an alternative covering law approach in trying to substitute one universalization by another. The other is to include a learning dimension, showing that after some period of learning, experimental subjects will not commit the 'mistakes' anymore and produce the predicted result. The importance of the Henrich et al. study lies in showing up a third solution: This is that the response pattern is systematically influenced by socially embedded interpretations of the subjects (e.g. in societies with cooperative hunting offers in the ultimatum game would also be higher). I think that this also introduces a third alternative to Guala's (2007) methodological evaluation of experimental economics: He distinguishes between 'testers' and 'builders' and emphasizes that 'builders' aim at transforming the context of an experimental game in order to make subjects performing it. He thinks that this does not invalidate the predictions of the model, as one can see this procedure as an attempt to isolate behavioural determinants, which, after all, actually appear to work, given the setting of the experiment. The Henrich et al. experiments show that collectives of experimental subjects might systematically create autonomous 'performances' of the models. This is what is expected in the mechanism approach, such as argued by Little (1992) who champions the idea of medium-level theoretical conceptions in the social sciences, with limited reach in space and time.
17. Although the learning argument would be the most straightforward one in dealing with these issues from the viewpoint of standard economic theory,

in fact even this only works under special 'performative' conditions, see Camerer (2003: 59f). I pointed to Guala's (2007) assessment in the previous footnote. This problem is an aspect of the issue of external validity of experiments which is certainly taken very seriously by experimental economists. But this results in a very strong impact of basic convictions and intentions of experimenters on the actual empirical strategies and interpretation of results, which I would see as another instance of performativity, in this case with reference to the collective or community of researchers.
18. See Hedström and Ylikoski (2010: 61f). For the original contribution, see Merton (1948: 195): 'The self-fulfilling prophecy is, in the beginning, a false definition of the situation evoking a new behavior which makes the original false conception come true. This specious validity of the self-fulfilling prophecy perpetuates a reign of error. For the prophet will cite the actual course of events as proof that he was right from the very beginning.'
19. Singer and Lamm (2009) provide a concise statement of this interaction between top-down and bottom-up processes in triggering empathy. It is particularly interesting because this is a clear case where we cannot say that a mental phenomenon supervenes on a neuronal structure, because the mental phenomenon involves extra-somatic mechanisms. On the consequences of this research for economics, see Kirman and Teschl (2010). Interestingly, they point to experimental evidence that emphatic behaviour even varies for the same individuals depending on specific interactions with others. On the biological foundations of in-group/out-group distinction, see Bowles et al. (2003).
20. For a survey of the ecological approach, see Yamagishi (2012). In a large number of experiments Yamagishi has shown that Japanese subjects only appear to act more collectivistic than Americans if they receive certain contextual clues. If the context is entirely anonymous and de-contextualized, they often even act less other-oriented than Americans. This contradicts a long tradition in social psychology (e.g. Triandis 1995) in assuming that culture imbues individuals with certain sets of internalized values that explain certain behavioural patterns in comparison to people from other cultures (for a survey in the context of economics, see Beugelsdijk and Maseland 2010).
21. It is important to notice that economists normally treat all incentives as equivalent to monetary incentives; in the context of experimental economics, this is most explicitly done so, as monetary pay-offs are seen as indirect indicators of utility. Beyond economics, the notion of incentive is much broader and includes, for example, praise, awards, prizes, fame, and so on. As is well known from psychological research, these incentives can work very differently on motivation than material incentives that are directly

targeted at producing a certain level of activity. I come back on this point below.

22. There are very complex constellations that need further scrutiny in terms of Peircian semiotics, as I have previously mentioned (footnote 13). Basically, every incentive is a physical object, namely a physically embodied stimulus. There are incentives in which object and sign are physically united such as in the case of extending bodily caress to a person as a positive gratification. In other cases, the sign is separate, such as bestowing a medal on a person, where the original incentive would be the psychological and social states that are expressed by that sign. Money raises very tricky issues here, as economists, but also some neuroscientists treat money as directly reflecting the underlying utility. Although this is regarded as a technical device that is limited to certain experimental settings, the use of money is normally extended far beyond them. That would imply that money plays the intricate role of a culturally conditioned 'primary reinforcer', coming close to an oxymoron (see Camerer et al. 2005: 35). In standard economic theory, to the contrary, money is treated as a sign (a 'veil') that represents other underlying incentives, which are the things money can buy (see the discussion in Harrison 2008: 306f).

23. A concise argument on this has been presented by Sliwka (2007), compare also Falk and Kosfeld (2006). Psychologists have shown that in such a setting, there are many degrees of freedom: For example, when the incentive system signals the dominance of cooperative types, this might induce more people to free-ride (see Chen et al. 2005).

24. There is ample psychological evidence of strong framing effects of money, as in priming experiments; for a survey, see Vohs et al. (2006). Framing effects can be various and differentiated (e.g. even framing with clean or dirty banknotes can make a difference in behaviour); as exemplary studies, see Yang et al. (2012). This literature also refutes the typical assumption in experimental economics that money directly reflects underlying utilities, see Amir et al. (2008).

25. Since the seminal survey of Deci et al. (1999), the general notion of a conflict between extrinsic reward and intrinsic motivation is well accepted, but rarely received in economics, with exceptions such as Frey (1997) or Falk and Kosfeld (2006). Most importantly, for our discussion of managerial incentive system in the next section, these effects are especially strong if extrinsic rewards are very large and fall into the same category as the goal pursued by the incentivized action (James 2005). Bonus systems for managers should have an especially strong negative effect on their intrinsic motivation.

26. As one example of the discussion, see the influential work of Bebchuk and Fried (2004); on the public debates, see Joutsenvirta (2013). This has

already triggered many regulatory responses, such as imposing caps on bonuses and strengthening the role of shareholders in fixing remuneration schemes for CEOs. But all these measures so far do not question the fundamental principles of these schemes.
27. The seminal contributions were La Porta et al. (1997, 1998) and the generalization by Djankov et al. (2003). Interestingly, in the latter contribution, contextualization creeps back into the analysis because the performance of certain legal systems is seen as being dependent on the stock of civic capital.
28. For a devastating empirical critique of the legal origins theory, see Siems and Deakin (2010). Aoki (2010: 71ff) is a good survey of the discussion.
29. This refers to the phenomenon that the investors' perspective tends to dominate the entire institutional design of the corporate sector, hence also changing the strategic orientation of business towards financial goals, see Krippner (2005). In Herrmann-Pillath (2013) I offer an interpretation of this in terms of performativity theory, including aspects such as the accounting and financial reporting institutions or the patent system.
30. Aoki (2010: 26ff). Aoki's theory can be related to formal mathematical approaches to firm structure that point towards positive externalities between production factors, thus creating supermodular production functions, see e.g. Milgrom and Roberts (1990). Interestingly, in practical application of this thinking, 'high commitment human resource management systems' would not take the shape of high-powered extrinsic incentives, see Roberts (2004: 174f).
31. This is an important issue in social ontology: Economics just accepts the idea that cognitive states are confined to individuals, hence brains, whereas in recent developments of cognitive science these are seen as being partly externalized, see e.g. Clark (2011). Again, this can only properly appreciated in a mechanism view.
32. These arguments have been already deployed in Aoki's (1988) classical comparison between the A-Firm and the J-Firm. In principle, the two governance schemes in the USA and Japan achieved similar performance levels at that time, because they were embedded into different institutional structures of the labour market, different distributions and contents of skills, and so on, hence were contextualized differently. However, it is also partly a question of technology which scheme works best: At that time, Aoki pointed towards automotive industry as an example for a good match with the Japanese model, whereas chemical industry might be better governed by the US model. This observation points towards the possibility of 'counterperformativity' (MacKenzie 2007), which is an important phenomenon in rendering performativity theory empirically meaningful.

33. Ghoshal (2005) accused business schools in educating students to become opportunistic agents, based on advanced theory. It is important to notice that in the light of performativity theory, this does not need to suppose that students actually 'become' more opportunistic, which is probably not the case empirically (Guala 2007). Ghoshal's reasoning matches with the aforementioned theory by Sliwka (2007) in that the education transmits information about the composition of types in the economy, which triggers strategic responses of individuals. Such effects can be leveraged by endogenous sorting of different types across market and non-market domains of the economy, see Kranton (1996).

References

Amir, On, Daniel Ariely, and Ziv Carmon. 2008. The Dissociation between Monetary Assessment and Predicted Utility. *Marketing Science* 27(6): 1055–1064.
Aoki, Masahiko. 1988. *Information, Incentives, and Bargaining in the Japanese Economy*. New York: Cambridge University Press.
Aoki, Masahiko. 2010. *Corporations in Evolving Diversity: Cognition, Governance, and Institutions*. Oxford: Oxford University Press.
Aunger, Robert. 2002. *The Electric Meme: A New Theory of How We Think*. New York: Free Press.
Bebchuk, Lucian, and Jesse Fried. 2004. *Pay Without Performance: The Unfulfilled Promise of Executive Compensation*. Cambridge, MA: Harvard University Press.
Beugelsdijk, Sjoerd, and Robbert Maseland. 2010. *Culture in Economics: History, Methodological Reflections, and Contemporary Applications*. Cambridge: Cambridge University Press.
Bhaskar, Roy. 1989. *The Possibility of Naturalism. A Philosophical Critique of the Contemporary Human Sciences*. New York: Harvester Wheatsheaf.
Bowles, Samuel, and Sandra Polanía-Reyes. 2012. Economic Incentives and Social Preferences: Substitutes or Complements? *Journal of Economic Literature* 50(2): 368–425.
Bowles, Samuel, Jung-Kyoo Choi, and Astrid Hopfensitz. 2003. The Co-evolution of Individual Behaviors and Social Institutions. *Journal of Theoretical Biology* 223: 135–147.
Callon, Michel. 2007. An Essay on the Growing Contribution of Economic Markets to the Proliferation of the Social. *Theory, Culture & Society* 24(7–8): 139–163.
Callon, Michel, Yuval Millo, and Fabian Muniesa (eds.). 2007. *Market Devices*. Oxford: Blackwell.
Camerer, Colin. 2003. *Behavioral Game Theory: Experiments in Strategic Interaction*. Princeton, NJ: Princeton University Press.

Camerer, Colin, George Loewenstein, and Drazen Prelec. 2005. Neuroeconomics: How Neuroscience Can Inform Economics. *Journal of Economic Literature* 43(1): 9–64.
Chen, Xiao-Ping, S. Arzu Wasti, and Harry C. Triandis. 2007. When Does Group Norm or Group Identity Predict Cooperation in a Public Goods Dilemma? The Moderating Effects of Idiocentrism and Allocentrism. *International Journal of Intercultural Relations* 31(2): 259–276.
Clark, Andy. 2011. *Supersizing the Mind. Embodiment, Action, and Cognitive Extension*. Oxford: Oxford University Press.
Craver, Carl F. 2007. *Explaining the Brain. Mechanisms and the Mosaic Unity of the Neurosciences*. New York: Oxford University Press.
Deci, Edward L., Richard Koestner, and Richard M. Ryan. 1999. A Meta-analytic Review of Experiments Examining the Effects of Extrinsic Rewards on Intrinsic Motivation. *Psychological Bulletin* 125(6): 627–668.
Demeulenaere, Pierre (ed.). 2011. *Analytical Sociology and Social Mechanisms*. Cambridge; New York: Cambridge University Press.
Djankov, Simeon, Edward Glaeser, Rafael La Porta, Florencio Lopez-de-Silanes, and Andrei Shleifer. 2003. The New Comparative Economics. *Journal of Comparative Economics* 31(4): 595–619.
El-Hani, Charbel Niño, Joao Queiroz, and Claus Emmeche. 2006. A Semiotic Analysis of the Genetic Information System. *Semiotica* 160(1–4): 1–68.
Elster, Jon. 1989. *Nuts and Bolts for the Social Sciences*. Cambridge and New York: Cambridge University Press.
Erlei, Mathias, and Wiebke Roß. 2014. Bounded Rationality as an Essential Component of the Holdup Problem. *Working Paper*, Clausthal University.
Falk, Armin, and Michael Kosfeld. 2006. The Hidden Costs of Control. *American Economic Review* 96(5): 1611–1630.
Fehr, Ernst, Michael Powell, and Tom Wilkening. 2014. Handing Out Guns at a Knife Fight: Behavioral Limitations of Subgame-Perfect Implementation. *Working Paper* 171, University of Zurich.
Frey, Bruno S. 1997. *Not Just for the Money. An Economic Theory of Personal Motivation*. Brookfield: Edward Elgar.
Ghoshal, Sumantra. 2005. Bad Management Theories are Destroying Good Management Practices. *Academy of Management Learning & Education* 4(1): 75–91.
Guala, Francesco. 2007. How to Do Things with Experimental Economics. In *Do Economists Make Markets? On the Performativity of Economics*, edited by Donald MacKenzie, Fabian Muniesa, and Lucia Siu, 128–162. Princeton, NJ: Princeton University Press.
Harrison, Glenn W. 2008. Neuroeconomics: A Critical Reconsideration. *Economics & Philosophy* 24(3): 303–344.
Hart, Oliver. 2009. Hold-Up, Asset Ownership, and Reference Points. *Quarterly Journal of Economics* 124(1): 267–300.

Hausman, Daniel. 1992. *The Inexact and Separate Science of Economics*. Cambridge and New York: Cambridge University Press.
Hausman, Daniel. 2013. Philosophy of Economics. In *The Stanford Encyclopedia of Philosophy* (Spring 2013 Edition), edited by Edward N. Zalta. Accessed November 1, 2015. http://plato.stanford.edu/archives/spr2013/entries/economics/
Hedström, Peter, and Petri Ylikoski. 2010. Causal Mechanisms in the Social Sciences. *Annual Review of Sociology* 36: 49–67.
Henrich, Joseph, Robert Boyd, Samuel Bowles, Ernst Fehr, Herbert Gintis, Richard McElreath, Michael Alvard, et al. 2005. 'Economic Man' in Cross-cultural Perspective: Behavioural Experiments in 15 Small-Scale Societies. *Behavioral and Brain Sciences* 28(6): 795–855.
Herrmann-Pillath, Carsten. 2010. A Neurolinguistic Approach to Performativity in Economics. *Journal of Economic Methodology* 17(3): 241–260.
Herrmann-Pillath, Carsten. 2012a. Institutions, Distributed Cognition and Agency: Rule-Following as Performative Action. *Journal of Economic Methodology* 19(1): 21–42.
Herrmann-Pillath, Carsten. 2012b. Towards an Externalist Neuroeconomics: Dual Selves, Signs, and Choice. *Journal of Neuroscience, Psychology and Economics* 5(1): 38–61.
Herrmann-Pillath, Carsten. 2013. Performativity of Economic Systems: Approach and Implications for Taxonomy. *Journal of Economic Methodology* 20(2): 139–163.
James Jr., Harvey S. 2005. Why Did You Do That? An Economic Explanation of the Effect of Extrinsic Compensation on Intrinsic Motivation and Performance. *Journal of Economic Psychology* 26(4): 549–566.
Joutsenvirta, Maria. 2013. Executive Pay and Legitimacy: Changing Discursive Battles Over the Morality of Excessive Manager Compensation. *Journal of Business Ethics* 116(3): 459–477.
Kirman, Alan, and Miriam Teschl. 2010. Selfish or Selfless? The Role of Empathy in Economics. *Philosophical Transactions of the Royal Society, B* 365: 303–317.
Kranton, Rachel E. 1996. Reciprocal Exchange: A Self-Sustaining System. *American Economic Review* 86(4): 830–851.
Krippner, G. 2005. The Financialization of the American Economy. *Socio-Economic Review* 3(2): 173–208.
La Porta, Rafael, Florencio Lopez-de-Silvanes, Andrei Shleifer, and Robert Vishny. 1997. Legal Determinants of External Finance. *Journal of Finance* 52(3): 1131–1150.
La Porta, Rafael, Florencio Lopez-de-Silanes, Andrei Shleifer, Robert Vishny. 1998. Law and Finance. *Journal of Political Economy* 106(6): 1113–1155.
Latour, Bruno. 2005. *Reassembling the Social. An Introduction to Actor-Network Theory*. Oxford et al.: Oxford University Press.

Little, Daniel. 1992. *Understanding Peasant China. Case Studies in the Philosophy of Social Science*. New Haven: Yale University Press.
Lycan, William G. 1999. *Philosophy of Language. An Introductory Text*. London: Routledge.
MacKenzie, Donald. 2006. *An Engine, Not a Camera: How Financial Models Shape Markets*. Cambridge, MA: MIT Press.
MacKenzie, Donald. 2007. Is Economics Performative? Option Theory and the Construction of Derivatives Markets. In *Do Economists Make Markets? On the Performativity of Economics*, edited by Donald MacKenzie, Fabian Muniesa, and Lucia Siu, 54–86. Princeton, NJ: Princeton University Press.
Maskin, Eric. 2002. On Indescribable Contingencies and Incomplete Contracts. *European Economic Review* 46(4–5): 725–733.
Maskin, Eric, and Jean Tirole. 1999. Unforeseen Contingencies and Incomplete Contracts. *Review of Economic Studies* 66(1): 83–114.
Merton, Robert K. 1948. The Self Fulfilling Prophecy. *Antioch Review* 8(2): 193–210.
Milgrom, Paul, and John Roberts. 1990. The Economics of Modern Manufacturing: Technology, Strategy, and Organization. *American Economic Review* 80(3): 511–528.
Muniesa, Fabian, and Michel Callon. 2007. Economic Experiments and the Construction of Markets. In *Do Economists Make Markets?: On the Performativity of Economics*, edited by Donald MacKenzie, Fabian Muniesa, and Lucia Siu, 163–189. Princeton, NJ: Princeton University Press.
Papineau, David. 2009. The Causal Closure of the Physical and Naturalism. In *The Oxford Handbook of Philosophy of Mind*, edited by Ansgar Beckermann, Brian P. McLaughlin, and Sven Walter, 53–65. Oxford: Oxford University Press.
Pinch, Trevor, and Richard Swedberg (eds.). 2008. *Living in a Material World, Economic Sociology Meets Science and Technology Studies*. Cambridge, MA: MIT Press.
Reutlinger, Alexander, Gerhard Schurz, and Andreas Hüttemann. 2015. "Ceteris Paribus Laws", The Stanford Encyclopedia of Philosophy (Fall 2015 Edition), Edward N. Zalta (ed.), http://plato.stanford.edu/archives/fall2015/entries/ceteris-paribus/
Roberts, John. 2004. *The Modern Firm. Organizational Design for Performance and Growth*. New York: Oxford University Press.
Salthe, Stanley N. 2009. The System of Interpretance: Naturalizing Meaning as Finality. *Biosemiotics* 1(3): 285–294.
Schmid, Michael. 2011. The Logic of Mechanistic Explanations in the Social Sciences. In *Analytical Sociology and Social Mechanisms*, edited by Pierre Demeulenaere, 136–153. Cambridge: Cambridge University Press.
Searle, John R. 1995. *The Construction of Social Reality*. London: Penguin.

Searle, J.R. 2010. *Making the Social World. The Structure of Human Civilization.* Oxford: Oxford University Press.
Short, Thomas L. 2007. *Peirce's Theory of Signs.* New York: Cambridge University Press.
Siems, Mathias M., and Simon Deakin. 2010. Comparative Law and Finance: Past, Present, and Future Research. *Journal of Institutional and Theoretical Economics* 166(1): 120–140.
Singer, Tania and Claus Lamm. 2009. The Social Neuroscience of Empathy. *Annals of the New York Academy of Sciences* 1156: 81–96.
Sliwka, Dirk. 2007. Trust as a Signal of a Social Norm and the Hidden Costs of Incentive Schemes. *American Economic Review* 97(3): 999–1012.
Triandis, Harry C. 1995. *Individualism & Collectivism.* Boulder, CO: Westview Press.
Tuomela, Raimo. 2007. *The Philosophy of Sociality.* Oxford: Oxford University Press.
Vohs, Kathleen D., Nicole L. Mead, and Miranda R. Goode. 2006. The Psychological Consequences of Money. *Science* 314(5802): 1154–1156.
Vromen, Jack. 2011. Routines as Multilevel Mechanisms. *Journal of Institutional Economics* 7(2): 175–196.
Yamagishi, Toshio. 2012. Micro–Macro Dynamics of the Cultural Construction of Reality. A Niche Construction Approach to Culture. In *Advances in Culture and Psychology: Volume 1*, edited by Michele J. Gelfand, Chi-yue Chiu and Ying-yi Hong, 251–308. Oxford and New York: Oxford University Press.
Yang, Qing, Xiaochang Wu, Xinyue Zhou, Nicole L. Mead, Kathleen D. Vohs, and Roy F. Baumeister. 2012. Diverging Effects of Clean Versus Dirty Money on Attitudes, Values, and Interpersonal Behavior. *Journal of Personality and Social Psychology* 104(3): 473–489.

CHAPTER 4

'Doing' Laboratory Experiments: An Ethnomethodological Study of the Performative Practice in Behavioral Economic Research

Juliane Böhme

4.1 INTRODUCTION

Studies in the tradition of laboratory constructivism have confirmed that the outcomes and subjects of scientific knowledge are being constructed by the practices of the scientists themselves (Knorr-Cetina 1984; Knorr-Cetina and Mulkay 1983; Latour and Woolgar 1979). Building on the theoretical tradition of Harold Garfinkel, Knorr-Cetina (2002) refers to these situational scientific practices as *ethnomethods*. In contrast to these classic studies, the economic laboratory experiments in this paper are built

---

I am grateful to the Berlin Social Science Research Center (WZB) for funding. I would like to thank Nina Bonge, Rustamdjan Hakimov, and the laboratory staff for teaching me how to act properly in the laboratory. I am especially grateful to Dorothea Kübler and Rustamdjan Hakimov for their openness to reflect about their own research practice and Michael Hutter who supported the sociological perspective in various stimulating discussions with our economic colleagues. Parts of the article base on a revisited version of Böhme (2015a).

J. Böhme
Berlin Social Science Center, Berlin, Germany

© The Editor(s) (if applicable) and The Author(s) 2016
I.A. Boldyrev, E. Svetlova (eds.), *Enacting Dismal Science*,
DOI 10.1057/978-1-137-48876-3_4

around a systematically different object of observation. Whereas classic laboratory studies look at how objects in natural science laboratories are being manipulated and constructed by the scientists, the 'objects' of experimental economic research are human actors. This difference is also reflected in the specific setting of the laboratory.

As in natural science, the economic laboratory must satisfy specific scientific criteria for their outcomes to be considered valid and valuable by the relevant scientific communities. After all, one general concern of laboratory-based research is to eliminate, or at least minimize, the influence of confounding variables by creating a controlled environment. In analogy to the terminology introduced by Klaus Amann, the laboratories of economic researchers may be regarded as 'laboratopes' (Amann 1994, 30). During the experimental process, the practice of the scientists and the material equipment of the laboratory create a specifically scientific and technically structured environment for the scientific object that economists are out to study: the decision-making of the rational actor.

In this paper, I argue that researchers produce the conditions for their own assumptions through practical action. Or as Fabian Muniesa and Michel Callon write: 'Economic experiments perform economic objects in a quite general sense. What experimenters describe is indeed produced by them in the experimental setting. They account for what they provoke. Experimental objects are both observed and fabricated—fabricated in order to be observed and vice-versa' (Muniesa and Callon 2007, 163).

The ethnomethodological perspective allows to understand the ethnomethods or specific practices as performative acts which are used to constitute the situation of a laboratory experiment. By means of a detailed description and analysis of what goes on in the laboratory, this article elucidates the first steps of the 'fabrication process' mentioned by Muniesa and Callon. We will see how the participants are bounded in their action and interaction and pushed to a specific (rational) behavior the researchers are out to study. Special emphasis is on the role of the economists' performative practices, which have a key influence on the construction of decision-making situations in the laboratory. But in addition to Muniesa and Callon, the empirical examples will show that also the participants and their expectations of normality play an important role in the construction process of the laboratory situation.

To explain the theoretical foundations of my argument, the first section is devoted to presenting the relevant key assumptions of ethnomethodology. The second section presents the empirical database and the methodological background. The third section features an analysis of experimental economists' epistemic assumptions, which are implemented as precautions in the experiments to increase the likelihood that participants define the situation as requested by the experimenters. Drawing on empirical examples, the forth section provides a detailed account of the typical course of an economic laboratory experiment and behavioral economists' common practices. By way of example, this account highlights the performative way in which researchers try to translate their assumptions and conceptions into a practical experiment, as well as the problems and conflicts that may arise when working with 'objects' with a will of their own. The last section offers a brief summary of the findings discussed throughout the article. Based on these findings, I elucidate the situation-based construction of a rational actor during an economic laboratory experiment.

4.2 Producing Situations of Limited Choice

The theoretical perspective of ethnomethodology is especially well suited for the purpose of this article. From a procedural standpoint, it enables us to show how the situational practices of researchers and participants lead to the simultaneous production and reproduction of a specific social order in the laboratory. I begin by presenting the relevant concepts of the ethnomethodological position. Next, these theoretical reference points are used to explain how this perspective can be used to elucidate the practical construction of the economists' actor model in the laboratory setting.

4.2.1 The Theoretical Perspective of Ethnomethodology

The basic assumption of ethnomethodology (Garfinkel 1967) is that our actions are not arbitrary but structured and ordered in a meaningful way. Drawing on Garfinkel, they can be described as group-specific *ethnomethods*. 'The activities whereby members produce and manage settings of organized everyday affairs are identical with members' procedures for making those settings 'account-able.' (Garfinkel 1967, 1–2) The specific practical ethnomethods have to be understood as performative as they play the crucial part in the simultaneous production and reproduction of the specific situation of the laboratory experiment.

Ethnomethodologists think of social reality as procedural reality. Rather than being some sort of objective entity, social reality evolves from actors' ongoing construction efforts. Along the same lines, Harvey Sacks and

Harold Garfinkel refer to social phenomena as 'doings' (Garfinkel and Sacks 1979, 148) to highlight the practices by which such phenomena are being produced.

From an ethnomethodological point of view, actors should not be seen as self-contained persons or monads but as socially *situated actors*. The situational practices performed by the actors determine what and who they are in the corresponding situation. In the words of Anne W. Rawls, 'The actor becomes a location for practices—instead of a container for motivations' (Rawls 2006, 21).

Following the tradition of 'breaching experiments' (Garfinkel 1967), ethnomethodological studies often put special emphasis on situations of crisis. Such moments reveal that actors have specific expectation in the proper course of action but they do not follow a deterministic role model in the sense suggested by Parsons. Instead of following predefined patterns, actors are in every situation involved in an ongoing and active process of sense-making. The practical methods that actors use to 'fix' the situations of crisis, disruption, or surprise offer insights in how this kind of situations 'normally' evolve (Garfinkel and Sacks 1979).

According to Garfinkel, the use of strong role model concepts reduces the actor to a 'cultural' or 'judgmental dope' (Garfinkel 1967, 67) who follows, robot-like, predefined role models based on her internalized values and norms. A way to construct such an actor is to disregard the fact that the use of words and symbols always has to be understood as happening within a specific language game, as described by Wittgenstein ([1953] 1971). Here, researchers incorrectly assume that their own language games are identical to those of the persons they study (Garfinkel 1967, 70). This is why the members of society are expected to behave exactly as researchers would wish.

For the following account of economic laboratory experiments, the idea of constructing an actor incapable of judgment is very relevant. The behavioral economic research methodology follows a model of rational action. But this model no longer matches the classic *homo oeconomicus* but rather Herbert A. Simon's (1957) notion of 'bounded rationality.' The central concern is to study the bounds of rationality in economic behavior, for example, the influence of trust, fairness, or risk evaluation in the decision-making process (Camerer 2003). But the fundamental theoretical assumption that people make goal-oriented decisions and act rationally is still regarded as a given; 'rationality cannot be disproven as it follows from the decision to view people as agents who pursue their goals' (Kübler

2010, 6). In this case, however, the limitation of choices brought about, according to the ethnomethodological perspective, by applying this kind of model is a desired effect and itself part of the methodology of laboratory experiments.

However, from an ethnomethodological point of view and as sketched out above, the rational decision-making appears as an outcome of a specific situational social order. The decision-making behavior of the rational actor is enforced and co-produced by means of the researchers' practical methods before and in the process of the experiment. My thesis is therefore that economists not only study but also (re-)produce this actor model and its defining elements. The economists' rational actor thus matches the practices of his creation and has to be viewed as an empirical phenomenon from the perspective of 'doing.'

If we assume the practices to be constitutive of the emergence of a situated actor, the detailed study of what goes on in economic laboratories will allow us to better understand the rational actor as the economist's object of inquiry.

4.3 Empirical Data

The following two sections are devoted to the presentation of empirical data and their interpretation. The third section shows how central behavioral economists' assumptions are translated in precautions in the course of the experiment, whereas section 4 focuses on the typical course of an experiment and the interaction in the laboratory.

The empirical observations and findings discussed here emerged from an interdisciplinary project. Having regard to the particularities of the laboratory setting (e.g. restriction of observation, prohibition of communication) different types of data were used and joined. I combined aspects from Grounded theory methodology with the ethnomethodological perspective to integrate data apart from the observed situation.[1] The data were collected by observation during 40 behavioral economic experiments in a German laboratory. I started with participant observations of different experiments. After a while I was practically introduced in the practice of the laboratory research by the staff of the laboratory and my project colleague. They taught me how to act properly as a member of the laboratory staff and involved me substantively in the conduction of different experiments. So in the process of the data collection, my position changed from participant observation to an observing participation. To supplement that information, I talked to experimental economists and research assistants and made audiotapes from project sessions were economists discussed the conception and results from an ongoing series of experiments. The data set involves additionally interviews with 100 participants, to collect more precise information regarding possible discrepancies in the interpretation of the laboratory situation.

The pool of participants available for research in the observed laboratory currently consists of about 4000 persons. Most of them are university students. Even if researchers make constant efforts to recruit new participants, the frequency of experiments necessitates that participants are involved in multiple experiments.

4.4 Economists' Epistemic Assumptions and Practical Precautions

According to the discussions I had with researchers performing laboratory experiments, the key concern when designing such experiments is to ensure that the experiments are comparable and that participants are highly motivated. Standardization, anonymization, and compliance with the rules are particularly important in that regard. Three key aspects to be considered when designing experiments are the physical or material environment of the experiment, the instructions, and the software (Guala 2007).

4.4.1 *The Experimental Laboratory as a Neutral Space*

Economists view the material environment of the laboratory as a neutral space (cf. Gieryn 2002). The term 'neutral' refers to the fact that all participants understand that space in the same way, and that the spatial basis it provides for decision-making is the same for everybody. Typically, each participant is seated between three partitions enclosing them at the front, left, and right sides, and separating them visually and acoustically from the persons seated next to them. Likewise, the workstations are made to look as identical as possible. In front of them, participants find a keyboard, a mouse, and the screen of their computer.

Using the technical equipment of the laboratory and following the need for a high degree of standardization in communications, the individual decision-making situations are commonly displayed on the computer screens. By using computer software specifically designed for conducting laboratory experiments, it is possible to provide participants with exactly the same information on all computer screens. In addition to presenting the information in a standardized format, z-Tree, the software program used in the observed laboratory also provides experimenters with the possibility of monitoring the progress of the experiment and the actions of the participants. The participants are anonymous for each other and know just about their own roles. The experimenters can check easily on their computer screen which participant is assigned with which role and what he is doing in the course of the experiment. The empirical examples will show the importance of this control option.

4.4.2 Decision-Dependent Monetary Incentives

Participants in economic laboratory experiments are paid depending on the decisions they make. This means that not all participants receive the same fixed amount of money. Using monetary incentives is standard in experimental economics in line with the 'Induced value theory' by Vernon Smith (1976). This theory includes a set of methodological rules for the design of experiments and aims explicitly at the manipulative character of laboratory experiments (Muniesa and Callon 2007). This is done for several reasons, which at the same time reflect key assumptions in the economic concept of actors. Arguably, the most popular reason is that monetary incentives are assumed to motivate participants to display optimal behavior. '[B]y inducing value using money payments, the experimenters need to rely only on the assumption that everybody likes having more money and nobody gets tired of having more of it' (Camerer 2003, 39).

Many of the economists I interviewed reported that all participants are always interested in money. They also said that without using decision-dependent financial rewards, they could never be sure of whether or not participants are simply lying or making arbitrary choices to speed up the experiment.

Furthermore, researchers intentionally use monetary motives to override other incentives, assuming that providing the extrinsic motivation of the financial incentive gives them better control over participants' motivation for action. 'Participants are paid according to their choices so that successful participants earn more money in an experiment than unsuccessful ones. Direct monetary incentives help to control the motives of the participants.' (Kübler 2010, 6)

Moreover, the remark that participants can make 'successful' choices provides crucial evidence for the hypothesis presented here. There are three aspects which influence how successful participants are in an experiment: luck, other participants, and the 'right' understanding of the game. To a certain extent, whether or not choices are 'successful' is often a matter of luck. This is especially true of experiments involving lotteries, because in such cases, participants can never safely predict the outcome of the draw. In some experiments, participants are playing together in a virtual mediated group. How much money they make depends in these cases on their own decisions as well as those of other participants. In the sense of maximizing financial profits, however, the term 'successful' also refers to the fact that participants understand the rules of the experiment, as explained to them by the economists, and develop suitable action strategies for making decisions based on these rules. The payment they can achieve essentially depends on whether or not they interpret the information they receive in the way anticipated by the economists. If participants fail to do so, their chances of making 'successful' choices in the experiment diminish, along with their potential earnings.

4.4.3   Framing Through Instructions

The psychologists Daniel Kahneman and Amos Tversky (1981) found that different phrasings of the decision-making situation can lead to significant differences in participants' decision-making behavior. This effect is called framing. Behavioral economists pick up this point and acknowledge that semantics can influence participants' decision-making process. Accordingly, the economic concept of framing assumes that the written instructions have a significant impact on participants' decision-making situation in an experiment.

The framing is understood as something that economists can actively control, typically by varying specific aspects of the written instructions or the setup. From this point of view, the framing of the experiment is constructed by the experimental economists. The instructions provide participants with detailed information about the decision-making situation and the roles they may be assigned during the experiment. They are also informed about the criteria by which the roles are assigned, for instance, whether the roles are assigned randomly or based on previous results, such as winning a game. Moreover, the specific rules that govern how much money participants can win in each of the decision-making situations are explained and typically illustrated with the help of examples or oral explanations.

One framing method often used in laboratory practice is to test participants' reading literacy and understanding of rules by giving them test questionnaires. These questionnaires feature sample decision-making situations similar to those presented in the subsequent experiment. Participants have to answer follow-up questions or make decisions regarding the predefined situation. After answering all questions, they indicate to a laboratory staff member that they are finished. The results are reviewed by one of the experimenters, and wrong answers are pointed out to participants, if necessary. Only after all participants have completed the questionnaire correctly do researchers begin with the part of data collection that will subsequently be used for scientific analysis. This example shows how this performative practice is used to increase the likelihood of participants adopting the language and behavioral games of the economists.

In this way, economic researchers succeed in making it more difficult for participants to deviate from the intended interpretation of a situation. For the practice of the experiment and the scientific claims of the laboratory-based experimental method in general, this is essential because it increases the chance of minimizing the interference of undesired confounders.

This is in line with Guala's observation (2005) that non-compliance with the typical experimental procedure will cause the peer group to sharply criticize the work in question or to downright ignore the findings of the study due to a lack of comparability.

4.5 Empirical Examples from the Recruitment Process and the Laboratory Experiments

The previous section discussed central economists' theoretical assumptions and showed how they are enacted as precautions in the practice of the experiments. In this section, I provide a detailed insight into the practice of economic laboratory experiments. The examples show how the practices of the actors contribute to a specific situational order in the experimental laboratory.

4.5.1 Promotion and Registration of Participants

Participants' expectations and prior knowledge have a decisive influence on the construction of the laboratory situation, as they become part of that situation as contextual knowledge. In my interviews, participants reported that they had specific expectations even before stepping into the laboratory for the first time. Therefore, when giving an account of how the situation builds up for the participants during the laboratory experiment, it is essential to also look at the steps taken prior to entering the experimental laboratory like the promotion for the experiments and the process of registration.

Early on when recruiting participants for the laboratory experiment, researchers explicitly point out that this kind of experiment is an easy way to make 'quick money.' On the handouts and posters used for recruiting new participants, the slogan *Spielend Geld verdienen* ('making money by playing') instantly grabs the reader's attention. The focus on the monetary incentive is also reinforced in the explanations that follow. 'No prior knowledge is required,' readers are told, to make a 'substantial amount' of money in an experiment. Many participants also hear about the experiments by word of mouth. Most recommendations came from fellow students or friends who had previously participated in a laboratory experiment themselves.

All of the participants I interviewed said the monetary incentive was their primary reason for participating in the experiment. The focus on financial rewards, which are emphasized in the ads for the experiment, is thus replicated in the expectations of potential participants and reflect the power of the implied expectations of the researchers.

If interested persons decide to take part in economic experiments, they have to register in a specifically designed database via the Internet. Registration is handled with the help of a specifically designed software application called ORSEE (Greiner 2015). This tool serves to depersonalize and standardize the interactions between participants and experimenters. Furthermore, the participant pool can be used to generate information and statistics, for instance, to invite specific groups of participants for individual experiments. Students registered in the database do not sign up for a specific experiment; rather, they receive invitations from the experimenters to take part in the experiments going on at the time. Before being able to sign up with ORSEE, however, prospective participants are required to agree to the terms and conditions of the experimental laboratory.

Only those who receive an invitation to an experiment and explicitly confirm that invitation are allowed to participate. This confirmation is viewed as a binding commitment that may only be revoked in exceptional and justifiable cases. If participants cancel too late or do not show up for the experiment, a negative entry will be added to their personal account. These penalty points lower the chances of being invited to further experiments. Once an account contains three negative entries, the account is deactivated. Prospective participants are informed that experimenters always admit more persons to the experiment than are actually needed. On experiment day, they will admit those who arrive first at the laboratory and can show proof to the laboratory staff that they are in fact the ones who have been invited. Those who arrive at the laboratory in time but fail to sign up before all slots in the laboratory are taken receive a small expense allowance. Furthermore, participants agree to comply with the rules defined in the instructions. Participants are typically paid in cash.

This description of the recruitment process shows that prospective participants are already confronted with the necessity and rigidity of compliance, as well as the consequences of non-compliance, before taking part in the actual experiments. Key aspects of the concept of the rational actor are already applied at this early stage.

The ORSEE software is used to accomplish this in a standardized manner. It is only by accepting the rules that participants can register for the experiments. Since admission to the experimental laboratory is reserved for invited participants, they are expected to accept these general conditions as the basis for action and to be aware of the consequences of non-compliance. Participants' reflexive reference to information they collected during the recruitment process becomes evident in the way the interactions between participants and laboratory staff members evolve. Thus, control, standardization, and the focus on monetary incentives are the key elements of the recruitment process.

4.5.2 *The Process of the Laboratory Experiment*

Whereas the account of the recruitment process was more focused on describing the relevant procedures, the empirical examples below are more concentrated on the actors' situated practices, ranging from the process of participants arriving in front of the lab to the administration of the specific experiments inside the laboratory. As the empirical examples show, the actors (re-)produce the rules that govern the experiments *in situ*, thereby creating the specific situational order. In doing so, they clearly make reference to knowledge gained or accepted during the recruitment process.

4.5.2.1 *Arriving at the Laboratory*

Prior to the experiment, the invited individuals arrive in the hallway in front of the laboratory. Most of them are quietly busy. A few minutes before the scheduled beginning of the experiment, a member of the experimenter team arrives, holding a list in his hand. His arrival causes the group to stir. The attendees quickly leave their seats and gather around the laboratory assistant—not forming a disciplined line but rather facing him in a semicircle. The assistant extends a friendly welcome to everybody, asking the attendees to come up to him one at a time for ID verification to make sure they really are the persons who were invited. When walking up to the laboratory assistant, most participants already carry their ID document in their hands to show it to him. The assistant has a clipboard in his hand with a list that participants sign to confirm their participation.

Once rules have been established and accepted by all participants, they are enforced very consistently. The following brief example shows how conscientiously rule compliance is reproduced by the actors during the laboratory experiment.

The participants had just entered the laboratory, and the door was closed behind them to begin with the experiment at the scheduled time. Then one young man briskly walked up to the laboratory assistant who was still standing in front of the door to the experimental laboratory. Without any greeting, the young man apologized for his tardiness right away. In the conversation he had with the assistant, the student offered many details to explain why he was late, imploring the assistant not to add a negative entry to his account. The discussion lasted for several minutes. Considering that it had only been a small delay, they agreed that while the student would not receive the €5 show-up fee, the negative entry would be removed from the list. The young man was extremely grateful for this, assuring that he would be more than punctual the next time.

The fact that the young man started apologizing and defending himself even before the laboratory assistant confronted him with his non-compliance, can be regarded as an indication that he activated the strong emphasis on compliance during the experiments as background knowledge in this situation, already anticipating the consequences of his actions. Likewise, the laboratory assistant's reaction indicates a reflexive reference to the standardized experimental procedures. There was no need to explain that the participant's late arrival would be sanctioned and that he would have received a €5 show-up fee if he had arrived on time, even if he had not been allowed to participate in the experiment. Rather, the laboratory assistant assumed that the invited student was aware of the rules of the experiment and the consequences of being late. Both sides in this action sequence referred to rules of conduct accepted by prospective participants during the recruitment process, and both used this knowledge in procedural ways to construct their interaction. Even if this episode is not part of an interaction inside the laboratory, it does provide a vivid illustration of how participants in the interaction are actively involved in producing and reproducing the situational order typical of the laboratory experiment. They play an important part in the performance of the economic researchers. Whereas the laboratory members, in their practical actions, make sure in various ways that participants comply with the rules and that non-compliance leads to clear sanctions, participants anticipate this behavior as being appropriate in this situation. In their negotiations, the interaction partners do not talk about whether or not the late arrival should be sanctioned but only about which kind and scope of sanction would be appropriate, given that it was only a small delay.

4.5.2.2 The Start of the Experiment

After all participants have verified their legitimacy, the laboratory assistant passes around a small bag for each of them to draw a numbered chip. Based on that number, each participant is randomly assigned a seat in the laboratory. After all participants have drawn a number, the door to the laboratory is opened, and all persons enter to take their assigned seats. Inside, participants are usually quick to orient themselves, meaning that everybody finds their seat shortly after entering. At their workstation, each participant finds a few sheets of paper containing written instructions for the experiment. Some participants start leafing through the instructions right after taking their seats. The members of the experimenter team gather at a separate table at the front end of the laboratory. Using the computer screen at that table, they can start the computer software needed for the experiment, monitor the progress of the experiment, and intervene in case of a disruption or crisis.

The experiment itself begins with a member of the experimenter team welcoming the participants. The content of this welcome is standardized. The participants are informed about the three essential rules guiding their behavior in the laboratory. They are not permitted to use smartphones or other technical devices. Furthermore, they are not permitted to communicate with each other in any way. If a participant has a question, he is supposed to raise his hand to attract the attention of the laboratory staff. A member of the experimenter team will then come to the participant's workstation to answer the question individually. Participants are informed about the consequences of non-compliance with the rules. They risk being excluded from participation and losing the payment they may have already earned. After receiving these directions, participants are asked to begin reading the written instructions.

After the rules have been communicated, participants start reading the instructions. Regardless of the characteristics of the specific experiment at hand, the introductory instructions are remarkably similar in all cases. The instructions begin by repeating the rules that were presented orally just a few moments earlier and then go on to once more point out the possible consequences of non-compliance.

This general introduction is followed by the instructions for the specific experiment about to take place. While participants are reading the instructions, the members of the laboratory team watch out for participants raising their hands to indicate they have a question.

4.5.2.3 Discipline and Punish
The members of the laboratory team are seated at a separate table at the front end of the laboratory. This is also where they retreat if no further activity is required on their part. The computer at their table is used for starting the z-Tree program. The anonymity that participants are guaranteed during the experiment refers to the fact that no connection can be made between the personal identity of the participants and the assigned role in the laboratory. Additionally, no participant in the room knows which roles have been allotted to the other participants. This rule does not apply to the laboratory staff, however. The experimenters can find out at any time which role is performed by which participant in the experiment.

The most important task to be fulfilled when conducting an experiment is making sure the experiment runs smoothly. The experimenters do this by using the software program to monitor the progress of the experiment. At any time, the software tells the experimenters which participant is doing what, and how much time has passed since this phase of the experiment started. Considering that participants' decisions are round-based in most cases, this is highly relevant, because all other participants have to wait until the last participant has entered his or her decision. If the experimenters notice that certain participants take much longer than the others, their responsibility is to approach these participants to find out whether there is a reason why they have not made their decision. In some phases of the experiments, participants are required to click an OK button. If the monitoring screen indicates that some participants have not yet made that confirmation although sufficient time has elapsed, the experimenters first remind all participants to click the OK button once it appears on their screens. If individual participants still don't comply with that request, the experimenter can use the available data to identify the workstations where these participants are seated and remind them individually to click the button.

The vehemence with which experimenters use their physical presence to reinforce informal rules is illustrated by the following empirical example:

In an experiment on minimum wages, participants were divided into groups of five. Each group consisted of one consumer, two company executives, and one employee of each company. In each round, the consumer had a fixed amount of money he could spend on ten goods. Whatever amount was left after making his purchases, the consumer could keep as a profit for himself. The companies had to offer their goods for a certain price without knowing the price their competitor would choose. Moreover, the consumer could see, prior to making his purchase, how much the employees of each company would be paid for each good sold. At the end of each round, the score was displayed to all group members, who had to confirm it by clicking the OK button. In the observed experiment, the participants who had taken on the role of company executives started not paying their employees any wage whatsoever. The way the program was set up, the participants acting as employees had no chance to do anything against that, because their part in the experiment was restricted to simply clicking the OK button after each round. After a few rounds, however, the experiment suddenly stalled. All participants were waiting. It was only with the help of the monitoring screen that experimenters were able to identify the participant who caused the experiment to stall. One of the participants who had assumed the role of employee refused to click the OK button and kept all other participants waiting for several minutes. The experimenters asked him to click the button now so that the experiment could continue. He did as he was told. But in the next round, there was another delay caused by the same participant, who again kept all the others waiting. Once more, one of the experimenters approached him, urging him to please stop interfering with the experiment from now on. For the rest of the experiment, one of the experimenters remained standing behind the said participant.

This kind of behavior also indicates a very high level of competence regarding the range of behaviors possible inside the laboratory. By doing what he did, the participant used the only option he had left in his assigned role as employee: choosing non-action as an expression of protest. Although the participant's intervention caused a factual disruption and a notable delay in the experiment, his violation of the rules was not an instance of non-compliance with the rigid laboratory rules. In terms of the economic language game, his action did not run counter to the economists' understanding of communication. Moreover, the instructions did not state any time limit for confirming the results of each round. As the participant could not be accused of non-compliance, he did not put his payment at risk. This example also illustrates the defining role of the experimenters' monitoring screen with regard to what goes on inside the laboratory. The software program's functionalities made it easy to identify the participant causing the delay and track him down in the laboratory. The experimenters' two oral requests to stop disrupting the experiment by delaying it can be understood as a rule created right there in that situation. The experimenter who positioned himself behind the back of the participant in question could use his physical presence to add extra emphasis to the new rule by directly monitoring the participant's compliant behavior.

Let's look at another example to see how easy it is to be excluded from an experiment due to an inconsiderate violation of the rules.

During a series of experiments on the endowment effect, participants were asked to play *Connect 4* on the computer. Teams of two players each were formed via the network. Playing the game, the players took turns placing their checkers. In case of a tie, the win went to the player who did not place the first checker. The teams were instructed to play until one of the two parties had scored four wins. The players were told that the winner of the group would win some sort of object as a prize. For technical reasons, it was not possible to deactivate the integrated chat function of the *Connect 4* game. To eliminate communication between the players as a possible confounding variable during the experiment, the instructions pointed out explicitly and emphatically that players were not permitted to use the chat function. If players violated that rule, the instructions went on, their opponent would be declared the winner of the group, and the person who violated the rule would have to leave the laboratory without receiving any payment. In one experiment, the following incident occurred:

One participant (P1) raised his hand and said that his partner wasn't reacting anymore. With the help of the monitoring screen, the experimenters were quickly able to identify the participant in question. That participant (P2) explained his actions by pointing out that his partner had sent a chat message, which is why he (P2) had ceased to react. The content of the chat message, however, did not refer to the object that could be won in the *Connect 4* game but rather to the fact that the current game would end up in a tie, suggesting that the two players simply start a new game. Yet that didn't change anything about the fact that participant (P1), who had used the chat function, had to leave the laboratory without payment, whereas the other participant was declared the winner of his group.

This sequence clearly illustrates the simultaneous production and reproduction of the situational order in the laboratory. It is only when the other actors start doing something that P1 becomes aware of his non-compliant behavior. His deviation from the rules is only constructed as such through the related actions of the other actors. The imposed sanction is legitimized by referring to the rules as shared background knowledge. P2 can tell by the actions of the experimenter that he has acted 'correctly' when ignoring P1's suggestion to start a new game. The experiment calls for compliant behavior in terms of the researchers' language game even if participants' situational assessment of the rule leads to individually different valuations. As pointed out earlier in the theoretical section, the empirical example shows how the actors in a given situation mutually construct each other through their practices.

As the empirical examples have shown, the laboratory staff works to overcome disruptions and 'fix' deviant participant behavior. The experimenters' interventions vary in magnitude, ranging from friendly comments to kicking participants out of the laboratory. In all of the 'crisis situations' described above, however, the situation is never as severe as to cause the experiment to break down. This is interesting evidence of the actors' situational competence. Both participants and experimenters are able to respond appropriately to disruptions, using ethnomethods to ensure the interaction can go on. Which rules remain valid in a specific situation and which are suspended because of the crisis is something that the actors negotiate and communicate on a per-situation basis during the interaction.

4.6 Conclusion and Outlook: The Situation-Based Construction of the Rational Actor

The specific situation of the laboratory experiment is designed in a way to create a friendly environment for the kind of rational agent's decision-making economists seek to study. Key aspects of the experimental design and economists' basic assumptions are translated into the situation-based framework of the laboratory situation by means of the experiment's material setting and the experimenters' so-called framing methods. These conceptual aspects were discussed in Sects. 4.3 and 4.4, where I showed how they are integrated into the experimental practice in the laboratory. My observations are in line with sociological findings about the performativity of economic research: 'Economic experiments perform economic objects, in a quite general sense [...] They account for what they provoke.' (Muniesa and Callon 2007, 163). This article focused on the practical construction of the (economic) rational actor model in the laboratory setting. I outlined some field observations to illustrate how economists not only produce laboratory situations in accordance with their research methods and the scientific rules of their epistemic community. I also show how these situations are challenged, tested, and sustained by the equally performative behavior of compliant or non-compliant participants, by carrot and stick through punishment and payment.

Standardization and control thereby emerge as the key elements in the design and practical implementation of laboratory experiments. As described above, this includes the spatial–material setting, the instructions, the software, and the use of monetary incentives, which create an equally performative scene for all interactions in the laboratory.

Building on an ethnomethodological reflection on the observations described above, the following section will show that the co-construction of the situation by experimenters and participants also produces the rational actor in the process of the experiments.

The actor that economists seek to study in the experiment is a very specific one. This actor is an anonymous decision-maker and needs visual and acoustic shielding from other persons to avoid unintended interferences. He interacts with experimenters and other participants just in the pre-structured ways given by the experimenters. Different representations of the decision-making situation in the written instructions have an impact on that actor. Controlling and explanatory techniques are used to increase the likelihood of actors understanding the instructions and rules in the way anticipated by the researchers. He is supposed to make decisions based on his motives. These motives are controlled by offering monetary incentives and decision-dependent payment. His interest in the monetary incentive doesn't decrease in the course of the experiment. That's why the central way to penalize this actor for non-compliant behavior is the potential loss of yielded profits.

Based on the ethnomethodological perspective's claim that actors are the result of practices rather than guided by fixed motives (Rawls 2006), the relevance of the monetary incentives, the instructions, and the visual and acoustic restriction through the material setup are established by the practices of the actors.

The use of the economic actor model and its empirical implementation in the experiments reflect the assumptions about the limited nature of the economists' actor model. Here, we see a striking connection to Garfinkel's criticism of the construction of an actor incapable of judgment. Doing so means doing exactly what Garfinkel criticized as an example of treating individuals as cultural judgmental dopes. When designing and evaluating the experiments, researchers apply this notion of an actor to design different variations of an experiment and compare them in terms of their different outcomes. According to the economists' reasoning, this is of essential importance if the experiments are to be successful and replicable.

That is why, in experimental practice, test questionnaires, examples, and additional explanations are used to increase the likelihood of participants understanding the instructions and rules in the sense intended by the researchers. Monetary incentives are used to reward compliant and prevent non-compliant behavior of participants. The empirical examples have shown in various ways—from recruiting participants to penalizing non-compliant behavior—how the monetary incentive is integrated into experimental practice and how it is used to support the compliance.

The ethnomethods that experimental economists apply in the laboratory to construct and analyze the rational actor are thus factually inseparable from the economic concept of the rational actor. In line with the procedural perspective of 'doing,' the way this rational actor is performed and commonly fabricated in the laboratory is a simultaneous production and reproduction of that phenomenon. What characterizes the economists' rational actor to be studied by means of laboratory experiments thus becomes evident in the experimental practice itself.

The practices of experimental economists are designed to construct a situation in which there is a higher chance of participants adopting the language and behavioral game induced by the economists, thereby enabling the researchers to study the rational actor. As the empirical examples have shown, order in the laboratory is being produced and reproduced on a situation-by-situation basis. Appropriate behavior is marked as appropriate because none of the experimenters feels a need to intervene. Deviant behavior is penalized and addressed with the help of typical methods and in a way that is appropriate in that particular situation. The actors apply certain practices that enable them to fix the situation and to maintain situational order.

Acknowledging that participants' choices are limited does not mean to negate the fact that the actors do have the potential to interpret situations through action, thereby making sense of them. Especially the crisis situations show that there will always be an 'overflow' (Callon 1998) between the framing of a situation and the connection to the world outside of the laboratory which can cause 'deviant' interpretations of the situation. But even if the actors are capable of engaging with situations in a creative manner, they are biased with regard to how they perceive their choices. As a consequence, some options seem to be appropriate, whereas others are marked as undesirable and deviant behavior by means of impending sanctions and control. Judgment also means being able to recognize the options that are not available in a specific situation and being able to choose between the limited alternatives.

As a result, experimental economists might succeed in creating a 'hospitable environment' (Guala 2007) for observing the rational actor. But by ensuring the scientific standards and rules of their epistemic community, they also impose a specific game, which must be accepted and played by the participants so that the experiment can take place successfully. This raises questions, which are also acknowledged by behavioral economists themselves: Accordingly, Colin Camerer points out that identifying the game that actors are actually playing in the laboratory is still among the top ten open questions in behavioral economics (Camerer 2003, 474–475). As I hope to have shown, the ethnomethodological perspective can bring light into laboratory settings and practices thereby turning the economists' question into a problem of performativity. From an ethnomethodological point of view, the question to be asked here is then how different situational practices in the experiment lead to different understandings of the game among participants.

Notes

1. For a detailed discussion of methodological aspects, see Böhme (2015b).

References

Amann, Klaus. 1994. Menschen, Mäuse und Fliegen. Eine wissenssoziologische Analyse der Transformation von Organismen in epistemische Objekte. *Zeitschrift für Soziologie* 23(1): 22–40.

Böhme, Juliane. 2015a. 'Doing' Laborexperimente: Eine ethnomethodologische Betrachtung der Praxis experimenteller Wirtschaftsforschung im Labor. *Berliner Journal für Soziologie* 25(1): 33–59.

Böhme, Juliane. 2015b. Kombination von Grounded Theory und Ethnomethodologie. In *Handbuch Grounded Theory—Von der Methodologie zur Forschungspraxis*, edited by Claudia Equit and Christoph Hohage. Weinheim: Beltz Verlag (in print).

Callon, Michel. 1998. An Essay on Framing and Overflowing: Economic Externalities Revisited by Sociology. In *The Laws of the Markets*, edited by Michel Callon, 244–269. Oxford: Blackwell.

Camerer, Colin. 2003. *Behavioral Game Theory: Experiments in Strategic Interaction*. Princeton, NJ: Princeton University Press.

Garfinkel, Harold. 1967. *Studies in Ethnomethodology*. Englewood Cliffs, NJ: Prentice-Hall.

Garfinkel, Harold, and Harvey Sacks. 1979. Über Formale Strukturen Praktischer Handlungen. In *Ethnomethodologie. Beiträge zu einer Soziologie des Alltagshandels*, edited by Elmar Weingarten, Fritz Sack, and Jim Schenkein, 130–176. Frankfurt am Main: Suhrkamp.

Gieryn, Thomas F. 2002. Three Truth Spots. *Journal of the History of the Behavioral Sciences* 38(2): 113–132.

Greiner, Ben. 2015. Subject pool recruitment procedures: Organizing experiments with ORSEE. *Journal of the Economic Science Association*, 1(1): 114–125.

Guala, Francesco. 2005. *The Methodology of Experimental Economics*. New York: Cambridge University Press.

Guala, Francesco. 2007. How to Do Things with Experimental Economics. In *Do Economists Make Markets? On the Performativity of Economics*, edited by Donald MacKenzie, Fabian Muniesa, and Lucia Siu, 128–162. Princeton, NJ: Princeton University Press.

Kahneman, Daniel, and Amos Tversky. 1981. The Framing of Decisions and the Psychology of Choice. *Science* 211: 453–458.

Knorr-Cetina, Karin. 1984. *Die Fabrikation von Erkenntnis. Zur Anthropologie der Naturwissenschaft*. Frankfurt am Main: Suhrkamp.

Knorr-Cetina, Karin. 2002. *Wissenskulturen. Ein Vergleich naturwissenschaftlicher Wissensformen*. Frankfurt am Main: Suhrkamp.

Knorr-Cetina, Karin, and Michael Mulkay. 1983. *Science Observed. Perspectives on the Social Study of Science*. London: Sage.

Kübler, Dorothea. 2010. Experimental Practices in Economics: Performativity and the Creation of Phenomena. *WZB Discussion Paper*. SP II 2010-01.

Latour, Bruno, and Steve Woolgar. 1979. *Laboratory Life: The Social Construction of Scientific Facts.* London: Sage.

Muniesa, Fabian, and Michel Callon. 2007. Economic Experiments and the Construction of Markets. In *Do Economists Make Markets?: On the Performativity of Economics*, edited by Donald MacKenzie, Fabian Muniesa, and Lucia Siu, 163–189. Princeton, NJ: Princeton University Press.

Rawls, Anne W. 2006. Respecifying the Study of Social Order—Garfinkel's Transition from the Theoretical Conceptualisation to Practices in Detail. In *Seeing Sociologically: The Routine Grounds of Social Action*, edited by Harold Garfinkel, 1–97. Boulder: Paradigm Publishers.

Simon, Herbert A. 1957. *Models of Man, Social and Rational: Mathematical Essays on Rational Human Behavior in a Social Setting.* New York: John Wiley and Sons.

Smith, Vernon L. 1976. Experimental Economics: Induced Value Theory. *American Economic Review* 66(2): 274–279.

Wittgenstein, Ludwig. [1953] 1971. *Philosophische Untersuchungen.* Frankfurt am Main: Suhrkamp.

CHAPTER 5

The Problem with Economics: Naturalism, Critique and Performativity

Fabian Muniesa

The idea according to which economics does contribute in a performative manner to the construction, enactment, initiation, transformation or maintenance of economic things has gained some relevance in the social sciences, but has also raised scholarly discomfort and criticism (e.g. MacKenzie et al. 2007).[1] What is this discomfort about? It is in part, I would like to argue here, about the unsettling of naturalism. I develop the hypothesis that such discomfort can serve as a useful vehicle to analyse naturalism in economic reason, or, more precisely, to explore some features of a somewhat naturalistic style that often characterizes the taking into consideration of economic things. The intellectual device that I use in order to tackle this question consists of a series of 'breaching thought experiments' in which the behaviour of economic reason is confronted to annoying situations (one being the claim that economics is performative) with the purpose of showing what is taken for granted when the naturalness of economic things is at stake.

I consider here 'economic reason' in a wide sense, and I refer with this expression to a variety of things: traits of modern economic thought and of economic science (i.e. economics), but also aspects of economic logic

F. Muniesa
Centre de Sociologie de l'Innovation (CSI),
Mines ParisTech (École des Mines de Paris), Paris, France

operating in economic reality, or characteristics of the modern critique of the economy or modern critique of economic thought as well. The mixing-up of all these things may generate confusion and ambivalence, but it is precisely this otherwise usual mixture of aspects—all equally modern—that I want to address. The notion of 'naturalism' is also taken in a very general sense: I employ it mainly in reference to the intellectual style of modern scientific thought and to the idea of the existence of natural laws, although I consider also, more prosaically, situations in which something economic may be referred to as being natural.

What I call 'breaching thought experiments' constitute here a tentative and candid intellectual methodology. These experiments resemble, in some way, the breaching experiments developed in the tradition of ethnomethodology (Garfinkel 1967). For the purpose of this demonstration, breaching experiments can be defined as a series of exasperating questions or weird interventions that aim at bothering a normal course of action in order to reveal what normality is made of, or at least to point to some features of interest. The idea here is to test the behaviour of economic reason when confronted to a few odd situations. These experiments are also thought experiments in the sense that they do not correspond to actual, empirically monitored events. But they are not fully imaginary, however. They are based on experience gathered in real conversations with economists or with scholars who criticize economics, in real observations of such conversations, in real exposure to economic scholarly publications and in real self-exercising of economic reasoning and of economic critique. The reader is kindly asked to add her own considerations to mine, as both a potential experimenter and a potential experimental subject. But, before pursuing with the experiments, I shall provide an introductory clarification on the performativity of economics and on naturalistic style in economic reasoning.

5.1 Performativity and Naturalism

Scholarly speaking, and although the notion of performativity is connected to a wide variety of academic concerns and intellectual traditions (Muniesa 2014), the precise topic of the performativity of economics is often defined as an emerging research program resulting from the penetration of science and technology studies into economic sociology (e.g. Fourcade 2007). The extent to which the natural sciences do shape the world they scrutinize has been explored at length in science and technology studies (e.g. Hacking 1983; Latour 1987; Pickering 1995; Galison 1997; see also Jensen 2004 for a cogent overview). This works for the social sciences too, and it is probably Michel Callon's proposal that best characterizes the move towards economics: studying the ways in which the sciences of the economy do shape their objects would be the first move towards a renewal of the sociological understanding of how economic things work (Callon 1998).

Empirical research such as the one undertaken by Donald MacKenzie on the role of financial theory in the construction of contemporary financial markets demonstrates the extent to which a sound sociological analysis of economic things needs including economics and its effects among its objects of inquiry (MacKenzie 2006, 2007). As more and more markets appear nowadays as made out of market sciences (economics at large, including finance, marketing, accounting and other market-enabling disciplines), this empirical take cannot but make sense. But Callon's formulation of this research direction points out some rather radical implications that challenge—to some extent and in clear resonance with actor–network theory—the usual tenets of economic sociology (Callon 2007b).[2]

Although it is more than reasonable to acknowledge the fact that economists, with their tools and theories, sometimes intervene in the construction of economic things (be they markets, firms, economies, currencies or other economic formations), to consider that usual economic things such as 'economic preferences', 'marginal utility', 'transaction costs', 'equilibrium prices', 'rational expectations', 'aggregate demand', 'credit risk' or 'cost of capital' are not naturally occurring phenomena but rather artificial things which are always the outcome of an intense work of constitution—a work that includes the sciences of the economy among its key ingredients—is probably a more disturbing idea, an idea whose disturbance is best summarized by the provocative adage that can be extracted from Callon's proposal: namely, that 'the economy is embedded not in society but in economics' (Callon 1998, 30). Further disturbance is added to this by the fact that the problem of truth and falsehood, a problem to which the sciences (economic or otherwise) are usually expected to be exposed to, is neatly disregarded, within this viewpoint, in favour of the problem of success and failure. This challenges indeed the efficacy of a purely epistemological critique of economics: the truth or falsehood of economics depends now on its capacity to construct worlds in which its claims can hold together, not on any natural adequacy of these claims to their external objects.[3] Performativity would thus hamper not only science but also, more fatally, the rational critique of science—and these annoyances echo, of course, the objections to constructivism that have often animated science and technology studies in the case of the natural sciences (Callon 1999). The idea of the performativity of economics has been indeed critiqued in these or similar terms, sometimes with an explicit reference to its connections to actor–network theory (e.g. Miller 2002; Fine 2003; Mirowski and Nik-Khah 2007). In substance, this idea, it is said, would remove the strength of an epistemological critique of economics (i.e. a critique capable of signalling a lack of truth in scientific statements), and also possibly of a sociological critique (i.e. a critique capable of signalling social, explanatory forces more fundamental and effective than the work of economics).

The cultures of scientific thinking and scientific practice, the attachment to ideals of natural inquiry and intellectual critique in modern thought and the connections of all this to the development of the modern world are at the centre of a number of contributions to the history of science and to the anthropology of scientific activities. Modern reason has been scrutinized in more than one way and put to the test of various forms of historical and anthropological contextualization. As it is aptly put in the promotional jacket of a notable contribution to the subject matter, 'objectivity has a history, and it is full of surprises' (Daston and Galison 2007). Particularly important contributions to this line of inquiry come from anthropology. The consideration of modern scientific thought in the light of an anthropological classification of the different modes of thought (and of identification of beings in particular) undertaken by Philippe Descola (2013) proves particularly useful for that task.[4]

Descola classifies, in a very structural fashion, the several ways in which human beings might consider their interiority, and this interiority's relations to external beings, especially to beings other than other human beings. Naturalism is, according to this classification, a structure of intellection characterized by a univocal and exterior nature. Within a naturalistic mode of intellection, there might be several interiorities, preferably human (i.e. human subjects), but all beings (including human beings but not only) share a similar physicality. The modern scientist can thus talk about multiculturalism (several cultures, several ways of thinking and of seeing things, several ways of experiencing human interiority), but never about 'multinaturalism' (since there is only one nature). But human beings have lived and still can live without partaking of this form of thought. In animism, another section of Descola's classification, all beings (and not exclusively human ones) are similar in the sense that they all share similar interiorities. But they are different in the sense that they have different physicalities. From an animist perspective (e.g. in Amazonian thought), everything has a soul, everything is a person. Trees have a soul, animals have a soul and rivers have a soul. And all souls are similar in kind. But everything might not share the same nature. A soul may have different bodies that live in different natures.[5] In animism, there is certainty about the universality of spirit, but there is uncertainty about the universality of body and matter.[6]

One important hypothesis defended by scholars interested in the particular style of 'Western' modern reason (whatever this means) is that the latter is plainly naturalistic. Human beings are strictly distinguished from other beings. They distinguish themselves because they have one kind of interiority that we call subjectivity and which might be idiosyncratic. But they all share among them and with other beings a similar physicality, in the sense that they share the same laws of nature. Bodies are bodies here and elsewhere. Molecules are molecules here and elsewhere. Radiation is radiation here and elsewhere. The self-evident outcome of that state of mind is modern scientific inquiry. Galilei's motto is crucial in this characterization of naturalism: the book of nature might not be easy to read, but there is surely only one and it is written in mathematical language, that is, a language prone to scientific reading. Authors such as Bruno Latour, however, have opposed meticulously this version of what modern thought is and of how it operates (Latour 1993, 2013). For Latour, naturalism corresponds to the picture modern science keenly provides of itself, but is at odds with what modern science really does. According to Latour, the archetypical modern thinker speaks with a forked tongue, praising naturalism, pretending to be a naturalistic-minded inquirer, but in practice not stopping from producing hybrids, from entangling human beings and other beings and from provoking nature rather than unveiling it. Such duplicitous manners constitute probably the main outcome of the symmetric anthropology of modern reason undertaken by Latour.

Is naturalism a fundamental characteristic of economic thought? Or is economics an instance of the modern forked tongue? My purpose here is not (and could not be) to try to settle this issue. It is, at best, to provide some elements that could help consider the case of economic reason with a few observations on the 'naturalistic style' often displayed in economics or about economics. The claim on the performativity of economics can intervene in this inquiry as an assertion that breaches the naturalistic style of economic thought, but also as a test of the forked tongue hypothesis. In what follows, I propose a series of situations (which I have referred to as 'breaching thought experiments') that allow characterizing several aspects of this question.

5.2 EXPERIMENT 1: NAME BOTH SCIENCE AND OBJECT

It is easy to recognize in economics a sort of a naturalistic style, which is of course acknowledged to a great extent in the literature. We may all have different cultures, opinions, beliefs, but we all share the same economic laws. Money is money here and elsewhere. Budgetary constraints are budgetary constraints here and elsewhere. Marginal utility is marginal utility here and elsewhere. We all may have different preferences, but we all certainly have such a thing as 'economic preferences' that can be taken into account economically and aggregated together into some sort of an economic calculation. Any sort of process, regardless of its particular point and scope, as soon as it is costly (and any process may be costly) is economic in nature and thus subject to economic analysis. Economic characteristics do characterize individuals, but also groups, families, countries, firms and also natural resources, ecosystems, animals or, why not, cells, neurons and computer programs. This seems naturalistic indeed: a reason that goes through all and unifies all, an economic nature that is transversal to all bodies and to all souls. Is economic reason the paramount naturalistic reason?

Let me point to a most curious index of naturalization that characterizes economic reason, an index that is actually more visible in French than in English. Although in the English vocabulary, a difference is often drawn between economics (the science) and the economy (the thing), in French the same word may be used to refer to both: *'économie'*. *'L'économie'* is 'the economy', but also 'economics' in the sense of the academic discipline. The later can also be referred to as *'sciences économiques'*, but *'économie'* corresponds to a fairly widespread use, especially among professionals of the discipline. Note the oddity: for the study of *'société'* (society), you have *'sociologie'* (sociology); for *'coeur'* (the heart) you have *'cardiologie'* (cardiology); for *'minerais'* (minerals) you have *'minéralogie'* (mineralogy); but for the study of *'économie'*, you have *'économie'*. In an empirical version, this first 'breaching thought experiment' could consist in playing, in the conversation, with what would have been a logical guess for the name of the science: *'Vous voulez dire économicologie'* ('You mean economicology').[7] A science that calls itself just like its object: this may look like an extreme symptom of naturalism, or maybe rather like a brilliant coup of naturalization.

Of course, such anecdotal comments should not stand in place of references to a long and fruitful tradition in the history of ideas that explores naturalistic style in economic reason. This tradition has studied at length the construction of the categories of modern economics, starting with the notions of economic individual, self-interest, utility, and so forth, including also the study of how mathematics and formalistic languages in general have allowed economics to emancipate, as a science, from moral philosophy (see, e.g. Dumont 1992; Dupuy 1992; Ingrao and Israel 1990; Demeulenaere 1996). But it is nonetheless interesting to stop at issues such as the ordinary naming of economics. Is economics the knowledge or the object of knowledge? In French, this question (our first 'breaching thought experiment') is in effect slightly annoying, and revealing. And perhaps in English too, especially in American English, a language in which a political speech on 'economics' can indeed be meant to be on the current state of affairs in the national economy or, conversely, praise for the importance of 'the economy' can indeed signify a call for more attention to scientific economic thinking.[8]

5.3 Experiment 2: The Object of Economics (Natural or Social)

Consider now economics (the science) as a whole and ask the question of its object. More prosaically, ask an economist: 'What kind of object does your science look at?' You may then introduce some annoying element and refine the question as follows: 'But do you study objects which are natural or which are social?' Insist: 'Is your science a social science or a natural science?'

Well, of course, we may easily say that economics is the study of the economy, and that the economy is a human invention, so the science that studies it is therefore a human or social science. However, the experiment is far from providing such a straightforward conclusion. When you tell an economist that her science should naturally side with the humanities or the social sciences, an expression of discomfort or of slight doubt may arise, especially among economists from a highly quantitative or mathematical tradition. Such kind of expression of doubt or discomfort may arise spontaneously, in multidisciplinary gatherings in which, say, economists and sociologists negotiate a common institutional tag. It is usual, for instance, to use labels such as 'economic and social sciences' in order to refer to scholarly institutional arrangements (e.g. academic departmental sections or research councils) that are to encompass both economics and other sciences such as sociology, anthropology, history or political science. But does this mean 'economics and the rest of the social sciences'? Or does this rather mean 'economics and other sciences which are different because they are social'? There is, indeed, a doubt.[9] Some economists would spontaneously praise for the difference, others would find that odd, others may just say: 'Well, yes, economics is a social science too indeed, but it is a different sort of social science because it is a hard science.'

There are myriad possible answers to that question. But many may carry some hesitation. Nuances, in any case, need to be put forward in order to make sense of a difference that does not seem to be quite comfortably acceptable. What is this hesitation about? Not exactly, I believe, about the object of economics as such. The object of economics is probably quite clear for economists as well as for other scholars: it is the economy, it is economic processes, it is economic behaviour. The hesitation comes when economics is asked to stick to one of two boxes: nature or culture, social or natural. Because economic things, even if they are things of culture (human things), are also perfectly natural in the sense that the laws they may follow are like the laws of nature—and explicitly not like those other laws we primarily refer to as politically instituted conventions.

This imaginary test is meant to produce exaggeration and, of course, does not make justice to the variety of approaches (including so-called 'heterodox' or 'critical' ones) that exist in economics, or to the fact that some specialties in sociology, political sciences or psychology may share similar features too. But it is now commonly accepted that the hard core of economics (i.e. its mainstream or more legitimized components) has been fighting to side with the hardest sciences, such as physics (Mirowski 1989). And the entanglements of economics with the hard sciences are not only a matter of shared use of scientific tropes. Training in physics or mathematics has become a usual feature (if not a requisite) of the curricula that lead to a brilliant career in the trading rooms of international investment banks. Would quantitative finance side with the social sciences or with the natural sciences? How would it behave in our first 'breaching thought experiment'? Will it actually try to go beyond this divide, just as the 'cyborg sciences' once tried to do? And what about other avant-garde forms of economics such as computational economics or network dynamics? Economics gives itself, as an object of inquiry, something that is visibly human. But economics prefers to describe itself as a natural science or rather as a 'general' science, with a transversal object called 'economy', an object beyond nature and culture, just as pioneering cybernetics invented for itself a similarly transversal object called 'information' (Mirowski 2002).

5.4 Experiment 3: Money in a Constructivist Situation

Let us explore further these strange features of the style of economic reason. The economy is probably one site in which the expression 'social construction of' is less meaningful. To say that the economy is socially constructed may be as pointless as saying that society is socially constructed: of course it is. Economic institutions are artificial by definition. Money is a cultural artefact, and so are the market, the factory and the firm. Economy is done, made up, not given in nature. Even economists from the hardest laissez-faire traditions can agree on this. But, by a strange loop of reason, economic categories suddenly appear as more natural than natural. Economic laws are not laws in the primary sense of the word, which means political rules instituted by human beings, but laws in the sense of the laws of nature, which are universal and independent from any political endeavour. This loop, this drift of economic reason, does not only happen among economists. Of course, they are the first to benefit from this effect of naturalization. But this loop is shared by everybody, in a certain sense, and shared specifically by critics of economics.

The setting of our third 'breaching thought experiment' is a constructivist situation: a scholarly conference in which radically constructivist or relativist perspectives are used in order to address objects which are usually considered as natural realities, such as physical space or time. This could be, for instance, a conference on science and technology studies.[10] In this setting, it is possible to attend lectures or presentations in which categories as hard as time and space (i.e. primary qualities, in the philosophical sense) are said to actually look universal only because of an intense work that accomplishes them as universal.[11] But, some attendees would convincingly explain, since this work is partial and contingent, this leads indeed to a multiplicity of forms of organizing spacing and timing, best referred to as verbs (Jones et al. 2004). Imagine a moment in which, against this constructivist background (which is indeed not naturalistic at all), the issue of money is raised. Prefer a situation in which money (or capital or markets) is critically presented as some universal machinery that creates abstraction and renders all things and beings commensurable and alienable, and which therefore informs, or constructs, particularly globalized and uniformed forms of timing and spacing. The breach is introduced by a redirection of constructivism to money, perhaps with a naïve remark such as: 'But I thought that money was the thing that was socially constructed, at least more than time and space!'

When economic things (money, capital, markets) appear as explanatory factors in radically constructivist accounts of supposedly natural things (space, time), one could expect an equitable use of constructivism. Actually, one could have thought of money as an easier target to relativism than time or space. There might exist several spaces and several times, but there surely exist several monies, several types of markets and several accounting methods (see Dodd 1994; Zelizer 1997; Hopwood and Miller 1994; Power 1996). And still, economic categories can intervene in a constructivist appraisal of the natural world in a much unconstructed fashion: as universal realities that provide a univocal explication of global unity. The continuity of time and space might be an illusion. But capital is the ultimate primary quality. The outcome of this somehow likely 'breaching thought experiment' is the remarkable resistance to constructivism of economic reasoning, the tendency of economics to side with explanatory variables instead of with constructed ones or, better, to stand as a fixed point around which revolves the rest of the world.

5.5 Experiment 4: The Question of Fiction and Reality

Now ask an economist: 'Are your models fictitious or real?' This is a test on the ambivalence of economics towards its object. Economics has often been accused of dealing with fictional objects.[12] This is particularly the case for economic theory in the neoclassical tradition and for purely model-based economic science. Microeconomic models or game-theoretical models deal with market configurations that are unreal in the sense that they are composed of minimalist actors who exchange minimalist goods with minimalist money in a minimalist setting, and that attain situations of equilibrium or disequilibrium that we also can legitimately call minimalist.

What do economists say to that? Many may complain against this critique and claim realism instead (realism of assumptions, realism of data fed into the models). But some (good ones) may also acknowledge the fictional status of economic models, and even add that fiction is not an unintended flaw of their science but a purposeful rational device.[13] The ambition of economic theory, will they answer, is not to describe what happens in the real world but to isolate and comprehend a mechanism that is precisely almost impossible to isolate 'in vivo': hence the need to abstract it, for example, to simulate or to model it. This answer, sophisticated but widespread among economists with sufficient epistemological curiosity, seems quite reasonable. But it comes with a strange supplement. The economist produces a theoretical fiction, develops a model or an experimental setting that describes the functioning of that fiction, deploys a number of implications and consequences of this functioning and, little by little, this deployment starts to navigate into the world 'out there', to circulate within regulatory bodies, consultancy firms, investment banks, government departments, and to flow in what we curiously call 'economic reality', as opposed to the presumably 'unreal' reality of economics. Of the many examples of this sort of movement from abstracted theorizing to operational implementation, perhaps the neoclassical theory from the Chicago School and the reconfiguration of the Chilean economy by the 'Chicago Boys' under Augusto Pinochet is a particularly salient one (Valdés 1995; see also Montecinos and Markoff 2009; Ariztía 2012). If addressed at these economists and their teachers, our 'breaching thought experiment' might have triggered an interesting set of well-structured but at some point slightly paradoxical reactions, wavering between a lecture on the distinction between normative and positive economics and a comment on the political usefulness of being scientifically right.

Is this another example of modernistic forked tongue? Do economists tell they unveil economic laws but then actually institute them? Even in the hardest laissez-faire traditions of contemporary neoliberal economics, there is a realist perception of the fact that markets are constructed and that economists may need to work as constructors if they want to achieve their policy project, as pointed out by Michel Foucault in the case of neoliberal economics (Foucault 2008). Perhaps the key to this experiment does not lie in the choice between reality and fiction (several compromises are possible in this respect) but in the position of the narrator as an author—be it of fictions or of realities, indiscriminately. The economist can claim authorship of her axiomatic models without much trouble. But she would probably prefer to fade out in favour of the economy itself as authors of economic realities. This ellipsis is particularly important to neoliberal approaches, since, according to these, markets are supposed to be more intelligent than economists.[14]

5.6 EXPERIMENT 5: ECONOMICS IS PERFORMATIVE

Let us now turn to a 'natural-occurring experiment': Michel Callon's programmatic call (Callon 1998) and some subsequent critical reactions.[15] I use some of the critics here, with all respect due, as the victims of one imaginary 'breaching thought experiment' on the polemical behaviour of economic reason. In particular, I use the critique put forward by Daniel Miller and by Philip Mirowski, two scholars working from different academic perspectives (the first is an economic anthropologist and the second is an economist and historian of science) but who do have in common an explicit critique of mainstream economic science and a sense of infuriation in their approach to performativity.

In his critique of Callon as well as in earlier work, Daniel Miller proposes a theoretical framework to tackle the impact that economists, their theories and their models might have in real economies (Miller 2002; see also Carrier and Miller 1998). Although this might seem comparable to Callon's proposal, Miller sees in Callon's viewpoint a threat: the research direction defended by Callon may hamper the sociological critique of economics and turn into a defense of the power of economics instead. For Miller, if the market that is envisioned by economists can have a real impact in economic reality, it is more as an ideological model than as an empirically operational tool. Economists produce views, models and doctrines, which remain essentially abstract. These may hold as viewpoints in order to justify action. But they cannot form a durable world. The reason is that economic reality is not like economists posit it, but is constituted instead by social bonds and power relations, that is, it is socially constituted. These are phenomena that only sound economic sociology or anthropology can analyse. But sociology then needs to emancipate from the illusion of economics: the illusion of the existence of detached rational agents in a world of calculation. Talking about the performative efficacy of economics in constructing such world of calculation would be to contribute to reproducing this illusion.[16]

The arguments of Mirowski and his co-author Edward Nik-Khah are comparable to Miller's, although not exactly equivalent (Mirowski and Nik-Khah 2007).[17] Science studies come here at the forefront, but rather as a tool to examine the ideas and epistemic constraints that govern the intellectual ventures and professional biographies of economists. One major contribution of Mirowski's history of economics is to show that economics (especially within neoclassical or associated paradigms) is essentially defective (e.g. Mirowski 2004). For Mirowski, Callon's notion of performativity suggests that, even being false, an economic theory may pretend to veracity just because of its pragmatic success. Again, this is the same as siding with the economists. Because economists can impose their economic machines they can also aim, with the help of Callon, at being scientifically right: this is probably what most infuriates Mirowski. If, by any chance, some economists or some devices coming out from their science get involved in some social engineering, such as the construction of a market, this is not at all due to any performative aspect of their science. It is, above all, a matter of power and economic interests. It is not economists who perform, it is the powerful. Callon, according to Mirowski, takes our critical eye away from this fact, away from the explanatory power of social forces—or economic forces, which seems to be the same anyway, since we seem to be dealing here with capitalism.[18]

These scholars, convinced of the interest of combining an examination of economics and a sociological critique of effective economic practices, are alarmed by an hypothesis that seems empirically reasonable but that can become an unsupportable threat to the critique of economics. My suggestion is that the alarm triggered by this test reveals some difficulties of the naturalistic style of economic reason. At the core of this dispute lies the crucial question of the truth of economic reasoning, a question that, as any other question about truth, may be indeed disturbed by any pragmatist idea (in the philosophical sense), as the idea of performativity is. The problem is that this critical resistance ends up enforcing a strange alliance between economic science and economic critique. Why? These critics need to face a difficult paradox. From a first claim that signals how necessary it is to criticize economics (this science being false and providing a flawed account of economic reality) follows a second one against its performative capacity (being so flawed, the science as such fails from having any effect on reality). In short, economics is wrong but does not matter. So why then should we waste time criticizing something that does not matter?

The answer, I believe, has to do with something (a style of thought) that these exemplary critical voices might share with the economists they criticize.[19] There is agreement on the fact that the aim of economic science should be to describe and comprehend the world (critically or not), but not to provoke it. The debate is on the kind of economic science that can do that rightly or wrongly. But, although there is disagreement on how to be positive about the stuff the economy is made of, there is conformity on the fact that the economy is out there, as an operating variable that needs to be captured. What Callon says—namely that there is no economic anything without a process of economization—cannot be easily admitted, perhaps because what is out there (let us call it 'nature') is ultimately thought to be already written in economic language.[20]

5.7 By Way of Conclusion

I believe that some naturalistic style intervenes at the surface of economics, but that the hypothesis of the modern forked tongue (claiming naturalism while blatantly performing) applies also quite well to the case of economic reason (Muniesa 2014, 35–41). This is something our five 'breaching thought experiments' contribute to clarify. The first experiment (on the naming of economic science) brought evidence of a naturalizing subconscious in economic academic parlance. The second experiment (on economics as social or natural science) revealed a highly unchallenged universalism, with an object that is highly general and undetermined. The third experiment (on economics in constructivist situations) demonstrated a high degree of resistance of economics to any kind of relativism or constructivism. The fourth experiment (on the fictitious character of economic theory) made explicit some ambivalence on the reality of the object of economics. The fifth experiment (on the performativity of economics) pointed to some traumatic features of the modern critical position when it comes down to economics.

Perhaps our fifth experiment focused too much on the potential behaviour of the critique of economics and failed to address the behaviour of economics itself. How would the paramount modern economist react to the idea, preferably formulated in a bold manner, that her science provokes the world it studies? Will she be shocked? Or would she rather remain indifferent?[21] She might just say something along the line of: 'Yeah, thanks, we knew already.' Adding perhaps: 'But if we do that it's because we're right.' Performative pride, wrapped up into a naturalistic epistemological layer? That is only a hypothesis, but a plausible and interesting one. When you say that the book of nature is written in economic language but then you get caught in the act with that book in one hand and a pen in the other, well, the wisest thing to do is probably to smile at the camera and say that, ok, you were writing it but you were writing it nicely. Overall, it is interesting to note that the performativity breaching experiment seems to be perceived as a shock more by critics of economics than by economists themselves. If we consider this test as a test that excites naturalistic style, this would mean that naturalism affects economic reason better when this reason is critical. This is serious, because it would mean that the critique of economic reason would be indeed more tied to the naturalization of economic categories than economics is. If true, this would be a bit sad—although hopefully not definitive.

Extracting the critique of economics from the epistemic anxieties of modern naturalism is certainly a difficult task. But it is a worthwhile one. Not because this would redress an intellectual tort—quite to the contrary—but rather because it can further critical imagination in the direction of experimental realism. Experimental critique indeed sees in performativity a deliberate methodological key, definitely not some sort of a demoralizing deterrence (Muniesa 2014, 127–130). In a sense, the 'breaching thought experiments' that have been sketched out in these pages could very well be considered as a fine, though rudimentary example of what I call experimental critique. That would amount to some kind of 'experimental economics'—but certainly not of the canonical kind (Guala 2005).[22] This would not be about testing the fit or misfit of economic reason in relation to economic reality, but rather about provoking states of anthropological shock in which the worldviews that control what 'economic' means are unsettled, debated and transformed.

Notes

1. The reflection that follows was initially elaborated as a contribution to the Colloque de Cerisy on 'The Historical Anthropology of Scientific Reason' organized by Philippe Descola and Bruno Latour (12–19 July 2006). It was also presented at the 'Markets, Economics, Culture and Performativity' Conference at Goldsmiths organized by Will Davies and José Ossandón (6 March 2007) and then transformed into a contribution to 'Performativities: Contexts, Domains, Perspectives', a publication project (sadly suspended) prepared by Silvia Posocco and Sadie Wearing. After sleeping for a few years, it gained the opportunity to reach the published side of the world as a contribution to this collection of essays prepared by Ivan Boldyrev and Ekaterina Svetlova. Acknowledgements are also due to funding provided by the European Research Council (grant no. 263529). I thank Daniel Beunza, Ivan Boldyrev, Michel Callon, Will Davies, Philippe Descola, Keith Hart, Petter Holm, Bruno Latour, Scott Lash, Javier Lezaun, Emilio Luque, Donald MacKenzie, José Ossandón, Paolo Quattrone, Ekaterina Svetlova, Silvia Posocco, Yamina Tadjeddine, David Teira, Manuel Torres and Sadie Wearing for their remarks on this unusual essay or for the conversations that contributed to the reflection.

2. Actor-network theory—a scholarly viewpoint of which Michel Callon is an active proponent—originated as both a materialist approach to the study of science and technology and a pragmatist critique of regular sociological explanatory categories (see Muniesa 2015).
3. Francesco Guala's phrasing conveys this idea remarkably well: 'Economic rationality is not like Newton's laws, which are supposed to be at work everywhere in the universe. It is a fragile property that must be carefully preserved by creating a hospitable environment' (Guala 2007, 147).
4. But see also the clarification provided by Marshall Sahlins (2008).
5. Eduardo Viveiros de Castro uses the notion of 'multinaturalism' to characterize this feature of Amazonian thought (Viveiros de Castro 1998, 2004; see also Latour 2004).
6. The structural classification proposed by Descola adds to naturalism and animism, two other forms of intellection, which are totemism and analogism. In naturalism, the universality of physicality is linked to the contingency of interiorities. In animism, the generalization of interiority is a counterpoint to the differentiation of physicalities. Totemism is characterized by a moral and material continuity of physicality and interiority. Analogism is the realm of multiple differences at both levels, and of multiple networks of correspondence that make the world readable as an ongoing chain of relations.
7. This instance of a 'breaching thought experiment' is based on a real conversation with a British academic on how to translate slightly ambiguous expressions like *'économie des conventions'* or *'économie alternative'*, for which both 'economics' and 'economy' may make sense (but mean entirely different things).
8. For useful examinations of the origins of the notion of 'the economy', see for instance Breslau (2003), Mitchell (1998, 2002, 2008) and Goswami (2004).
9. This second instance of a 'breaching thought experiment' is based on one actual discussion at the seminar of an interdisciplinary academic society which includes economists, sociologists, anthropologists and political scientists as members and which hosts a monthly research seminar in Paris on the 'social studies of finance'. A clarification was needed to convince one economist (who actually made a point of speaking 'as an economist') that *'sciences sociales'* was short for *'sciences économiques et sociales'*, not a nasty way to exclude economics. The name of the ESRC (the British Economic and Social Research Council) can also serve as a blatant demonstration.
10. This instance of a 'breaching thought experiment' is inspired by observations at one panel discussion at the annual meeting of the Society for Social Studies of Science held in Paris in 2004.

11. A particularly helpful introduction to the analysis of the role of metrology in the construction of universality is O'Connell (1993).
12. On the 'scholastic fallacies' of economics, see for instance Bourdieu (1997, 2005). On the problems of criticizing the unrealism of assumptions in economics, see Cartwright (1999).
13. This fourth 'breaching thought experiment' is based on memories from the first year of the undergraduate programme in economics at the Universidad Autónoma de Madrid (I then had to redirect preferences to sociology).
14. I owe to Petter Holm a particularly brilliant interpretation of neoliberal economics in the light of Right Said Fred's debut song 'I'm too sexy': the music stops abruptly after we hear 'I'm too sexy for this song'.
15. This last instance of a 'breaching thought experiment' is inspired by the discussions that took place during a workshop on 'The Performativities of Economics' held in Paris in August 2004. A number of papers presented at the workshop evolved into contributions to MacKenzie et al. (2007), others were part of Callon et al. (2007).
16. A follow-up of this discussion can be read in a series of reactions and of further clarifications (Callon 2005; Miller 2005; see also Barry and Slater 2005). An accurate appraisal is offered by Holm (2007).
17. An almost identical version of the argument is published as Mirowski and Nik-Khah (2008).
18. The empirical parts of the critique by Mirowski and Nik-Khah focus on an article by Francesco Guala on the role played by economics (game theory and experimental economics) in the construction of spectrum auctions (Guala 2001). A further exchange is available in Edward Nik-Khah (2006) and Guala (2006). See also Callon (2007a), Nik-Khah (2008) and Muniesa and Callon (2009).
19. I put here the topic of shared academic socialization and scholarly habits aside.
20. If we play with Descola's structural categories, we could think of the role of Callon in this 'breaching thought experiment' as impersonating the menace of analogism over naturalism, that is, the menace of a style of intellection that would be attentive to varied correspondences between economists and economies, both imitating each other, engendering each other.
21. In a critical review of MacKenzie et al. (2007) published in the *Journal of Economic Literature*, David Colander (a reputable economist) says among other things that he does not understand the notion of performativity very well, that he dislikes it and finds it irritating, that proponents in that field think this topic is new but in reality it is not, that the point is about signalling a contradiction in economics but that there is no such contradiction,

that most economists are indifferent to science studies and would not care about this discussion, and, finally, that economics should perform more and better (Colander 2008).
22. I refer instead the reader to the tradition of 'provocative containment' examined in Lezaun et al. (2013). I owe to Javier Izquierdo the idea that cultural pranks can operate as vehicles for economic inquiry (Izquierdo Antonio 2010).

REFERENCES

Ariztía, Tomás (ed.). 2012. *Produciendo lo Social: Usos de las Ciencias Sociales en el Chile Reciente*. Santiago de Chile: Ediciones UDP.
Barry, Andrew, and Don Slater (eds.). 2005. *The Technological Economy*. London: Routledge.
Bourdieu, Pierre. 1997. Le Champ Économique. *Actes de la Recherche en Sciences Sociales* 119(1): 48–66.
Bourdieu, Pierre. 2005. *The Social Structures of the Economy*. Cambridge: Polity Press.
Breslau, Daniel. 2003. Economics Invents the Economy: Mathematics, Statistics, and Models in the Work of Irving Fisher and Wesley Mitchell. *Theory and Society* 32(3): 379–411.
Callon, Michel. 1998. The Embeddedness of Economic Markets in Economics. In *The Laws of the Markets*, edited by Michel Callon, 1–58. Oxford: Blackwell.
Callon, Michel. 1999. Whose Imposture? Physicists at War with the Third Person. *Social Studies of Science* 29(2): 261–286.
Callon, Michel. 2005. Why Virtualism Paves the Way to Political Impotence: A Reply to Daniel Miller's Critique of The Laws of the Markets. *Economic Sociology European Electronic Newsletter* 6(2): 3–20.
Callon, Michel. 2007a. An Essay on the Growing Contribution of Economic Markets to the Proliferation of the Social. *Theory, Culture & Society* 24(7–8): 139–163.
Callon, Michel. 2007b. What Does It Mean to Say that Economics is Performative? In *Do Economists Make Markets? On the Performativity of Economics*, edited by Donald MacKenzie, Fabian Muniesa, and Lucia Siu, 311–357. Princeton, NJ: Princeton University Press.
Callon, Michel, Yuval Millo, and Fabian Muniesa (eds.). 2007. *Market Devices*. Oxford: Blackwell.
Carrier, James G., and Daniel Miller (eds.). 1998. *Virtualism: A New Political Economy*. Oxford: Berg.
Cartwright, Nancy. 1999. *The Dappled World: A Study of the Boundaries of Science*. Cambridge: Cambridge University Press.
Colander, David. 2008. Review of 'Do Economists Make Markets?' *Journal of Economic Literature* 46(3): 720–724.

Daston, Lorraine, and Peter Galison. 2007. *Objectivity*. New York: Zone Books.
Demeulenaere, Pierre. 1996. *Homo Oeconomicus: Enquête sur la Constitution d'un Paradigme*. Paris: Presses Universitaires de France.
Descola, Philippe. 2013. *Beyond Nature and Culture*. Chicago, IL: University of Chicago Press.
Dodd, Nigel. 1994. *The Sociology of Money: Economics, Reason and Contemporary Society*. Cambridge: Polity Press.
Dumont, Louis. 1992. *Essays on Individualism: Modern Ideology in Anthropological Perspective*. Chicago, IL: University of Chicago Press.
Dupuy, Jean-Pierre. 1992. *Le Sacrifice et l' Envie: Le Libéralisme aux Prises avec la Justice Sociale*. Paris: Grasset.
Fine, Ben. 2003. Callonistics: A Disentanglement. *Economy and Society* 32(3): 478–484.
Foucault, Michel. 2008. *The Birth of Biopolitics: Lectures at the Collège de France, 1978–1979*. New York: Palgrave Macmillan.
Fourcade, Marion. 2007. Theories of Markets and Theories of Society. *American Behavioral Scientist* 50(8): 1015–1034.
Galison, Peter. 1997. *Image and Logic: A Material Culture of Microphysics*. Chicago, IL: University of Chicago Press.
Garfinkel, Harold. 1967. *Studies in Ethnomethodology*. Englewood Cliffs, NJ: Prentice-Hall.
Goswami, Manu. 2004. *Producing India: From Colonial Economy to National Space*. Chicago, IL: University of Chicago Press.
Guala, Francesco. 2001. Building Economic Machines: The FCC Auctions. *Studies in History and Philosophy of Science, Part A* 32(3): 453–477.
Guala, Francesco. 2005. *The Methodology of Experimental Economics*. New York: Cambridge University Press.
Guala, Francesco. 2006. Getting the FCC Auctions Straight: A Reply to Nik-Khah. *Economic Sociology European Electronic Newsletter* 7(3): 23–28.
Guala, Francesco. 2007. How to Do Things with Experimental Economics. In *Do Economists Make Markets? On the Performativity of Economics*, edited by Donald MacKenzie, Fabian Muniesa, and Lucia Siu, 128–162. Princeton, NJ: Princeton University Press.
Hacking, Ian. 1983. *Representing and Intervening: Introductory Topics in the Philosophy of Natural Science*. Cambridge: Cambridge University Press.
Holm, Petter. 2007. Which Way is Up on Callon? In *Do Economists Make Markets? On the Performativity of Economics*, edited by Donald MacKenzie, Fabian Muniesa, and Lucia Siu, 225–243. Princeton, NJ: Princeton University Press.
Hopwood, Anthony G., and Peter Miller (eds.). 1994. *Accounting as Social and Institutional Practice*. Cambridge: Cambridge University Press.
Ingrao, Bruna, and Giorgio Israel. 1990. *The Invisible Hand: Economic Equilibrium in the History of Science*. Cambridge, MA: MIT Press.

Izquierdo Antonio, Javier. 2010. *Marcianos, Melanesios, Millonarios, Mochileros y Murcianos: De la Perdición Económica o el Turista Espacial.* San Fernando de Henares: Fiesta.
Jensen, Casper Bruun. 2004. A Nonhumanist Disposition: On Performativity, Practical Ontology, and Intervention. *Configurations* 1(2): 229–261.
Jones, Geoff, Christine McLean, and Paolo Quattrone. 2004. Spacing and Timing. *Organization* 11(6): 723–741.
Latour, Bruno. 1987. *Science in Action: How to Follow Scientists and Engineers through Society.* Cambridge, MA: Harvard University Press.
Latour, Bruno. 1993. *We Have Never Been Modern.* Cambridge, MA: Harvard University Press.
Latour, Bruno. 2004. *Politics of Nature: How to Bring the Sciences into Democracy.* Cambridge, MA: Harvard University Press.
Latour, Bruno. 2013. *An Inquiry into Modes of Existence.* Cambridge, MA: Harvard University Press.
Lezaun, Javier, Fabian Muniesa, and Signe Vikkelsø. 2013. Provocative Containment and the Drift of Social-Scientific Realism. *Journal of Cultural Economy* 6(3): 278–293.
MacKenzie, Donald. 2006. *An Engine, Not a Camera: How Financial Models Shape Markets.* Cambridge, MA: MIT Press.
MacKenzie, Donald. 2007. Is Economics Performative? Option Theory and the Construction of Derivatives Markets. In *Do Economists Make Markets? On the Performativity of Economics*, edited by Donald MacKenzie, Fabian Muniesa, and Lucia Siu, 54–86. Princeton, NJ: Princeton University Press.
MacKenzie, Donald, Fabian Muniesa, and Lucia Siu (eds.). 2007. *Do Economists Make Markets? On the Performativity of Economics.* Princeton, NJ: Princeton University Press.
Miller, Daniel. 2002. Turning Callon the Right Way Up. *Economy and Society* 31(2): 218–233.
Miller, Daniel. 2005. Reply to Michel Callon. *Economic Sociology European Electronic Newsletter* 6(3): 3–13.
Mirowski, Philip. 1989. *More Heat than Light: Economics as Social Physics, Physics as Nature's Economics.* New York: Cambridge University Press.
Mirowski, Philip. 2002. *Machine Dreams: Economics Becomes a Cyborg Science.* New York: Cambridge University Press.
Mirowski, Philip. 2004. *The Effortless Economy of Science?* Durham, NC: Duke University Press.
Mirowski, Philip, and Edward Nik-Khah. 2007. Markets Made Flesh: Performativity, and a Problem in Science Studies, Augmented with Consideration of the FCC Auctions. In *Do Economists Make Markets? On the Performativity of Economics*, edited by Donald MacKenzie, Fabian Muniesa, and Lucia Siu, 190–224. Princeton, NJ: Princeton University Press.

Mirowski, Philip, and Edward Nik-Khah. 2008. Command Performance: Exploring What STS Thinks It Takes to Build a Market. In *Living in a Material World: Economic Sociology Meets Science and Technology Studies*, edited by Trevor Pinch and Richard Swedberg, 89–128. Cambridge, MA: MIT Press.
Mitchell, Timothy. 1998. Fixing the Economy. *Cultural Studies* 12(1): 82–101.
Mitchell, Timothy. 2002. *Rule of Experts: Egypt, Techno-Politics, Modernity*. Berkeley, CA: University of California Press.
Mitchell, Timothy. 2008. Rethinking Economy. *Geoforum* 39(3): 1116–1121.
Montecinos, Verónica, and John Markoff (eds.). 2009. *Economists in the Americas*. Cheltenham: Edward Elgar.
Muniesa, Fabian. 2014. *The Provoked Economy: Economic Reality and the Performative Turn*. Abingdon: Routledge.
Muniesa, Fabian. 2015. Actor-Network Theory. In *The International Encyclopedia of Social and Behavioral Sciences*, edited by James D. Wright, Vol. 1, 2nd ed., 80–84. Amsterdam etc: Elsevier.
Muniesa, Fabian, and Michel Callon. 2009. La Performativité des Sciences Économiques. In *Traité de Sociologie Économique*, edited by Philippe Steiner and François Vatin, 289–324. Paris: Presses Universitaires de France.
Nik-Khah, Edward. 2006. What the FCC Auctions Can Tell Us About the Performativity Thesis. *Economic Sociology European Electronic Newsletter* 7(2): 15–21.
Nik-Khah, Edward. 2008. A Tale of Two Auctions. *Journal of Institutional Economics* 4(1): 73–97.
O'Connell, Joseph. 1993. Metrology: The Creation of Universality by the Circulation of Particulars. *Social Studies of Science* 23(1): 129–173.
Pickering, Andrew. 1995. *The Mangle of Practice: Time, Agency and Science*. Chicago, IL: University of Chicago Press.
Power, Michael (ed.). 1996. *Accounting and Science: Natural Inquiry and Commercial Reason*. Cambridge: Cambridge University Press.
Sahlins, Marshall. 2008. *The Western Illusion of Human Nature: With Reflections on the Long History of Hierarchy, Equality and the Sublimation of Anarchy in the West, and Comparative Notes on Other Conceptions of the Human Condition*. Chicago, IL: Prickly Paradigm Press.
Valdés, Juan Gabriel. 1995. *Pinochet's Economists: The Chicago School in Chile*. Cambridge: Cambridge University Press.
Viveiros de Castro, Eduardo. 1998. Cosmological Deixis and Amerindian Perspectivism. *Journal of the Royal Anthropological Institute* 4(3): 469–488.
Viveiros de Castro, Eduardo. 2004. Exchanging Perspectives: The Transformation of Objects into Subjects in Amerindian Ontologies. *Common Knowledge* 10(3): 463–484.
Zelizer, Viviana A. 1997. *The Social Meaning of Money: Pin Money, Paychecks, Poor Relief, and Other Currencies*. Princeton, NJ: Princeton University Press.

CHAPTER 6

Performativity Matters: Economic Description as a Moral Problem

Philip Roscoe

6.1 Introduction: Why Performativity Matters

Would an economist be upset if 'accused' of designing markets? It seems unlikely in the light of Alfred Roth's work on barter markets for transplant organs (Roth et al. 2005) and his subsequent Nobel Prize for innovations in market design, or the much trumpeted success of Ken Binmore's mobile spectrum auctions (Binmore and Klemperer 2002). On the contrary, economists seem to delight in their success as designers of markets. This poses a problem for the sociological study of markets and performativity—at least if that is all that performativity has to say, for performativity 'simply loses its radicalism' (Frankel et al. 2015), repeating the truism that market designers work on markets. Moreover, to limit performativity to the building of markets lays the thesis open to an easy critique: that the infinite permutations of the social are simply too complex to be presented as the outcomes of a single economic theory, and that performativity accounts are little more than victor's histories as told by the economists themselves (Mirowski and Nik-Khah 2007). Yet social scientists do have much to say about the role of economics in the constitution of the social: the 'anthropology of markets' research programme has drawn attention

P. Roscoe
Department of Management, University of St Andrews, Scotland, UK

to the socially constituted nature of market agency, and to the social and organisational processes that contribute to 'economisation' and the formation of markets (Çalışkan and Callon 2009). The cornerstone of this analysis is the performativity thesis which, when taken seriously, implies much more than just economists as builders of markets: that economics itself constitutes the economy, that the economy is 'embedded in' economics, and, perhaps most importantly of all, that the economic agent is a product of economics (Callon 1998).

In this chapter, I seek to elaborate on the concept of performativity, not simply as market design, but as the careful configuration of social life along the lines predicted by economic theory. I will argue that the processes of description in which economic modelling and simulation specialises are performative not only of organisational settings but also of individual rationalities and behaviours. On this basis, I will seek to connect the concept of performativity to a rich tradition of thinking critical of market arrangements as iniquitous, commodifying, and even contrary to human flourishing (MacIntyre 1981; Sandel 2012). It is not my intention to develop this critique, so much as to indicate how performativity offers a theoretical and empirical means of connecting the sociological study of the economy to such philosophical arguments. As it is uninteresting to say that economists build economic objects, our attention should instead focus on the framing, overflowing, and reframing that occur as they do so. Our lens must slip from the market itself to the organisational settings it configures and the behaviour it engenders; away from the trivial observation that a market designer builds markets to the weightier truth that in building markets she restructures society. For we must, in the end, ask what kind of world we wish to see performed (MacKenzie 2006).

The literature of the anthropology of markets has remained mute on the topic of ethics. Despite the existence of a recognisable critical narrative in the social sciences concerning the problems with markets and marketisation (Polanyi 2001 [1944]; Sandel 2012; Roscoe 2014) market studies, which deals with so many pressing contemporary concerns, has never allowed itself to take sides. Certainly it is the case that the founders of science and technology studies—from which the anthropology of markets has sprung—were keen to break with existing critical sociological theory. Yet positions have softened over the years: Latour, whose differences with his critically inclined predecessors were never understated (Schinkel 2007), has taken up a strong position on the subject of climate change and the anthropocene (Latour 2013). Perhaps, in its hastiness to disassemble the 'social' (Latour 2007) and the 'economic'

(Callon 1998) market studies has left itself no firm ground upon which to assemble its critique.

Its silence is all the more uncomfortable as economics does not shy away from involvement in the political and moral—austerity, taxes, social security, immigration, education, and many others are ethically charged issues where economic interventions have substantially dictated policy. Cost-benefit analysis and the study of trade-offs are often the basis of explicit normative appeals. For example, when discussing responses to global warming, Robert Mendelsohn, Professor of Environmental Economics at Yale, argues that 'the ethical justification for intentionally overspending on selective projects with low rates of return is weak indeed' (Mendelsohn et al. 2008, 309). Equally, Horst Albach, the pre-eminent scholar of business ethics in Germany, argues decision theory and calculating trade-offs automatically give rise to 'ethics' when appropriately applied (Hühn 2014, 529, 537).

If performativity were only to imply that economists build markets, or intervene in policy, perhaps the moral codes of economics would matter less. We might take refuge in the well-worn distinction between fact and value, and comfort ourselves in the relative scarcity of empirical cases documenting 'genuine'—what MacKenzie (2006) calls 'Barnesian' performativity. But it is increasingly recognised that fact and values are mutually constitutive, overlapping, and intertwined (Dussauge et al. 2015). I extend that claim to argue that much of the moral work is done in the 'utterance' itself. In this essay, therefore, I offer a bare-bones account of performativity as centring on the act of *description*—the primary task of economic theory. Description, by this account, carries illocutionary force. Following Austin (1962) and more recently Muniesa (2014), I argue that description alone represents a substantial enough instance of performativity to make us take note of moral quandaries that it produces; descriptions, as Muniesa puts it, 'provoke', act, and present us with a 'new ontological deal'. Descriptions are facts, acts of classification with consequences in the world (Bowker and Leigh Starr 1999; Pollock and D'Adderio 2012); they are complicit in the act of economisation, for they happen at the boundaries, in 'the agonistic field, where the delimitation-bifurcation between the economy and politics is constantly being debated and played out' (Callon 2010, 165).

To say that economic utterances are complicit in economisation is to claim that they performatively recast aspects of the social as economic, and are governed by a particular form of instrumental–rational authority. The performativity thesis suggests a subordination of critical discourse through the construction of economic modes of action; it is what the critical theorist Judith Butler (2010) calls 'a hermeneutic phenomenon' where the answer to the question (or at least the manner in which the answer must be specified) is determined in advance. So, for example, economic calls for austerity must be met, not by arguments based on justice, rights, or notions of jubilee and forgiveness, but by other economic arguments. If the only response to a strongly normative economic claim is a counter claim made in the same language, we are offered little possibility for critique. Economic arguments, in short, demand economic answers, deflecting attention from other means of accessing difficult problems (Roscoe 2013). Moreover, if taken seriously, it involves the substitution of one set of normative arrangements with another—the construction of rational economic calculations of worth and ethical action to replace existing claims and justifications. Finally, the performative reclassification, by means of description, of an activity as economic radically changes the nature of social interactions and of the goods and virtues available to social actors participating in that activity. Critical narratives have shown economic interactions to be instrumental, means–ends rational, commodifying, and corrosive of virtue (MacIntyre 1981; Sandel 2012; Roscoe 2014); if performative descriptions constitute such social practices, then performativity itself presents a difficult moral problem, for performativity implies that theorists and market builders are complicit in all of the above. At the same time, echoing Butler (1997), the recognition of performativity's moral force gives us a basis for enacting social change—a problem performatively recast as opportunity.

My argument proceeds as follows: first of all, I will explore how social scientific description constitutes reality, via the work of Law and Urry (2004) and of Austin (1962) and Butler (2010). Following Butler, I examine how 'hermeneutic' performativity weakens the critical capacity of social scientists. Finally, I explore performativity and the reconstruction of social relations. Throughout I illustrate with examples, both from the market studies literature and from my own empirical studies of online dating and organ transplantation.

6.2 Economics Describes

Let us consider first of all a point on which there must be universal agreement: that economics describes. But what does it mean to claim that economics describes? Moreover, what does economics do *in* describing? It is clear that economics has consequences both in and for society; as with all social sciences, economic methods 'participate in, reflect upon, and enact the social' (Law and Urry 2004, 392) wherever they are invoked. But political arguments based on GDP or of deficits, while they exemplify the interactions of state and social science, do not in themselves counter the assumptions of empiricist realism: that there is a world to be discovered which exists prior to and independently of the process of discovery, and that the world can be unproblematically separated from any knowledge we might gain of it. Law and Urry press the case further. The social sciences, they argue, 'have effects; they make differences; they can help bring into being what they also discover' (ibid. 393). Durkheim's investigation of suicide is a case in point, transforming the phenomenon into an analytic category, a national problem, and a potential site of political intervention. It follows that there are multiple possible realities attached to multiple available research processes, and that choices of reality become political matters; that 'every time we make reality claims in social science, we are helping to make some reality more or less real'(ibid. 396). Just as Durkheim's investigation helped to demarcate the 'social' through the use of novel statistical measures, so the practices of economic investigation carve out the 'economy' as a distinct site of economic expertise.

What are the transformations in performances of the social, then, if we choose to describe it is a specifically *economic* way? That depends, of course: such a question can only be answered by empirical work of the kind in which the anthropology of markets specialises. Let me offer an example. Shiona Chillas and I have argued that online dating is an example of the performative construction of a market, driven by an economic model of relationship formation as utility maximising, rational matching, and underpinned by positivist social science methods (Roscoe and Chillas 2014). We explored how online dating instantiates abstract categories such as 'love' and 'happy marriage' into forms tangible enough to be sold on subscription. As with other instances of market design—such as Holm and Nielsen's (2007) study of fishing quotas—economic theory is able to enrol other kinds of scientific knowledge into its performative network. In the case we studied, positivist psychology lends a hand. An entrepreneur and an (equally entrepreneurial) psychologist set to work to establish the basis of a happy marriage, through the discovery of key factors underlying stable long-term relationships. In order to identify these factors, they conducted large-scale surveys of married couples in the USA. The surveys were detailed and included a standard measure of marital happiness used in the social sciences (Spanier 1976). This asks, for example, about the frequency of holding hands or arguing with spouses. Factor analysis across the population identified the factors that could be linked with couples scoring in the upper quartiles of marital happiness, with happiness measures taken as a proxy for long-term stability. These factors, of course, form the basis of the site's commercial offering: they are social scientific descriptions of the basis of a happy marriage.

These entrepreneurs' investigation is predicated on exactly the kind of naive realism that Law and Urry identify. The methods assume that there is, indeed, an ideal of a happy marriage, of which all actually existing marriages are but shadows flickering on the wall of the cave. Moreover, they assume (and our interviewees stated) that such an ideal is linked to personality traits which are fixed, and therefore stable enough to be analysed as causal mechanisms. There is no consideration of interdependence between investigation and its object, not even that the ongoing research process might have consequences for participants—perhaps the reflexive undertaking of the individual completing the questionnaire to hold hands with their next partner more often and argue less frequently. The knowledge gained can be separated from its object, processed, repurposed, and applied for commercial gain, without any apparent effect upon the ontological object of the happy marriage. Yet, if we recognise that social scientific methods constitute the things that they discover, it is clear that this cannot be the case; at the very least, the social scientific investigation constitutes the happy marriage as an object of scientific investigation and intervention, and as an object bearing certain characteristics.

In describing the happy marriage, our entrepreneurial pair has constituted it as an analytic object, and a site of intervention and commercial opportunity. In a second move, their project of matching describes a relationship as a maximising partnership of existing traits. Here we can see the shadows of a most economic understanding of relationships, as a bargain settled in advance (Becker 1973). Finding partners for individuals becomes a taxing computational problem, an exercise in algorithmic matching of the state of affairs as it is now; people are no longer things in themselves but bundles of attributes to be instrumentally partnered. There is a double economisation at work here. First of all, the economic notions underlying matching surface in the language the industry employs to describe it: eHarmony's founder, Neil Clark Warren, has been quoted as saying 'in successful relationships similarities are like money in the bank. Differences are like debts you owe.' (Gottlieb 2006). Second, the algorithmic matching processes used within the databases to operationalise pairings are those pioneered by market designers, such as Roth, to the extent where dating sites produce algorithmically stable outcomes (Hitsch et al. 2010).

Altogether, a particular reality has been brought into being. It is one where a happy marriage exists as a specialised knowledge, and can be operationalised by economic protocols. As Law and Urry (2004) might suggest, this world is equally valid, and equally real as any other socially and discursively constructed understanding of partnership. Butler (2010) points out that such performatives proffer an ontological quandary: what was there before? Perhaps a happy marriage was rather like obscenity, as the old joke runs: one knew it when one saw it. More likely it was, like pre-Durkheimian suicide, embedded in a very particular web of discursive and material relations, and that those too are the subject of certain empirically available performatives. That is exactly the point. Studying performativity gives us the ability to unpick 'metaphysical presumptions about culturally contested categories' (Butler 2010, 148) and these twenty-first-century descriptions *do* have consequences. Through a series of descriptions, partnership is radically reconfigured. Whatever it was before, it has become something else, an analytic object brought into being through the apparatus of social science and operationalised in the same manner. The use of economic theory and social science methods has fundamentally reconstituted the social relations of meeting, matching, and partnership. I will return to this theme later in the chapter; first of all, we must consider the performative nature of description in more detail.

6.3 Performative Descriptions

Discussions of economic performativity have seldom focussed on description. MacKenzie is sceptical of performativity as a purely linguistic phenomenon. His 'Barnesian' performativity suggests feedback loops driven by material practices and instrumentation (MacKenzie 2006). An exception is Muniesa (2014), who anchors his discussion of performativity in pragmatism, particularly the notion of reality as an act of effecting—or 'effectuation'—and of signification as an act. He argues that 'descriptions add to the world... they are all facts, things that happen, events' (ibid. 18). In the case of financial markets, to take Muniesa's example, these descriptions constitute the real, developed through representations and reflexive action. The outlandish derivative contracts underlying the credit crisis of 2008 were not only blessed by economics—a standard critique of the discipline's engagement with the crisis (Turner 2012)—but also constituted by economic methods. It was the calculations of value at risk, the Gaussian copula, and others that gave substance to these ideas, fleshed out, and made them tradable. Financial objects, although 'both descriptions and objects of descriptions, are very, very real' (Muniesa 2014, 20), a real built by networks of relations (Law and Urry 2004).

The emphasis on description seems at first to counter the intention of Austin (1962), who early in his lecture series established a distinction between constative and performative utterances. Some phrases describe; others, notably promises, perform the intended act at the time of being uttered. Mäki (2013) maintains that performativity claims in economics should be limited to promises (such as trades and verbal agreements) that require no further implementation. Even in such a limited sense, however, performativity depends upon the interplay of speech acts and those who hear, read, or see them. Cochoy (2015) captures this semantic ballet in his study of the 'Myriam' billboards. In August 1981, posters appeared on the Paris underground featuring 'Myriam', an attractive woman in a bikini, and the words 'On September 2, I remove the top'. The promise is, in the strictest sense, a performative. But as Cochoy shows, it is the promise and the audience reaction that constitutes the performative: the combination of a linguistic performance, appropriate conditions of felicity (such as appropriate authority and credibility), and the social logics challenged by the promise of bare breasts and even nudity—for on September 2 Myriam promises to 'remove the bottom'. On 4 September the trick is played out. The billboard featured a naked woman with her back to the camera and the caption 'Avenir, the bill poster who keeps its promises'. There is, as Cochoy makes clear, a 'magic' to this promissory performativity, a magic that depends on the social conditions of felicity into which the performative is uttered (MacKenzie 2007; Mäki 2013).

I would suggest, however, that there is more to performativity than simple promises. It is worth revisiting Austin's (1962) original distinction between the illocutionary and the perlocutionary utterance, where the former suggests doing *in* saying, and the latter *by* saying. Both are contrasted to the locutionary utterance, or simple statement. Austin's intention is to unsettle the distinction between the speaker and the act of speech, which is implicit in an everyday conception of statements or persuasion. In Austin's classification, the locution is 'he said to me, shoot her' (ibid. 101, his example!); the perlocution is 'he persuaded me to shoot her'; while the illocution is 'he urged (ordered, or advised) me to shoot her'. Only in the latter case is the work of the phrase done in its utterance: the perlocutionary merely reports on unspecified means of persuasion (perhaps he kidnapped a loved one, or offered a bounty).

There is a tendency in market studies to view the performativity of theories as perlocutionary. Theories, according to this view, act by persuasion. They are utterances that may (or may not) cause things to happen in the world, for example, by indicating opportunities for profit or highlighting risk. Such is the case in MacKenzie's work, or Svetlova's (2012) discussion of the performative power of the discounted cash-flow. She suggests that the ability of the model to determine the shape of the world depends upon institutional arrangements, particularly the 'calculative culture' of individual asset management firms. While some firms use such models in a rigorous manner, others treat their outputs as starting points for discussion, or work with the model to achieve an outcome in line with existing opinions and expectations. Therefore, an appropriate calculative culture becomes a 'condition of felicity' for perlocutionary performativity; performativity only takes place if the firm wants it to. I fear that such a reading of performativity strips it of much of its power, eroding the basic claim that linguistic performativity occurs, whether one wants it to or not. Austin, I think, would also find this reading less interesting, precisely because the connection between the perlocutionary and the happening in the world is tenuous and dependent upon other factors:

> for clearly *any*, or almost any, perlocutionary act is liable to be bought off, in sufficiently special circumstances, by the issuing, with or without calculation, of any utterance whatsoever [...] you may, for example, deter me [...] from doing something by informing me [...] what the consequences of doing it would in fact be' (Austin 1962, 109–110).

Austin is most interested in the work of illocutionaries. These, he says, have 'a certain (*conventional*) *force*' (ibid. 109, my emphasis). He eventually finds in *every utterance* some degree of illocutionary force. Such an illocutionary utterance may be felicitous or otherwise, but Austin's point, so far as it is accessible at all, is that saying is always doing. In stating, we are always doing something:

> Once we realise that what we have to study is *not* the sentence but the issuing of an utterance in a speech situation, there can hardly be any longer a possibility of not seeing that stating is performing an act. Moreover, comparing stating to what we have said about the illocutionary act, it is an

act to which, just as much as to other illocutionary acts, it is essential to 'secure uptake' (Austin 1962, 138).

Illocutionary utterances are acts which take place in the world, securing uptake and offering meaning in individual situations. Importantly, truth and falsehood elude them: It is impossible to say whether the statement 'France is hexagonal' expressed in a school geography class, is true or false. It is merely 'rough', adequate, and fit for purpose. What matters, it seems, is the *conventional force* associated with the illocutionary, implying repeated, understood, and pre-existing linguistic resources.

What does Austin mean by conventional? Simply the language that has gone before. Thus, economic description is a cumulative, conventional process. Repeated illocutionary acts establish, bring into being, and stabilise; the construction of economic categories through illocutionary utterance is a spatially distributed and temporally iterative processes (Butler 2010). The social construction of the world is not performed anew with each speech act; instead, each act contains within it the accumulated power and authority of those utterances that have gone before (Karl 2013). The speaking subject is, therefore, recognised as an effect of the speech that produces it: iterative, citational, and circular. Focusing on the way that a financial model is used by asset managers, for example, ignores the many, many performatives that have gone into constructing the financial world that they inhabit. It seems relatively unremarkable to say that financial market actors are economic agents—yet it is, in fact, quite remarkable to discover carefully crafted financial or organisational rationality in action. Karl (2013) shows how Butler's account of performativity allows us to understand how economics offers a causal logic that can bring financial markets into being and at the same time claim authority over them. Paraphrasing Butler, when an economic description is made, for example, it is not simply that a subject performs a speech act; 'rather a set of relations and practices are constantly renewed, and agency traverses human and nonhuman domains' (2010, 150).

In summary, focussing on description as a performative act offers a version of the performativity thesis that is both theoretically meaningful and empirically robust. It allows us to understand the recursive, citational practices by which economic theory can simultaneously constitute and claim authority over the economy. It can complement existing investigations into the perlocutionary force of models and theories by drawing attention to the state of the world brought about by the description itself.

It helps unpack the claim that the economy is 'embedded in' economics (Callon 1998) and to understand how the economy may be maintained as a place of economic rules and economic rationality: an ongoing purification through the sheer power of description.

6.4 DESCRIPTION, PERFORMATIVITY, AND THE CRITICAL VOICE

So we see that speech acts have an illocutionary force, accumulating power through repeated iteration and citation. Economic descriptions are speech acts, performances of reality embedded in 'dense and extended sets of relations'. As the example of online dating mechanisms shows, descriptions are nature–culture hybrids (Latour 1993) where ends are folded into means (Latour and Venn 2002). To put it more simply: economic descriptions have moral content, hybridised and invisible among the disciplines' supposedly value-neutral models. Once economic models are in place it is very difficult to move arguments beyond their axioms, and it is hard to find an 'outside' on which to base critique (Roscoe 2013). Butler calls this a 'hermeneutic' reading of performativity, suggesting that the 'theory that enquires into the phenomenon establishes in advance what the phenomenon can and will be, and so participates in the making of what it finds' (Butler 2010, 152). In other words, the use of economic methods of analysis to describe a certain question or problem performatively cast that problem as an economic one, to be settled by economic methods.

An example of this hermeneutic nature of economic description is offered by an experiment conducted to determine the efficient allocation of transplant organs (livers) in the UK (for a detailed account see Roscoe 2015). Transplantation is an ethically fraught process, and allocation is closely monitored. In June 2009, the group of clinicians responsible for the supervision of liver transplantation agreed to develop a new, national scheme for the allocation of these organs, based entirely on clinical evidence of survival rates, and predicated on the assumption that public resources, in this case, organs for transplantation, should be used for maximum benefit—a reasonable enough assumption, perhaps, until it is recognised that any calculable definition of maximum benefit immediately excludes other, non-calculable (and popular) concerns such as justice (Ubel and Loewenstein 1996), sympathy, or right of rescue (Tong et al. 2010). It focussed on trade-offs, achieving the maximum cost–benefit outcomes from each liver, and was based on the agreement that those benefits—

potentially defined in many different ways—should be understood in terms of survival outcomes. It proposed a national allocation protocol that aims to maximise the national benefit of any liver donated, calculated on the basis of the total years of life saved at a population level.

To determine this protocol, the advisory group conducted a 'thought experiment' on allocation policy, which tested three differing allocation schemes: a need-based scheme; a survival-based, or best outcome, scheme; and a 'transplant benefit' scheme representing the net gain per patient, or estimated survival with a transplant, less estimated survival on the waiting list. Basing allocation on survival measures alone sees mortality shifted pre- or post-transplant: a best outcome approach, offering organs to the healthiest and youngest candidates on the list produces huge gains in post-operative survival, but results in high waiting list mortality; a need-based, or sickest-first, approach improves waiting list mortality at the cost of lower post-operative survival. The population life years approach, on the other hand, visualises total life expectancy on both sides of the operation, across the whole patient group. An allocation regime can then be chosen on the basis of the greatest contribution to population life expectancy.

The population life year approach, a 'thought experiment', is a novel form of description. A new reality, described by this measure, is assembled through complex relations of scientific factors—all with their associated measuring techniques, clinical records of survival and mortality, and complex statistical simulations. As with online dating, economics enrols other kinds of knowledge from the medical and social sciences in order to model and describe possible outcomes. At its heart, however, it is predicated upon economic claims; it is a cost–benefit, input–output model, based on utilitarian efficiency and rational trade-offs. Normative claims about the most appropriate way to organise one aspect of the social are embedded scientific relations, such that ends are inseparable from the means. Transplant allocation is a site of conflicting normative demands, invoking justice, fairness, ownership, and obligation (Roscoe 2015). The population life year measure trumps these with its normative assertion that the most appropriate use of resources is the one that will deliver most benefit, and that benefits should be measurable in terms of absolute years saved.

At the time of my study, the population life year simulation remained an experiment; it may gather force and sweep aside other measures, or it may remain a simulation on the statisticians' screens. Whatever the outcome, the experiment matters. These new, ethically charged descriptions, having been imagined and uttered into the world, make visible a different way of interrogating healthcare and offer up a world that is different from what went before. They have provoked, in Muniesa's words, a 'new ontological deal'. Parallel arguments may be drawn from studies of the valuation of nature (Fourcade 2011), or from my own account of the economic modelling of prices for cadaveric organs, and the $1000 cadaver (Roscoe 2013). Another famous example is the battle over the economist Nicholas Stern's choice of discount rate in his climate change report (Stern 2007); vicious arguments over technicalities, laden with explicit ethical claims, obscured the utility maximising framework taken up by the whole report and crowded out other possible considerations. It is this technical argument that made possible for Robert Mendelsohn et al. (2008) to remark that there is no ethical basis for investment in projects facing uncertain rates of return.

Every act of economic calculation gives rise to new descriptions, and these descriptions are performative. The allocation simulation shows how descriptions recast a problem in economic terms, shutting out some ethical claims, while privileging others. Nevertheless, recognising the performative nature of economic description offers a way into this hermeneutic problem, allowing us to pick away at the 'metaphysical presumptions' of such categories (Butler 2010, 148) and offering us a space in which we can begin to assemble a critique, should we wish, to do so.

6.5 Performing Economic Relations

Callon (1998, 2010) understands the economy as a clearly demarcated arena of the social world. In the economy, economic rules are followed and economic things done. It may at first seem tautological to define a social space by the activities which are themselves characterised by that space. But performativity offers a different perspective: it is the recursive and citational nature of economic speech which constructs the economy both as a site identifiable through economic actions, and as a space where economic actions are the appropriate form of social relations, where 'economic things are held stable and meaningful by economic words' (Cochoy et al. 2010, 141). Acts of classification and description demarcate the agonistic boundary between the economy and other social arenas; for Callon the economy must be constantly purified, its overflows managed and reframed. I have argued that the act of economic description is enough to breach this boundary, and to shift the social relations in question into the economic arena, where they become subject to the economic rules presented in the description.

What of individuals and their agency? People can choose how to act. Does this not have a bearing upon the eventual working out of a performative? Esposito (2012) considers the illocutionary construction of the social world as unproblematic compared with the radical uncertainty which sets in when individuals begin to exercise agency in deciding whether to participate in a theory. Yet this is where performativity really matters, for at the heart of Callon's programme we find the claim that economics constructs the economic agent; that the cardinal assumption of economic theory, the existence of the instrumentally rational, maximising actor (Townley 2008), is the product of economic theory itself.

Again, as a general claim, this may appear tautologous, but the concept of performativity allows us to investigate the processes of configurations through which the economic agent is organised and constructed. In other words, it provides a motivation for the kind of empirical work in which market studies excel; while economics strives for generality and theory, the performativity thesis requires us to examine the economic agent as an 'agencement' of the material and the discursive, of competencies and embodied skills (Callon 2007, 142). Thus, we have a mutually constitutive relationship between economic agency, evaluative or calculative competence, and ethics. This returns us to the problem of performativity. For economic accounts of competent valuation suppose that the agent, and the agent's knowledge, can be unproblematically separated from the world. But the data which the economic agent must evaluate are themselves descriptions which are bound up in multiple performativities, and the calculative resources upon which the agent must call are also products of, and productive of, economic and scientific theories. Agents, as I have argued, are caught up in a hermeneutic web of performative descriptions which allows no outside. Once an act is constituted as economic, it will be enacted according to economic rules, economic valuations, and economic norms.

As noted above, there are ready narratives in the social sciences for those who wish to critique the steady march of markets. Philosophical criticisms of economic relations argue that the proliferation of the economic converts social ties into instrumental ones and encourages a preoccupation with individual self-interest (Sandel 2012). Kantian perspectives suggest that economic relations are predicated on willingness to exchange and therefore demonstrate our disregard for uniqueness and dignity (Walsh 2001); economic social relations commodify persons and diminish individual dignity. MacIntyre (1981) argues that economic relations are emotivist, subversive of means–ends relationships, and fundamentally corrosive of human flourishing and the development of social goods.

Such narratives become more compelling at an empirical level. Recognising the performativity of economics offers us a means of understanding exactly how social relationships may be reconfigured into instrumental, economic exchanges, how individuals may be commodified and may commodify themselves, and how the development of social goods may be retarded. In the case of online dating, for example, the competence of actors to self-interestedly determine possible matches depends upon computer systems which are themselves performative of 'quality' in a potential partner. Online interfaces implement particular categories of understanding and accounting for the body and for personality, creating a 'standard body' (Jeacle 2003); journalistic accounts of what succeeds online (e.g. Webb 2013) suggest that they create a 'standard personality' as well. Users make individual rankings of the relative value of these categories and are encouraged, therefore, to establish the relative merits of different categories (e.g. hair colour versus hair length), and their value. The searcher (of either gender) is constituted as the one who controls, selects, and manipulates potential matches from the available pool. Selection decisions are made by the agencement of user and online interface: the economic agent rationally and instrumentally maximising her preferences. At the same time, these devices performatively enact what categories and qualities are perceived as important. The evaluative practices that must be employed on a dating site are inseparable from the process of commodification by which others are rendered into the material for commercial exchange. The user of the online dating site may exercise agency, but configured as a 'cyborg-dater' in an agencement structured by economic axioms and social-scientific methods, it is an agency of a very specific kind. Recognising the performativity of economic descriptions and tracing their subsequent translations through human agency and material devices allows us to present a compelling account of the economic structure of one particular set of social relations.

My argument, then, is that performativity has moral consequences, and that research should not refrain from recognising them. In the case of the organ allocation experiment, the methods described above radically reshape the nature of care (Roscoe 2015). From the predicate that maximum utility should be gained from each liver transplant, we arrive soon enough at the allocation by survival benefit proposed under the steering group's thought experiment. With transplantation framed in this way, the good clinician is committed to the needs of the population, rather than individual patients. The organ must be directed where it can do the most 'good', where the definition of 'good' is settled by economic and medical modelling and embedded in the allocation algorithm; it can only arrive at the right recipient through rigorous compliance to the evaluative framework demanded by the allocation calculations. Good practice becomes good measurement, reporting, and a dispassionate, even arm's-length, handling of the patients in one's immediate care. Just as the descriptions underlying online dating radically reshape the basis of a new partnership, so the allocation models transform the nature of care; for those who see the basis for human virtue and flourishing in partnership and care (MacIntyre 1981; Roscoe 2014), such a transformation is one of real ethical significance.

6.6 Concluding Remarks

I began this essay with a call—not mine alone—for a performativity thesis that retains its radicalism, and does more than just repeat what economists already know: that market designers design markets. Such radicalism, I have argued, should pay attention to the overflows and the reframings—the reshaping of society that accompanies the construction of economic arrangements in a particular space or activity. Few feathers will be ruffled by the statement that economists make markets. But the claim that economic descriptions are performative—and here I include models, theories and assumptions, as well as the knowledges they eventually produce—*does* come as a surprise to the economist. The discipline of economics is predicated on the existence of a world beyond its postulates. As Esposito (2012, 104) notes, 'mainstream economics is ill-equipped to deal with the circumstances in which the relevant information is produced by the very behaviour of the observers'. I have elaborated an account of the performativity of economic description, following Austin (1962), Butler (2010), and Muniesa (2014) as a means of understanding how economics can at once constitute the activities as economic, claim authority over them, and at the same time present those activities in such a way as to preclude other moral or ethical claims, what Butler terms a 'hermeneutic' reading of performativity. Economic descriptions constitute the social and so have an inherent ethical freighting. They are not detached scientific facts, but active performatives, laden with normative force and moral consequence.

Anthropologies of markets have examined how performatives travel through socio-material agencements, and how the eventual perlocutionaries are worked out in 'real life'. Perhaps in doing so, these studies have lost sight of the power of description as an utterance alone. Revisiting Austin and Butler, in conjunction with Callon's (1998) account of economic performativity, serves to remind us that the acts of classification and framing made possible by language, and the rhetorical authority at work in determining the particular set of rules and norms by which an act or a decision should be governed, are bound up in the moment of description itself. Yet performativity studies, despite dealing with a politically and ethically charged topic, have shied away from ethical engagement and political critique. We researchers have not yet taken up the emancipatory potential offered by recognising, and thus unseating the 'metaphysical presumptions' (Butler 2010) of economics and the economic. In this essay, I have begun to show that the performativity thesis can speak to established critical narratives within the social sciences, and—most importantly—can do so without losing its empirical and theoretical grounding. Here, I suggest, is the real radicalism of the performativity thesis.

REFERENCES

Austin, John. 1962. *How to Do Things with Words. The William James Lectures Delivered at Harvard University in 1955*. Oxford: Oxford University Press.
Becker, Gary S. 1973. A Theory of Marriage: Part I. *Journal of Political Economy* 81(4): 813–846.
Binmore, Ken, and Paul Klemperer. 2002. The Biggest Auction Ever: The Sale of the British 3G Telecom Licences. *The Economic Journal* 112(478): C74–C96.
Bowker, Geoffrey C., and Susan Leigh Starr. 1999. *Sorting Things Out*. Cambridge, MA: MIT Press.
Butler, Judith. 1997. *Excitable Speech*. Abingdon: Routledge.
Butler, Judith. 2010. Performative Agency. *Journal of Cultural Economy* 3(2): 147–161.
Çalışkan, Koray, and Michel Callon. 2009. Economization, Part 1: Shifting Attention from the Economy Towards Processes of Economization. *Economy and Society* 38(3): 369–398.
Callon, Michel. 1998. The Embeddedness of Economic Markets in Economics. In *The Laws of the Markets*, edited by Michel Callon, 1–58. Oxford: Blackwell.
Callon, Michel. 2007. An Essay on the Growing Contribution of Economic Markets to the Proliferation of the Social. *Theory, Culture & Society* 24(7–8): 139–163.

Callon, Michel. 2010. Performativity, Misfires and Politics. *Journal of Cultural Economy* 3(2): 163–169.
Cochoy, Franck. 2015. Myriam's 'Adverteasing': On the Performative Power of Marketing Promises. *Journal of Marketing Management* 31(1–2): 123–140.
Cochoy, Franck, Martin Giraudeau, and Liz McFall. 2010. Performativity, Economics and Politics. *Journal of Cultural Economy* 3(2): 139–146.
Dussauge, Isabelle, Claes-Fredrik Helgesson, Francis Lee, and Steve Woolgar. 2015. On the Omnipresence, Diversity, and Elusiveness of Values in the Life Sciences and Medicine. In *Value Practices in the Life Sciences and Medicine*, edited by Isabelle Dussauge, Claes-Fredrik Helgesson, and Francis Lee, 1–30. Oxford: Oxford University Press.
Esposito, Elena. 2012. The Structures of Uncertainty: Performativity and Unpredictability in Economic Operations. *Economy and Society* 42(1): 102–129.
Fourcade, Marion. 2011. Cents and Sensibility: Economic Valuation and the Nature of 'Nature'. *American Journal of Sociology* 116(6): 1721–1777.
Frankel, Christian, Jose Ossandon, and Trine Pallesen. 2015. Markets for Collective Concerns. Paper presented at the EGOS Colloquium, Athens, Greece, July 2–4.
Gottlieb, Lori. 2006. How Do I Love Thee? *The Atlantic Monthly*. Accessed November 1, 2015. http://www.theatlantic.com/magazine/archive/2006/03/how-do-i-love-thee/304602/
Hitsch, Günter J., Ali Hortaçsu, and Dan Ariely. 2010. Matching and Sorting in Online Dating. *The American Economic Review* 100(1): 130–163.
Holm, Petter, and Kåre Nolde Nielsen. 2007. Framing Fish, Making Markets: The Construction of Individual Transferable Quotas (ITQs). In *Market Devices*, edited by Michel Callon, Yuval Millo, and Fabian Muniesa, 173–195. Oxford: Blackwell Publishing.
Hühn, Matthias. 2014. You Reap What You Sow: How MBA Programs Undermine Ethics. *Journal of Business Ethics* 121(4): 527–541.
Jeacle, Ingrid. 2003. Accounting and the Construction of the Standard Body. *Accounting, Organizations and Society* 28(4): 357–377.
Karl, Alissa G. 2013. 'Bank Talk': Performativity and Financial Markets. *Journal of Cultural Economy* 6(1): 63–77.
Latour, Bruno. 1993. *We Have Never Been Modern*. Cambridge, MA: Harvard University Press.
Latour, Bruno. 2007. *Reassembling the Social: An Introduction to Actor-Network-Theory (New Edition), Clarendon Lectures in Management Studies*. Oxford: Oxford University Press.
Latour, Bruno. 2013. *An Inquiry into Modes of Existence*. Cambridge, MA: Harvard University Press.

Latour, Bruno, and Couze Venn. 2002. Morality and Technology: The End of the Means. *Theory, Culture & Society* 19(5–6): 247–260.
Law, John, and John Urry. 2004. Enacting the Social. *Economy and Society* 33(3): 390–410.
MacIntyre, Alasdair. 1981. *After Virtue: A Study in Moral Theory*. London: Duckworth.
MacKenzie, Donald. 2006. *An Engine, Not a Camera: How Financial Models Shape Markets*. Cambridge, MA: MIT Press.
MacKenzie, Donald 2007. Is Economics Performative? Option Theory and the Construction of Derivatives Markets. In *Do Economists Make Markets? On the Performativity of Economics*, edited by Donald MacKenzie, Fabian Muniesa, and Lucia Siu, 54–86. Princeton, NJ: Princeton University Press.
Mäki, Uskali. 2013. Performativity: Saving Austin from MacKenzie. In *Perspectives and Foundational Problems in Philosophy of Science, The European Philosophy of Science Association Proceedings*, edited by Vassilios Karakostas and Dennis Dieks, 443–453. Berlin: Springer.
Mendelsohn, Robert, Thomas Sterner, U. Martin Persson, and John P. Weyant. 2008. Comments on Simon Dietz and Nicholas Stern's Why Economic Analysis Supports Strong Action on Climate Change. *Review of Environmental Economics and Policy* 2(2): 309–313.
Mirowski, Philip, and Edward Nik-Khah. 2007. Markets Made Flesh: Performativity, and a Problem in Science Studies, Augmented with Consideration of the FCC Auctions. In *Do Economists Make Markets? On the Performativity of Economics*, edited by Donald MacKenzie, Fabian Muniesa, and Lucia Siu, 190–224. Princeton, NJ: Princeton University Press.
Muniesa, Fabian. 2014. *The Provoked Economy: Economic Reality and the Performative Turn*. Abingdon: Routledge.
Polanyi, Karl. [1944] 2001. *The Great Transformation*. Boston, MA: Beacon Press.
Pollock, Neil, and Luciana D'Adderio. 2012. Give Me a Two-by-Two Matrix and I will Create the Market: Rankings, Graphic Visualisations and Sociomateriality. *Accounting, Organizations and Society* 37(8): 565–586.
Roscoe, Philip. 2013. On the Possibility of Organ Markets and the Performativity of Economics. *Journal of Cultural Economy* 6(4): 386–401.
Roscoe, Philip. 2014. *I Spend Therefore I Am*. London: Penguin Viking.
Roscoe, Philip. 2015. A Moral Economy of Transplantation: Competing Regimes of Value in the Allocation of Transplant Organs. In *Value Practices in the Life Sciences and Medicine*, edited by Isabelle Dussauge, Claes-Fredrik Helgesson, and Francis Lee. Oxford: Oxford University Press.
Roscoe, Philip, and Shiona Chillas. 2014. The State of Affairs: Critical Performativity and the Online Dating Industry. *Organization* 21(6): 797–820.

Roth, Alvin E., Tayfun Sönmez, and M. Utku Ünver. 2005. A Kidney Exchange Clearing House in New England. *American Economic Review* 95(2): 376–380.
Sandel, Michael. 2012. *What Money Can't Buy*. London: Allen Lane.
Schinkel, Willem. 2007. Sociological Discourse of the Relational: The Cases of Bourdieu & Latour. *The Sociological Review* 55(4): 707–729.
Spanier, Graham B. 1976. Measuring Dyadic Adjustment: New Scales for Assessing the Quality of Marriage and Similar Dyads. *Journal of Marriage and Family* 38(1): 15–28.
Stern, Nicholas. 2007. *The Economics of Climate Change: The Stern Review*. Cambridge: Cambridge University Press.
Svetlova, Ekaterina. 2012. On the Performative Power of Financial Models. *Economy and Society* 41(3): 418–434.
Tong, Alison, Kirsten Howard, Stephen Jan, Alan Cass, John M. Rose, Steven Chadban, Richard D. Allen, and Jonathan C. Craig. 2010. Community Preferences for the Allocation of Solid Organs for Transplantation: A Systematic Review. *Transplantation* 89(7): 796–805.
Townley, Barbara. 2008. *Reason's Neglect*. Oxford: Oxford University Press.
Turner, Adair. 2012. *Economics After the Crisis: Objectives and Means*. Cambridge, MA: MIT Press.
Ubel, Peter, and George Loewenstein. 1996. Distributing Scarce Livers: The Moral Reasoning of the General Public. *Social Science and Medicine* 42(7): 1049–1055.
Walsh, Adrian. 2001. Are Market Norms and Intrinsic Valuation Mutually Exclusive? *Australasian Journal of Philosophy* 79(4): 525–543.
Webb, Amy. 2013. Hacking the Hyperlinked Heart. *The Wall Street Journal*, January 14. http://online.wsj.com/article/SB10001424127887323374504578217973101313736.html

CHAPTER 7

The IS–LMization of the General Theory and the Construction of Hydraulic Governability in Postwar Keynesian Macroeconomics

Hanno Pahl and Jan Sparsam

7.1 Introduction

The concept of performativity has stimulated an interesting strand of research in economic sociology as well as in neighboring areas of inquiry. Instead of criticizing mainstream economics along the lines of its highly unrealistic axiomatic or its mathematical excesses, emphasis is put on the various ways in which economic knowledge might influence or co-constitute its very object, even by statements that are considered to be purely descriptive. At the same time, the concept has evolved to accommodate subsequent critiques. Especially strong versions of performativity are said to propose an unrealistic and sometimes affirmative picture, over-estimating the role of economics (as outlined by economists themselves) and suppressing other influential factors. The text at hand contributes to these discussions by entering the still largely uncharted terrain of performativity and macroeconomics, combining theoretical reasoning with an

H. Pahl (✉) • J. Sparsam
Sociology Department, University of Munich, Munich, Germany

illuminating historical period. Our main intention is to shed some light on the question: What are the gains and limitations of the performativity perspective when the field of interest is not a single market or trading technique, but a vast, complex, and occasionally diffuse field, consisting of various macroeconomic forces as well as competing political players? To provide an, however impartial, answer, we will draw on the example of the impact of Keynesianism on German policy-making.

We set the stage with a short discussion of the literature on economics' performativity, including the respective objecting voices (part 2). Next, we turn to the history of economic ideas, reconstructing—in broader sketches—how the complex and multilayered narratives of Keynes's *General Theory* were transformed into the epochal IS–LM model and how this mathematically formalized and visually appealing 'little apparatus' (Hicks 1937, 156) served as an organizing cognitive landscape for the emerging field of (Keynesian) macroeconomics. The main task is to illustrate the process of economists creating an object of perception and keeping it stable, thus establishing what was later labeled 'Hydraulic Keynesianism' (Coddington 1976), including a straightforward guide of how to govern the economy (part 3). These remarks can be seen as a prerequisite for performativity analysis or a first stage, asking about the peculiar structure or format of the supposedly performative knowledge. The following section addresses the diffusion of this 'IS-LMised' (Young 1987, 94) version of Keynes's *General Theory* into policy circles in West Germany in the 1960s as a case in point (part 4). Compared to the USA or Great Britain, the history of Keynesian economics in Germany is less well investigated. On the one hand, the influence of the IS–LM model (and cognate models) in framing economic policy can clearly be identified, for instance, with regard to Karl Schiller's[1] concept of *Globalsteuerung* (overall control) and the *Act to Promote Economic Stability and Growth* (*Gesetz zur Förderung der Stabilität und des Wachstums der Wirtschaft*). On the other hand, our example shows the inappropriateness of oversimplistic, strong, and mono-causal variants of performativity theory: There are too many factors at work to clearly identify and single out individual chains of causation. In the concluding section, we place our case in the context of performativity theory in more detail, stressing the critical components of our inquiry as well as offering some methodological suggestions for subsequent research (part 5). This includes first a classification of our findings with regard to the categories used in performativity studies and second touches again on the question which kinds or formats of (economic) knowledge are better suited for a 'performative career' than others.

7.2 Performativity and the Macroeconomy

With his notion of performativity, Callon not only helped to draw the attention of economic sociologists to economics as a social phenomenon, he also made a much more rigorous point, that economics is accountable for designing the economy, or, in his early and frequently cited words, 'performs, shapes and formats the economy, rather than observing how it functions' (Callon 1998, 2). The basic idea is that the world is 'economized' by economics in a constitutive way: the possibility to experience the economy, speak of it in the way we do, and act economically in its different meanings derives from the fact that economics (co-)creates the objects of scientific inquiry (Çalışkan and Callon 2009, 370), or, in a more drastic description, 'the economy does not exist before economics performs it' (Callon 2007, 328). Thus, the role of economics as a science is not limited to analytical or descriptive tasks; it also encompasses constructive or productive features. Therefore, economic theories, models, and algorithms are not to be assessed as adequate if they merely correspond with an encountered economic reality. Rather, it is assumed that economics 'actualizes' its knowledge (ibid., 320). In summary, the notion of performativity implies that the economy in the empirical, real world falls into place more or less according to the economy drafted in the model world of economics.

One of the most prominent empirical analyses so far is MacKenzie's (2006) work on the performativity of the Black–Scholes–Merton model of option pricing, suggesting various modes or degrees of performativity: 'Barnesian performativity' describes a convergence between the model world and the real world because of the application of techniques stemming from economics. In contrast to 'generic performativity', meaning the simple usage of economics, and 'effective performativity', economics having a constitutive but diffuse impact on reality, the Barnesian type is much more radical in its consequences. It aims to demonstrate the 'incorporation' of economic models 'into algorithms, procedures, routines, and material devices' in economic contexts (ibid., 19). MacKenzie's example of the Black–Scholes–Merton formula shows at least the occurrence of effective performativity, but also detects full-fledged Barnesian performativity. In his view, such a strong form of performativity is in play if economics is literally evoking the effects deduced from its models. The Black–Scholes–Merton model's strong performativity can be concluded from 'a homology between the way the model was tested econometrically and options market prices based on the model' (ibid., 256). In the course of the implementation of the model in the world of finance, some of the (formerly unrealistic) assumptions would have become 'truer'. For example, portfolio management, according to the formula, reduced existing transaction costs, approximating the model's fixed zero transaction costs (ibid., 258).[2]

The notion of performativity is ever changing. Since its first inception, it was developed to cope with the diverse incarnations and aspects of economics as well as its different effects on economic reality. It has increasingly inspired sociological research of economics, but also has evoked a plethora of objections, of which two major ones are important for our contribution. First, it has been argued that in performativity theory the constitutive character of economics is overemphasized. Mäki (2013) doubts the implied monocausality of strong variants of performativity and claims that the constitution of economic objects always refers to practices, discourses, and social structures beyond economics. Most of the critics of performativity already agree with the finding that the argument of Callon et al. hinges on the question of the generalizability of performativity. Furthermore, generalizing performativity would create a tautology: 'any process of market building becomes, by definition, an instantiation of economics' (Santos and Rodrigues 2009, 992). This entails perceiving the economy as a reflection of its abstract depiction in economics. It naturally follows that the story the performativity approach is telling about the general workings of markets exactly resembles the story told by economists (Mirowski and Nik-Khah 2008, 96). This first objection is flanked by a second one aggravating the problems of the performativity approach. In particular, Fine (2005, 100) and Mirowksi and Nik-Khah (2008, 98) have emphasized Callon's undifferentiated perspective on economics. Thus, it can be questioned if Callon's treatment of every actor being involved in the economy counting to 'economics at large' (Callon 2007, 335–336) can handle the obvious and more subtle empirical distinctions of, and relations between, differently engaged economists: academics as 'confined economists' and non-academic actors deploying economic knowledge 'in the wild' (ibid.) as well as the social varieties within those groups.[3]

Overall, performativity theory in the vein of Callon tends to blank out reverse effects of constitution: the impact of the economy, society, culture, and so on, on economics. Not only are the actual requirements of the production of economic knowledge important to explain economics, but also the larger societal context in which economics and the economy as social and cultural practices are generally situated. This especially holds true if the analytical focus is significantly widened. This brings us to an adjacent question to answer our central one about the gains and limitations of the performativity approach: Which differences have to be considered analyzing the impact of macroeconomics on the economy, compared to the highly specific submarkets in analyses like the ones normally explored by representatives of performativity theory? Our contribution draws on the fact that the complex arrangements of and between macroeconomics and economic policy-making do not generally welcome explanations stressing definite and monocausal performativity. Instead, we want to suggest looking at the actual empirical effects of distributed theories and policies, and to ask to what extent macroeconomic governance is even possible. Therefore, we want to highlight some aspects of our example to argue for empirical research of the effects of macroeconomics.

The starting point of our discussion is the ambiguity in the literature concerning the question if there ever was a 'Keynesian Revolution' in Great Britain. Authors like Tomlinson (1981) disagree on this, emphasizing the non-Keynesian character of many actually exercised policy strategies. Booth (1983), however, affirms such a revolution and emphasizes Tomlinson's narrow definition of the notion of 'Keynesian'. The crucial point in this controversy is that the statement 'There has (not) been a Keynesian Revolution in economic policy-making in Great Britain in the 1940s' depends highly on the (canonized but contested) definition of Keynesianism, a specific (paradigmatic and political) idea of the interference of economics and policy-making, an own (implicit or explicit) concept of what the economy *is* and how it *works*, and, in the end, which one of these aspects is seen to be more decisive or even primary.[4] In this light, to take a leap and claim that Keynesianism was performed by British economic policies in the wartime leads to a simplified and unidirectional explanation, thereby disregarding the complex path-dependency of policy-making, the 'stickiness' of ideas and the persistence of social structures, the struggles for disciplinary and political authority as well as the ambiguity of theory, models, and even economic action.

7.3 FROM KEYNES'S *GENERAL THEORY* TO THE IS–LM MODEL: THE CONSTITUTION OF KEYNESIAN ECONOMICS AND THE PROLIFERATION OF HYDRAULIC GOVERNABILITY

Keynes's (1936) *General Theory* is often said to be the cornerstone and founding document of macroeconomics. Although macroeconomic topics were surely addressed prior to its publication, it was due to Keynes's intervention that macroeconomics was henceforth widely regarded as a separate branch of economics, not necessarily identical in its foundations and methods to the well-established and dominant microeconomic frameworks. The book was welcomed in the 1930s 'to fill the yawning gap between economic analysis and the real-world problem of the Great Depression', because for many (economists as well as policy-makers) it offered 'a plausible explanation and a feasible course of action' (Hoover 1988, 9). Opposing the dogma of the so-called *law of markets* ('Say's law') according to which every supply creates its own demand, Keynes pointed to the possibility of underemployment equilibria. The *General Theory* widened the 'range of possible stabilization policies to include fiscal as well as monetary measures' (Mehrling 1998, 299), setting an agenda for a more systematic account of state intervention. At the same time, Keynes's oeuvre was difficult reading, with complex and interlaced lines of thought that were hard to pin down. Although the use of formal reasoning in economics had risen since the interwar period (Morgan and Rutherford 1998; Yonay 1998), Keynes himself—despite using mathematics in certain instances—'refused to use a mathematical model to summarize the argument as a whole' (Backhouse 1997, 34). As Backhouse (ibid.) assumes: 'To construct a formal model was to attempt to specify exactly what was and what was not to be included in the analysis—to be "perfectly precise". But if the world was vague and complex, such an approach was inappropriate.' Keynes's vision of the capitalist economy relied heavily on the uncertain future paths of investments, promoting concepts like *animal spirits* that were hard to model in a rigid, equilibrium-based manner.

Immediately after the publication of the *General Theory*, many attempts were made to illustrate Keynes's basic message in a more formal manner. The most influential lines of thought emerged from a colloquium held by the *Econometric Society* in September 1936. The main focus of this meeting was directed toward the Keynesian claim that the submitted theory was more general than the classical–neoclassical tradition,[5] declaring the latter to be a special case within his framework. What came to dominate macroeconomic thinking in the 1950s and 1960s under the label of *Keynesian economics* was, for the most part, a popularization and extension of a line of thought originally published in a text titled *Mr. Keynes and the Classics* (Hicks 1937).[6] It was the IS–LM model presented in this text, and not the *General Theory* itself, that became the 'organizing theoretical apparatus of the emerging discipline of macroeconomics' (De Vroey and Hoover 2004, 3) and that counted as '*sine qua non* of macroeconomics' (Laidler 1999, 303).

John Hicks, the inventor of the IS–LM model, was not the only participant in the colloquium (and close-by discussion circles) who relied on simultaneous equations and a general equilibrium framework to pin down what was assumed to be Keynes's core message. As Young (1987) has shown in great detail, Roy F. Harrod and James E. Meade, as well as a couple of other economists, made very similar attempts at formalization. As Laidler (1999, 304) puts it: '[T]he basic model was Harrod's, the notation Meade's, but the geometry was Hick's; and it was that geometry which gave him and, a little later, Hansen so wide an audience.' Thus, the model was not so much the idiosyncratic idea of a single person, but rather the outcome of an obvious way of approaching and tackling macroeconomic questions when being academically socialized within mathematical general equilibrium theory. Hicks (1980, 142) later said that he developed the idea for the IS–LM model in the context of work he had been doing 'on three-way exchange, conceived in a Walrasian manner', referring to his book *Value and Capital* that was published in 1939. In this book, Hicks dealt with the foundations of Walrasian general equilibrium theory to construct more manageable models usable for policy analysis. Vercelli (1999, 4) notes: 'Therefore it came natural to him to represent the bulk of GT [General Theory, H.P./J.S.] in a small-scale semi-aggregate GE [General Equilibrium, H.P./J.S.] model and compare it with an analogous GE model of Walrasian inspiration in order to isolate and discuss the differences between them'.

In a first step, Hicks transformed the presumed core message of the *General Theory* in three equations: $L = G(i, Y)$, $I = F(i)$, $I = S(Y)$, and compared these equations with a classical (Walrasian) conception, written down as $L = kY$, $I = F(i)$, $I = S(i, Y)$.[7] While Keynes regarded his theory as a general approach that incorporated the perspective of the (neo)classical tradition as a special case, Hicks treated both the (neo)classical (Walrasian) tradition and the Keynesian conception as special cases within the same overarching mathematical framework. This admittedly amalgamates certain aspects of both conceptions, but at the same time excludes all those that do not fit into a system of simultaneous equations. In a second step, and this is another key feature of what later became the cornerstone of Keynesian macroeconomics, Hicks pushed further 'the discussion of the differences between Keynes and the classics without losing touch with economic intuition through a graphic method based on a further simplification of the model' (ibid., 6). By analogy with the first equation of the system, 'which expresses a relationship between income and the rate of interest under the assumption of equilibrium in the market for money, the reduced form which may be obtained from the second and the third equations by equating in equilibrium investment and savings also implies a relationship, generally different from the first one, between the same variables. This permits a simple representation in a two-dimensional Cartesian diagram of the macroeconomic equilibrium as the intersection of two curves: the LM that takes account of the equilibrium constraints arising in the market for money and the IS that takes account of the equilibrium constraints arising in the market for goods. The differences between Keynes and the classics is now reflected by the different assumptions on the slope of the two curves' (ibid.).

Critics later labeled the developments inaugurated by the IS–LM model with denotations like *bastard Keynesianism* (Robinson 1975), because— as will be shown below—it fostered not only a selective but sometimes even upside-down reading of Keynes's thoughts. Nevertheless, the IS–LM model proved to be a very effective way of organizing and propagating economic knowledge, with regard to both policy and academia: Being able to literally make visible the differences between Keynes and the classical– neoclassical tradition in a manner suitable for research, as well as teaching and policy experiments, it paved the way for science-backed modes of economic expertise. The graph shown below (adopted from Snowdon and Vane 2005, 107) depicts the model to map the ranges and effects of expansionary fiscal policy. The starting point at i_1Y_1, the first intersection of the IS curve and the LM curve, shows a state of equilibrium of the economy (in the goods market and in the market for money) with less than full employment. According to the mechanics of the model, expansionary fiscal policy shifts the IS curve to the right, from position IS_1 to position IS_2, and results in an increase in the equilibrium rate of interest (from i_1 to i_2) as well as in the equilibrium level of income (from Y_1 to Y_2). The total demand can be further increased—the flatter the LM curve the steeper the IS curve. In the limiting case of a vertical LM curve, fiscal policy has no effect—this is the so-called classical range—because it is in accordance with pre-Keynesian assumptions. In this case, altering the money supply will lead to changes in the overall price level (inflation, higher rates of interest), but not an increased level of output. In the second limiting case, a horizontal LM curve, fiscal policy has a maximum effect on increasing total demand, this is the so-called liquidity trap (cf. ibid., 106–107) (Fig. 7.1).

Michaelis (2013, 2) passes on the following anecdote to demonstrate the far-ranging academic socialization with the IS–LM model: Being asked what would happen if someone woke him at three o'clock in the morning, asking about the effects of expansionary monetary policy, Robert Solow answered that he would—picturing it in his mind's eye—shift the LM curve to the right. Keynes himself did not comment much on the IS–LM model, but there is some evidence that he at least appreciated it for strategic rea-

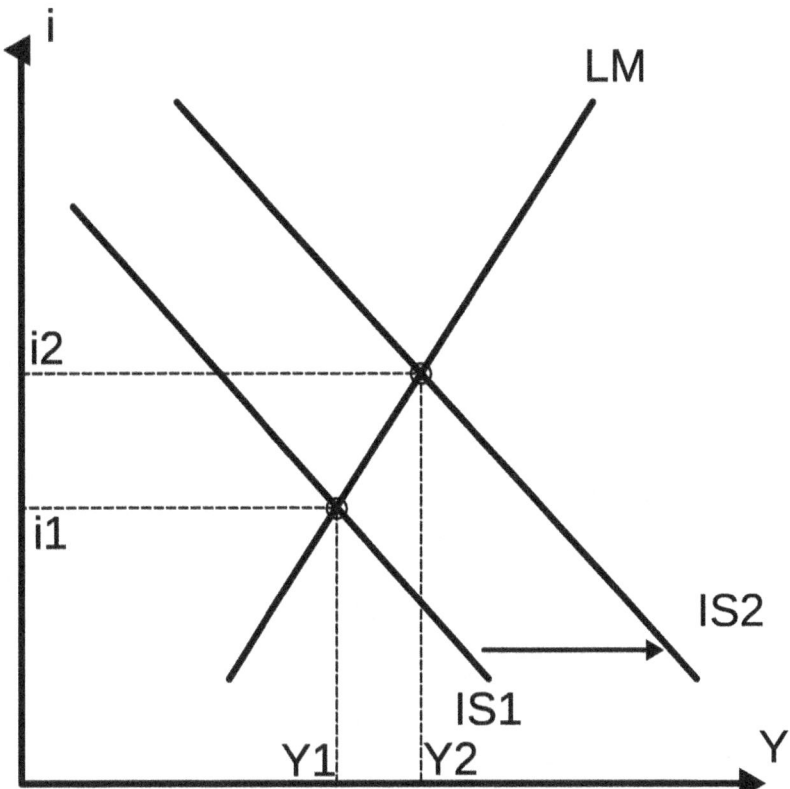

Fig. 7.1 The IS-LM Model

sons: 'Keynes's approval of Hicks's interpretation of his work was primarily based on the fact that the IS–LM model was able to capture the importance of effective demand, the possibility of underemployment equilibrium, and the important role of fiscal policy to achieve and maintain full employment' (Kaboub 2010, 343).[8]

As mentioned above, it was the IS–LM model that became the cornerstone of Keynesian macroeconomics after World War II in several aspects[9]:

(1) It served as a catalyst for the quickly emerging 'worldwide industry in econometric forecasting and policy analysis' (Mariano 2008, 1), with Lawrence Klein's *An Econometric Model of the United States, 1929–1952* (Klein and Goldberger 1955) being the first in a long line of econometric applications. 'For the first time', as de Vroey and

Malgrane (2010, 18–19) have commented on these developments, 'governments had at their disposition a quantitative macrodynamic general equilibrium model that they could use to help in the elaboration of their policy.' Later, these early econometric models served as a foundation to build ever more disaggregated and detailed models of the economy that included hundreds of variables and equations (Brookings Model, Wharton Model).

(2) The IS–LM model was conceptually expanded, most notably through an integration of a labor market and attempts for microfoundations, setting the stage for what was later called neoclassical synthesis (Modigliani 1944). Mundell (1963) and Fleming (1962) developed open-economy variants of the model to incorporate discussions of foreign trade and exchange rates.

(3) Along these lines, the model also functioned as a common ground to debate contested viewpoints: 'The Hicksian IS/LM model became the ground on which the postwar intellectual battles were fought. Because the model seemed to suggest that the difference between the Classical and Keynesian views was about slopes of curves and speeds of adjustment, the battles were fought with statistics, and as a consequence macroeconomics became much more empirical than it had been previously'(Mehrling 2006, 71).[10]

Many participants assumed that macroeconomics had found a definite form and was ready to proceed as a normal science: 'I think that most economists feel that short-run macroeconomic theory is pretty well in hand […]. The basic outlines of the dominant theory have not changed in years. All that is left is the trivial job of filling in the empty boxes, and that will not take more than 50 years of concentrated effort at a maximum' (Solow 1965, 146). The model introduced and domesticated—so to speak—the subsequently accepted forms of scientific dispute, disciplining, but also limiting, what could be said.[11] The primary example for the latter feature can be found in the discussions about the Phillips curve that have taken place since the late 1950s: The invention and alteration of the Phillips curve show the transformation and the bundling of economic problems in a model, providing controllable measures for policy-making. The classic Phillips curve constructs a correlation between nominal wages and unemployment (Phillips 1958) and has been modified by Samuelson and Solow (1960) to show a "trade-off" between inflation and unemployment. According to Humphrey's (1985, 9) synoptic view of the history of the curve, the model has mainly served as a "menu of policy choices"—the term coined by Samuelson and Solow (1960, 192). Computational choices have shaped the perception of the feasibility of policy-making. In turn, the curve has been revised consulting empirical data, but has also been varied to be compliant with policy requirements and the development of economic discourse. In the 1960s, 'the Phillips curve appealed to policy-makers because it provided a convincing rationale for their apparent failure to achieve full employment with price stability–twin goals that were thought to be mutually compatible before Phillips' analysis' (Humphrey 1985, 5).

7.4 Keynesian Economics at Work? The Case of West Germany in the 1960s

The emergence and proliferation of the 'IS-LMized' version of Keynes's economics was part of a broader development in economics, including the construction of categories of national accounting, increasingly sophisticated forms of econometric measurement, and general equilibrium theorizing as an overall framework. With regard to cognitive aspects, one can speak of an interlocking of various components that, while different in origin, were now reconfigured as mutually reinforcing parts of a new scientific culture. This was especially true in the emerging field of econometrics, 'Keynesianism was like a heavenly blessing' (Yonay 1998, 192), because it drew attention to questions of macroeconomic development and stability. In this matter, statistical knowledge seemed to be able to provide a definite basis for decision-making. Initially being only one among other special branches in economics Walrasian general equilibrium theory now occupied center stage. To characterize the influential approach put forth by the Cowles Commission in the 1940s, Boumans (2005, 75) speaks of a 'combination of the Walrasian method, which attempts to construct a mathematical skeleton of system, and econometrics, to put empirical flesh on the bones of the system'.

Categories of national accounting, although contested within economics, quickly became important benchmarks after World War II. Bos (2007, 20) emphasizes their significance as an 'empirical frame of reference for thinking and communicating about national economies', culminating in a status of 'universal facts and language'.[12] These developments also lead to reconfigurations in the internal structure of the discipline: Morgan and Rutherford (1998) speak of a shift from interwar pluralism to postwar neoclassicism. The mode of segmental differentiation that is typical for most of the other disciplines in the social sciences until today, does not match with economics which features a rigid center–periphery configuration (discriminating between orthodoxy and heterodoxies). Most important for our account is the way in which the (cognitive) object of inquiry was transformed in the course of these developments. Not long ago, the Great Depression drastically revealed the scientific and political impotence of economics, while mathematical modeling gave rise to a far more optimistic picture of the governability of economic affairs: 'The economy had been turned into a 'thing' whose behavior could be described (through national accounts), modeled into equations, tested, predicted, and acted upon' (Fourcade 2009, 85). During the 1950s and 1960s, this technocratic vision of control was sustained. Lawrence Klein, working on an econometric underpinning of Keynesian macroeconomics, was no exception with his statement, that '[t]here is no reason why intelligent economic planning cannot be of just the correct amount, that amount which gives permanent full employment and stable prices'(1966, 180).

The role West Germany played in these developments is twofold. On the one hand, the country was a latecomer with respect to the development and implementation of modern macroeconomics and econometric modeling. Problems with gathering data and data compatibility in the war-shaken territory, as well as various strong ideological reservations against quantitative research and science-led economic planning made Germany an inappropriate candidate for a macroeconomic control vision and economic fine-tuning (Heilemann 1981, 69–70). On the other hand, economic recovery was the focus of the early West German 'reason of state', with 'Ordoliberalism' being a solid building block of a new economy-centered self-confidence after World War II (Foucault 2008). While Keynes's thoughts (original or neoclassically transformed) were not represented in the early phase of recovery (the Adenauer-Erhard era),[13] Keynes as a person was widely known and appreciated in German policy circles, due to his participation in the Versailles peace conference after World War I, where he strongly criticized the peace treaty and the high levels of reparations (a position he put forth in a number of influential publications, for instance in *The Economic Consequences of the Peace* [Keynes 1920]). Between the wars, Keynes served as an unofficial adviser of the German Government to stabilize and rebuild the economy (Dillard 1985, 116).

The first major influence of Keynesian economics can be detected in the act (passed in 1963) that appointed the creation of a *Sachverständigenrat zur Begutachtung der gesamtwirtschaftlichen Entwicklung* (German

Council of Economic Experts). A central passage in the wording outlines the objectives of the council as follows: 'The council shall portray in his reports the particular overall economic development and its foreseeable future path. In doing so, it shall examine how—within the framework of a market economy—a stable price level, a high level of employment, an equilibrium in international balance of payment, and stable and appropriate growth can simultaneously be achieved'.[14] Four years later, in 1967, similar propositions were made in an even more prominent and influential place: The *Gesetz zur Förderung der Stabilität und des Wachstums der Wirtschaft* (*Act to Promote Economic Stability and Growth*) is often interpreted in the corresponding literature as the 'most Keynesian legislation of the post-war era' (Dillard 1985, 124–125). It also featured the four goals mentioned above, now directed at political decision-makers, but also provided the government with a rich arsenal of instruments for macroeconomic guidance, placing the manipulation of aggregate demand via governmental revenues and spending in a central position (Nützenadel 2005, 310).

After the bill was passed, it received widespread and enthusiastic support from most societal segments, including such diverse groups as unions, the federation of employers, the press, and even conservative intellectual circles, including proponents of Ordoliberalism (ibid., 312–313). While the 1950s had seen a continuous phase of economic growth, the mood of crisis spreading in 1967 reminded many observers of the global economic crisis of 1929: A consensus was in place that to avoid a recurrence of the Brüning Government failures (worsening the depression), the state must be able to counteract possible economic downturns, if necessary (ibid., 313–314). With respect to the four goals mentioned in the *Act*, Dillard (1985, 124) proclaims: 'The most Keynesian of these is, of course, the high-employment goal, which has its American counterpart in the Employment Act of 1946'. He further mentions: 'Notable is the absence of an annually balanced budget among the legislated aims of macro policy.' Fiscal policy now explicitly became 'part of anticyclical policy. Under the 1967 law the federal government was authorized to raise or lower income taxes by as much as 10 percent of the tax. Repayable surcharges on personal and business income tax could be assessed in boom years to dampen effective demand. These surcharges would be refunded when needed to stimulate the economy with more spending. Unbalanced budgets came to be acknowledged as devices to stimulate a lagging economy' (ibid., 125–126).

The most important individual in Germany advocating the new vision and policies was the economist Karl Schiller, minister for economic affairs (1966–1972), and later the minister of finance (1971–1972). He promoted his concept of *Globalsteuerung* not as a replacement of the formerly dominant approach of the 'Freiburg school' (Ordoliberalism), but as its extension. Microeconomic policies aimed at fostering and rationalizing competition had to be complemented by macroeconomic policies managing effective demand via countercyclical fiscal policy (Eicker-Wolf 2003, 90).

In two special reports (*Sondergutachten*) released by the German Council of Economic Experts in 1967 and 1968, a prioritization among the four goals is evident. The first special report states at the beginning: 'Of the goals set forth in the law of the council of economic experts, [...], the council regards the goals of a high level of employment and of stable and appropriate growth to be the most pressing at this very moment' (Sachverständigenrat... 1967, 260). The council report especially counters 'nonsensical measures of reduction' as taken into consideration by federal states (*Bundesländer*) and communities (ibid., 261). It emphasizes a domestic lack of demand as well as underused productive capacities (ibid., 263). The provisions were accompanied by strong ambitions to include the bargaining partners into the project of *Globalsteuerung*, demanding a stability-conformist wage policy to restrict upward trends of prices and wages (ibid., 265). The second special report asserts that the expansion of demand is still too weak, claiming domestic excess supply (Sachverständigenrat... 1968, 119). It states: 'Whatever immediate measures are taken, the limits for the new indebtedness of the federal state must be relaxed.' In 1967, two economic stimulus packages (of 2.5 billion D-Mark in January and 5 billion in July) were passed, the Bundesbank lowered the key interest rate and followed an expansionary route (Eicker-Wolf 2003, 91–92). As early as 1968, the German economy was back on a stable growth path, with an unemployment rate below 1% in 1969. While the general public often attributed the quick recovery to the stimulus packages, most research on the episode is far more skeptical, pointing to other factors that fostered the economic recovery (for instance, export growth) and to lags in the impacts of deficit spending (Heise 2007, 101–102).

The late 1960s were, with regard to the 'life-cycle' of the neoclassical synthesis and of 'Keynesian' economic policy, a rather bad starting point. The mid-1970s saw a quick decline in the hegemony of Keynesian economics, in both science and policy. The occurrence of stagflation led to doubts about a trade-off between unemployment and inflation (as depicted by the Phillips curve).[15] The oil price shocks (1973) led to disturbances on the supply-side that the Keynesian paradigm was ill-equipped to deal with (Turgeon 1996, 79). More conservative economic paradigms gained influence, including Monetarism in the policy arena, while the Rational Expectations School (*New Classical Macroeconomics*) led the most far-reaching attack on methodological grounds (Lucas critique). In Germany, the Deutsche Bundesbank switched to a monetarist policy of money supply control in 1974 (Eicker-Wolf 2003, 98–99). In his 1975 report, the *Sachverständigenrat* officially declared a crisis of the concept of *Globalsteuerung*, switching to more supply-side-oriented actions (Sievert 2003, 37).

7.5 Discussion

Having started with a short outline of performativity approaches and their critique, mentioning possible difficulties to apply the perspective to questions of macroeconomics and overall economic systems, we proceeded with our case: Although the *General Theory* set the stage for macroeconomics and large-scale governmental intervention, it was an IS–LMized version of Keynesian economics that played the major part in subsequent academic discourse, also fostering the emergence of somewhat mechanistic policy visions. The IS–LM model, in this respect, can be regarded as an *immutable mobile* (Latour 1986), a term coined to designate 'representational objects that can be transported from one place to another without changing their original form, such as maps and numbers produced in laboratories. These objects can leave where they were produced and be accumulated in one place along with those obtained in different locations' (Takami 2014, 184). De Vroey and Malgrane (2011, 4) accentuate two main virtues of the IS–LM model, first 'its ability to model economic interdependence in a simple and intuitive way […]. Even in its most elementary form, it lends itself to drawing cogent real-world inferences. The second main virtue of the IS–LM model is its plasticity. It constitutes an architecture that is general enough to allow a more-or-less unlimited diversity of specifications. This plasticity also extends to policy implications, since friends and foes of Keynesian policy alike can use it to promote or refute policy prescriptions'. Next, referring to German economic policy conceptions and actions in the 1960s, some evidence was given that— although for a rather short period (ca. 1966–1973)—economic policy-making and legislation had a distinctively Keynesian flavor—Keynesian in the sense of IS–LMized short-run macroeconomics.

We want to conclude by addressing two topics. The first one—more methodologically concerned and more provisionally articulated—again turns to the question of performativity theory and macroeconomics. Here we address the suitability of established categories of performativity studies for the case at hand. The second topic concerns the difference it makes with respect to policy prescriptions that Keynes's verbal *opus magnum* was incorporated—via Hicks and others—in a general equilibrium framework. While these developments were driven by a search for more rigorous mathematical foundations for economic theory, they also contained some (implicit and precarious) political consequences. The availability of sophisticated alternatives to hydraulic readings of Keynes on the one side, but their much less successful influence on policy on the other, should encourage to consider the processes of the 'material incorporation of ideas into scalable devices—or the change of ideas through devices' (Henriksen 2013, 483) to be included into performativity analyses.

7.5.1 Again: Performativity and Macroeconomics

Referring to the three degrees or modes of performativity distinguished by MacKenzie that we briefly introduced in Sect. 2, one can surely speak of 'generic performativity', describing cases 'in which an aspect of economics [...] is used in economic practice' (MacKenzie 2007, 55–56)—in our case in political-economic practice. Although the IS–LM model itself might not have been the direct and immediate object of reference, the mechanistic vision incorporated in the model can clearly be found in Schiller's concept of *Globalsteuerung*. But things become less clear-cut if we turn to 'effective performativity', designating 'cases in which the use of economics "makes a difference": for example, economic processes in which economics is drawn upon are different from those from which it is absent' (ibid., 56). As shown above, it is contested whether the economic stimulus packages of 1967 helped to counter the recession or whether other forces (like export growth) were more crucial factors. It seems unlikely that deeper investigation will be able to reach a unanimous conclusion. Furthermore, German economic policy quickly changed to more supply-side-oriented economics in the 1970s, often being mixed with ongoing financial stimuli. In both cases, our aforementioned skepticism regarding the complexity of macroeconomic affairs comes fully into play, as it is virtually impossible to single out individual chains of causation. Finally, the strong case of Barnesian performativity is difficult to consider regarding our case: As stated above, the IS–LM model functioned as a highly flexible device, designed to situate 'Keynesian' policy prescriptions within the context of (neo)classical prescriptions. Unlike the Black–Scholes–Merton formula analyzed by MacKenzie, the question of whether homology emerged between the model and economic reality, making the assumptions of the model truer, is meaningless in this case.[16] Tracing back the formation of the historically specific culture of economics is nevertheless an important factor to make sense of the actualization of scientific thought, because one can assume that the 'full performative potential of macroeconomics is only realised when a consensus exists regarding both *how the economy works* and *how its dynamics can be managed or controlled*' (Braun 2014, 53). The 'Keynesian' consensus on these matters was supposedly 'bastardized' very early on. Hagemann (2009, 98–99) suggests that through the influence of Erich Schneider, president of the *Institut für Weltwirtschaft* (Institute for World Economy) in Kiel after World War II, the German reception of the *General Theory* was initially a version in the vein of the neoclassical synthesis.[17] Following Henriksen (2013, 483), performativity analysis should include as an important topic the 'struggle for devices' by 'focusing on economic models as tools that actors use to forge paradigm shifts, rather than merely as devices for the promotion of certain market behaviors, which has been the main focus of previous performativity research.'

However, to further extrapolate from a consensus in economics (if ever possible) to the reality of economic policy-making is an explanatory shortcut that must be avoided. It was only touched upon in our contribution that policy-making takes place in a broader social context where economics is just a part of it. But it should at least be clear that we cannot derive what is economic and how the economy works by looking at economic discourse alone (Slater 2002, 237, 245). It is a long journey to a policy implication, contrived at the desk of the scientist, debated in advisory committees, distributed to decision-makers and processed through red tape, to become operative, if at all. Most importantly, economic policy-making does not appear as the sole implementation of 'pure' theory, but its actors interpret and combine the epistemic modules according to the encountered state of affairs in the field of politics. The trivial yet crucial point seems to be that to describe programs of management and control (i.e. policy) found in economic models means neither that those are necessarily perceived in policy context nor that they are executed partly, entirely or exactly as targeted in the specific model. They are not inevitably the basis for specific modes of governance or steps in specific practices. They do not even have to be the cause of specific effects, be it of those forecasted by the model or, in the spirit of MacKenzie's 'counterperformativity' (2006, 19), *ex negativo* all the other consequences not included in simulations and policy experiments.

As mentioned above, even Schiller's concept of *Globalsteuerung* was not meant as a substitute to the prevailing vision of Ordoliberalism, but as a macroeconomic supplement to it, affiliating to the idea of social market economy. Olaf Sievert (2003, 35), former member of the *Sachverständigenrat*, also remembers the first evaluations being a peculiar mix of microeconomics-cum-Keynes. In these examples we see that policy regards and policy-making are not materializations of specific academic schools of thought, but rather eclectic and adapted to needs other than scientific ones, even if they are formatted by economic discourse in a quite rigid manner. Bringing all this to account, we think it is necessary to differentiate between specific social fields processing economic ideas, including the perpetuation of the entire 'methodological horrors' scientists are confronted with: indexicality, inconcludability, and reflexivity (Woolgar 1993, 32–33). That is why we think that for an exhaustive understanding of performativity we have to open Callon's black box of 'economics at large'. Without being able to elaborate this perspective sufficiently, one might think of Wansleben's (2013) account on formal economic models used by analysts in currency markets. He shows that even if formal models are needed for the construction of consistent forecasts, the used models are often incompatible with the realities currency analysts are facing: 'econometric modelling is important, but for the production of consistent rather than accurate forecasts: models create durable, reliable and accountable ways of forecasting within a bank. However, econometric models are incompatible with a dynamic, theme-, and trend-driven market culture. Therefore, analysts take econometrics only as an anchor and then generate their own forecasts, which they call "views": views are directional forecasts (as opposed to point forecasts), they are handmade (arrived at by qualitative judgments), and they include non-econometric data. Analysts construe a view as a relational positioning within a field constituted by the competing views of other analysts' (ibid., 12). In quite an analogous manner, we assume, does the 'translation' (Callon) of models from the academic subfields in economics work in policy subfields.

7.5.2 Keynesian Economics and the Economics of Keynes, Then and Now

Around the same time the *Act to Promote Economic Stability and Growth* was passed in Germany and Keynesian economics in general 'was at its zenith' (Howitt 2002, 1), Axel Leijonhufvud (1968) published a groundbreaking study *On Keynesian Economics and the Economics of Keynes*, in which he questioned the dominant interpretation of the *General Theory* and declared the IS–LM model to be fatally flawed.[18] Contrary to other critiques of the IS–LMized version of the *General Theory*, namely by authors that belong to the heterodox school of Post-Keynesian economics, Leijonhufvud remained largely within the domain of the neoclassical tradition, keeping his critique—although radical in its consequences—accessible to the mainstream.

The original Keynesian mode to account for unemployment referred to the volatility of output, the latter being thought of as a result of fundamental uncertainty of investment decisions as well as of imperfect informational structures in and between markets. But these ideas could not be fitted into the general equilibrium framework nearly everyone had subscribed to (see Braun 2014, 59), because the Walrasian world of deterministic simultaneous equations offered no place for uncertainty, information loss, and historical time. What was done instead was to impose wage and price rigidities on a standard neoclassical model of (auctioneer-guided) perfect competition, obscuring Keynes's original account.[19] Leijonhufvud explicitly mentions the huge gap between Keynes's (as well as his own) agenda and the scientific vision his fellow economists subscribed to when he characterizes the Walrasian endeavor (and subsequent attempts to formalize the *General Theory*) in the following manner: 'This kind of Newtonian conception of what the economic system is like works very well in equilibrium economics. In the study of economic fluctuations, unemployment, and money, however, it tends to bias one's perception of the nature of the problem in a particular direction. When the huge machine does not work as it is supposed to (one tends to infer) it *must be* either because someone has thrown a spanner in the works—"monopolists and unions fix prices"—or because the cogs are slipping someplace—"savers and investors do not respond to interest incentives"' (1968, 395).[20]

To the contrary Leijonhufvud's argument implied 'that wage and price adjustment, which economists generally portray as stabilizing market forces, can sometimes be destabilizing, and that there are other market forces, which are usually ignored in macro theory, that are destabilizing. Otherwise the massive wage adjustments that took place during the Depression would have restored full employment rather than leading to an escalation of unemployment' (Howitt 2002, 2–3). This research agenda maximally opposes both the neoclassical tradition with its reliance on perfect coordination and self-correcting capacities of markets as well as the hydraulic-Keynesian vision of a state that is potent to counter liquidity traps through deficit spending. As Pernecky (1992, 127) outlines this alternative: '(1) imperfect information and disequilibrium trading are prevalent, (2) disequilibrium causes "wrong" (i.e. non-equilibrium) price and quantity signals to be sent, (3) individuals are constrained in their attempts to achieve their "notational" or planned levels of demand, and (4) quantity adjustments rather than price adjustments predominate. Disequilibrium in the labor market reduces income and thus constraints consumption in the product market with feedback effects. No auctioneering process is available to rectify the problem'. What we have here—in an embryonic state (looking back from today)—is a design that considers the complexity of the real-world economy.

Why do we, in the light of our preceding discussion, refer to this episode? It is not to again point solely to the fact that IS–LM is not a proper representation of the main lines of the *General Theory*. Tracing back the pathways of economic knowledge from a sociological perspective should not be a mere exegesis. In the end, what Keynes really meant is not too important in and of itself.[21] Important, however, is what we can learn from the episode of IS–LMization with regard to the mode mainstream economics is proceeding. With respect to the debates on performativity, one line of critique has accused the proponents of oftentimes taking an uncritical stance toward the self-descriptions of economics: 'The effect of the performativity idea on that literature is to have sociologists repeating and recapitulating economists own stories and never challenging their accounts. They never compare what they say they do with what they really do' (Mirowski 2013). In the same manner, Nik-Khah concludes that—contrary to what was announced—'neither Guala nor Callon have actually followed any economists around [...]; what they followed instead is a subset of the economists' own self-serving accounts published after the fact' (2006, 16). While advocates of performativity see economic facts as a manifestation or materialization of economic theory, Nik-Khah views them—here in the case of the telecommunications frequency auctions analyzed by both Guala and Nik-Khah—as 'a curious amalgam of technical achievement and crude politics', underlining 'the pivotal role of the telecoms in orchestrating the outcome' (ibid., 19).

However, things may actually be in the example above, in our case, referring to the IS–LM model is at the same time descriptive and critical: Following the process of the construction and (more rudimental) circulation of the model reveals interesting insights into both the way of the proceedings of macroeconomics as well as politics. Compared to its success story, Leijonhufvud's alternative perspective was never laid down in a definite and catchy mathematical model. While having contributed to the erosion of the hegemony of the neoclassical synthesis in the early 1970s, the disequilibrium approaches did not succeed in providing a viable alternative, according to the standards the discipline was willing to adapt to. Abandoning the Walrasian auctioneer, one can assume, created too many degrees of freedom and too much contingency and complexity for mainstream macroeconomics to be acceptable, with respect to both modeling and policy instruction.[22] Instead, the *Rational Expectations Revolution* quickly took over (Hoover 1988), offering ever more rigid modeling techniques based on general equilibrium theory (New Classical Macroeconomics, real business cycle models), supplemented with a popular vision of the market as an engine of truth.

Shortly thereafter in the late 1970s, a new generation of Keynesian economists (New Keynesian economics) emerged, accounting for various frictions to be included into state-of-the-art equilibrium models, relaxing the assumption of market clearing, but sticking to the rational expectations hypothesis (to avoid being vulnerable to the so-called Lucas critique, cf. Gordon 1990). In this respect, (economics') history repeats itself. The general equilibrium framework is a sort of 'historical *a priori*' (Foucault 1972, 127) of modern mainstream economics, being continuously refined technically as well as augmented with various (macroeconomic) frictions. At the same time, it functions as an implicit image of the economy, thus always incorporating a performative flavor. As De Grauwe (2010, 480) points out with regard to the latest generation of New Keynesian models: 'In the DSGE models now favored by central banks, business cycle movements in output and prices originate from price and wage stickiness. In order to reduce this kind of volatility more flexibility in prices and wages are required. That is why many central banks call for more flexibility. In a more flexible world, central banks will not be called upon so often to stabilize output, and thereby set price stability at risk'.

Of course, dynamic stochastic general equilibrium modeling (DSGE) models are a highly flexible device, just like the IS–LM model was in the past. Following the economic turmoil of 2007 ff., even more frictions are being added to the basic models, making them the jack-of-all-trades device of contemporary macroeconomics. Nevertheless, the underlying vision constantly conveys a certain, questionable picture of how decent markets are supposed to function. While real-world equivalents to the Walrasian auctioneer might (or might not) be successfully implemented in various niches—an endeavor actively promoted by research areas like *mechanism design* and *market design* (Boldyrev 2013)—it seems both unlikely and undesirable to us to assume that the economy as a whole can and should be molded according to the premises of general equilibrium theory. As Debreu (in Feiwel 1987, 243) once declared, characterizing the undertaking to outline the mathematical structure of general equilibrium theory: 'In providing existence one is not trying to make a statement about the real world, one is trying to evaluate the model.' Arrow (in Colander et al. 2004, 298), the second key figure in the history of modern equilibrium theorizing, was even more explicit: 'I came into my work, as indeed most theorists in the early1940s did, with the idea that competitive equilibrium was not a good description of the economy. Therefore, I wanted to clear up what the theory was, but that doesn't mean I found it a useful description of the economy'.[23]

Notes

1. The former minister for economic affairs (1966–1972) and finance minister (1971–1972) in Western Germany.
2. Nevertheless, MacKenzie would not go as far as to validate economic actors adjusting to the anthropology of *homo economicus* (MacKenzie 2006, 263). The performativity of the 'anthropological program' of economics is suggested by Callon (2007, 343–344). For a comment from an anthropological perspective, see Miller (2002).
3. A third, more historically oriented argument that is quite simple and striking stipulates that the market existed long before (neoclassical) economics was able to perform it (Slater 2002, 244). According to Callon, an agent other than neoclassical economics must have ruled economic discourse at that time because 'when economics (or economized) elements are already there it means that economics (at large) has already been that way' (Callon 2007, 328).

4. Other important contributions to the debate can be found in the comparative approaches by Hall (1989) and Wattel (1985).
5. Keynes used to speak of classical economics in a somewhat idiosyncratic manner, including much of what would be labeled as neoclassical economics today. If regarded from a methodological point of view, one would probably stress the differences between classical economics, based more or less strictly on a labor theory of value, and neoclassical economics, referring to marginalism. Keynes, however, was more interested in the political positions of traditional economics, a perspective that downplays the conceptual/methodological differences between the two branches.
6. Fourcade (2009, 160) resumes the events in the following manner: 'Keynes's economics was exported from Britain to the United States in the 1930s, it was then marketed back to Europe as "Keynesian economics" in the 1940s and 1950s'. Solow (1984, 14) asserts that 'to a large extent, the IS-LM model for almost 50 years has been Keynesian economics'.
7. With L denoting the aggregate demand for money (which is, in equilibrium, identical to M, the aggregate supply of money), i being the nominal rate of interest, I designating aggregate investment, and Y aggregate income. The variables refer to nominal quantities, but, due to the assumption of fixed prices, also relate to changes in real variables (Vercelli 1999, 4–5).
8. Some more skeptical aspects of Keynes's attitude towards the IS–LM model (for instance regarding the inability of the model to include expectations) are mentioned in Tily (2010) and Kriesler and Nevile (2002).
9. Morgan and Rutherford (1998, 15–16) point to some important social aspects of a more formalized macroeconomics: 'Although Keynesianism might have been thought dangerously close to Marxism, an IS–LM diagram probably looked innocuous to an outsider, and statistical numbers such as those of Mitchell had long held their own neutral status as data. 'Economics expressed in geometry, algebra, or numbers could be a good self-defense in the cold war days and pass muster in the classroom as well as in the government.'
10. See Bordo and Schwartz (2003) on the use of the IS–LM model in the monetarist discourse.
11. Even the most distinguished critiques of Keynesian economics at least appreciate the turn to a more model-based science that resulted from deploying the IS–LM model, as, for instance, Lucas and Sargent's (1997 [1979], 271) statement shows appreciating: 'the econometric framework by means of which Keynesian theory evolved from disconnected qualitative 'talk' about economic activity into a system of equations which could be compared to data in a systematic way, and provide an operational guide in the necessarily quantitative task of formulating monetary and fiscal policy.'

12. Speich (2011) draws a connection between the process of decolonization and the decline of the French and British empires to explain why national accounting gained momentum after World War II and highlights the role played by international organizations like the UN.
13. Richter (1999, 9) mentions some earlier German policy-documents bearing the hallmarks of the IS–LM model, for instance, a report (published in 1949) by the *Wissenschaftlicher Beirat bei der Verwaltung für Wirtschaft* (Academic Advisory Council of the Administration of Economic Affairs).
14. The legislative text is available at: http://www.sachverstaendigenrat-wirtschaft.de/fileadmin/dateiablage/Sonstiges/Gesetz_SRW.pdf. All quotes from German documents are translated by us.
15. In the 1970s, the discussion about adaptive versus rational expectations resulted in modifications of the Phillips curve, which, combined with the 'natural rate of unemployment' hypothesis and the 'acceleration'-hypothesis, led to a significantly altered 'menu' of policy-implications: The options of adjustment of the parameters in the long term are thereby notably reduced (Humphrey 1985, 13–14). Eventually, under the influence of the disputed policy ineffectiveness hypothesis, stabilization attempts were rendered useless.
16. This might be different with reference to the US case. As we said, the heyday of Keynesianism in Germany and its subsequent influence was a rather short episode. Drawing on literature that deals with policy effects of Keynesianism in the US (see for instance DeLong (1997) or Hetzel (2013)), one might argue that the successful implementation of Keynesianism-inspired policies in the 1950s and early 1960s ultimately led to undermining their preconditions (a case that might be framed as a shift from effective performativity to counter-performativity).
17. See also Schneider's own statement: 'What Keynes really meant first became obvious due to two articles by Hicks and O. Lange in which the mathematical framework of the Keynesian construction has been revealed' (1959, 208, own translation). His Hicksian reinterpretation has been proliferated by his voluminous and widely read textbook (Richter 1998, 1).
18. A quite similar critique had already been given in Robert Clower's (1965) *The Keynesian Counter-Revolution: A Theoretical Appraisal*. Some years later, both economists co-authored the paper *The Coordination of Economic Activities: A Keynesian Perspective* (Clower and Leijonhufvud 1975), further elaborating a line of thought that was later referred to as disequilibrium economics.
19. That is one reason why Minsky (1975, 55) declared: 'Keynes without uncertainty is something like Hamlet without the prince'.
20. It is no wonder that with Leijonhufvud's intervention, the above-mentioned question of general and special theories took another turn: 'Keynesian economics was not […] concerned with the special case of

when there was some barrier to the adjustment of wages so that markets cleared within a socially acceptable period: it was classical economics, with its assumption of an auctioneer who could ensure that markets were always in equilibrium, that was the special case' (Backhouse and Boianovsky 2013, 46).
21. This is also true for his followers. Even Hicks (1980, 152) himself became pretty skeptical about his model over the years, famously designating it as a 'classroom gadget'.
22. Of course, the ideas outlined by Leijonhufvud did not disappear completely. Today, complexity visions can be found in various (more or less) prominent approaches that radically abandon the Walrasian auctioneer—ranging from Akerlof and Shiller's (2009) *Animal Spirits* to agent based macro-models (Tesfatsion 2006).
23. See Düppe (2012) for a lengthy account on Arrow and Debreu's central paper. The same could probably be said of Walras, for even his original account differs significantly from the discursive artifact of the same name that was generated in the course of the mathematization of economics in the second half of the 20th century (as Walker 2006 has shown in some detail).

REFERENCES

Akerlof, George A., and Robert J. Shiller. 2009. *Animal Spirits. How Human Psychology Drives the Economy, and Why It Matters for Global Capitalism*. Princeton, NJ: Princeton University Press.
Backhouse, Roger E. 1997. The Rhetoric and Methodology of Modern Macroeconomics. In *Reflections on the Development of Modern Macroeconomics*, edited by Brian Snowdon and Howard R. Vane, 31–54. Cheltenham, UK: Edward Elgar.
Backhouse, Roger, and Mauro Boianovsky. 2013. *Transforming Modern Macroeconomics. Exploring Disequilibrium Microfoundations, 1956–2003*. New York: Cambridge University Press.
Boldyrev, Ivan 2013. Ökonomische Maschinen: Zur Performativität der Gleichgewichtstheorie. In *Wirtschaftswissenschaft als Oikodizee? Diskussionen im Anschluss an Joseph Vogls Das Gespenst des Kapitals*, edited by Hanno Pahl and Jan Sparsam, 77–90. Wiesbaden: Springer VS.
Booth, Alan. 1983. The 'Keynesian Revolution' in Economic Policy-Making. *The Economic History Review*, New Series 36(1): 103–123.
Bordo, Michael D., and Anna J. Schwartz. 2003. IS-LM and Monetarism (NBER Working Paper Series, 9713). http://www.nber.org/papers/w9713.pdf.
Bos, Frits. 2007. Use, Misuse and Proper Use of National Accounts Statistics. *National Accounts Occasional Paper*, NA-096.

Boumans, Marcel. 2005. *How Economists Model the World into Numbers*. New York: Routledge.
Braun, Benjamin. 2014. Why Models Matter: The Making and Unmaking of Governability in Macroeconomic Discourse. *Journal of Critical Globalisation Studies* 7: 48–79.
Çalışkan, Koray, and Michel Callon. 2009. Economization, Part 1: Shifting Attention from the Economy Towards Processes of Economization. *Economy and Society* 38(3): 369–398.
Callon, Michel. 1998. The Embeddedness of Economic Markets in Economics. In *The Laws of the Markets*, edited by Michel Callon, 1–58. Oxford: Blackwell.
Callon, Michel. 2007. What Does It Mean to Say that Economics is Performative? In *Do Economists Make Markets? On the Performativity of Economics*, edited by Donald MacKenzie, Fabian Muniesa, and Lucia Siu, 311–357. Princeton, NJ: Princeton University Press.
Clower, Robert W. 1965. The Keynesian Counter-Revolution: A Theoretical Appraisal. In *The Theory of Interest Rates. Proceedings of a Conference Held by the International Economic Association*, edited by Frank H. Hahn and Frank Brechling, 103–125. London: Macmillan.
Clower, Robert W., and Axel Leijonhufvud. 1975. The Coordination of Economic Activities: A Keynesian Perspective. *American Economic Review* 65(2): 182–188.
Coddington, Alan. 1976. Keynesian Economics. The Search for First Principles. *Journal of Economic Literature* 14: 1258–1273.
Colander, David C., Richard P.F. Holt, and John B. Rosser. 2004. *The Changing Face of Economics. Conversations with Cutting Edge Economists*. Ann Arbor, MI: University of Michigan Press.
De Grauwe, Paul. 2010. Top-Down Versus Bottom-Up Macroeconomics. *CESifo Economic Studies* 56(4): 465–497.
De Vroey, Michel, and Pierre Malgrange. 2011. The History of Macroeconomics from Keynes's General Theory to the Present. *Institut de Recherches Economiqueset Sociales de l'Universitecatholique de Louvain Discussion Paper*, 2011-28. Accessed November 2, 2015. http://sites.uclouvain.be/econ/DP/IRES/2011028.pdf.
DeLong, J. Bradford. 1997. America's Peacetime Inflation: The 1970s. In *Reducing Inflation. Motivation and Strategy*, edited by Christina Romer and David Romer, 247–280. Chicago: University of Chicago Press.
Dillard, Dudley. 1985. The Influence of Keynesian Thought on German Economic Policy. In *The Policy Consequences of John Maynard Keynes*, edited by Harold L. Wattel, 116–127. Basingstoke: Macmillan.
Düppe, Till. 2012. Arrow and Debreu De-Homogenized. *Journal of the History of Economic Thought* 34(4): 491–514.
Eicker-Wolf, Kai. 2003. *Vom Hydraulischen Keynesianismus Zur Radikalen Politischen Ökonomie (RPÖ). Keynesianische Wirtschaftspolitische Konzeptionen*

in der Bundesrepublik Deutschland Nach dem Scheitern der Globalsteuerung. Metropolis: Marburg.
Feiwel, George R. 1987. Oral History II: An Interview with Gerard Debreu. In *Arrow and the Ascent of Modern Economic Theory*, edited by George R. Feiwel, 243–257. New York: New York University Press.
Fine, Ben. 2005. From Actor-Network Theory to Political Economy. *Capitalism Nature Socialism* 16(4): 91–108.
Fleming, Marcus J. 1962. Domestic Financial Policies Under Fixed and Under Floating Exchange Rates. *IMF Staff Papers*, 9.
Foucault, Michel. 1972. *The Archaeology of Knowledge*. Translated by A. M. Sheridan Smith. New York: Pantheon.
Foucault, Michel. 2008. *The Birth of Biopolitics: Lectures at the College de France, 1978–1979*. New York: Palgrave Macmillan.
Fourcade, Marion. 2009. *Economists and Societies. Discipline and Profession in the United States, Britain, and France, 1890s to 1990s*. Princeton, NJ: Princeton University Press.
Gordon, Robert J. 1990. What is New-Keynesian Economics? *Journal of Economic Literature* 28(3): 1115–1171.
Hagemann, Harald. 2009. Zur frühen Rezeption der *General Theory* durch deutschsprachige Wirtschaftswissenschaftler. In *Aus gesamtwirtschaftlicher Sicht. Festschrift für Jürgen Kromphardt*, edited by Harald Hagemann, Gustav Horn, and Hans-Jürgen Krupp, 71–104. Marburg: Metropolis.
Hall, Peter A. 1989. *The Political Power of Economic Ideas, Keynesianism Across Nations*. Princeton, NJ: Princeton University Press.
Heilemann, Ullrich. 1981. *Zur Prognoseleistung ökonometrischer Konjunkturmodelle für die Bundesrepublik Deutschland*. Berlin: Duncker & Humblot.
Heise, Arne. 2007. Karl Schillers 'verspäteter Keynesianismus'. Zur politischen Ökonomie des Stabilitäts- und Wachstumsgesetzes von 1967. *Berliner Debatte Initial* 18(6): 92–105.
Henriksen, Lasse F. 2013. Economic Models as Devices of Policy Change: Policy Paradigms, Paradigm Shift, and Performativity. *Regulation & Governance* 7(4): 481–495.
Hetzel, Robert L. 2013. The Monetarist-Keynesian Debate and the Phillips Curve: Lessons from the Great Inflation. *Federal Reserve Bank of Richmond Economic Quarterly* 99(2): 83–116.
Hicks, John R. 1937. Mr. Keynes and the Classics: A Suggested Interpretation. *Econometrica* 5(2): 147–159.
Hicks, John R. 1980. 'IS-LM': An Explanation. *Journal of Post Keynesian Economics* 3(2): 139–154.
Hoover, Kevin D. 1988. *The New Classical Macroeconomics. A Sceptical Inquiry*. Oxford: Blackwell.
Howitt, Peter. 2002. A Dictionary Article on Axel Leijonhufvud's On Keynesian Economics and the Economics of Keynes: A Study in Monetary Theory. (Draft

of an article to be translated into French and published in the Dictionnaire des grandesœuvreséconomiques, edited by Xavier Greffe, Jérôme Lallement, and Michel deVroey, to be published by Éditions Dalloz). http://www.econ.brown.edu/fac/Peter_Howitt/publication/Dalloz.pdf

Humphrey, Thomas M. 1985. The Evolution and Policy Implications of Phillips Curve Analysis. *Federal Reserve Bank of Richmond Economic Review*. Accessed November1, 2015. https://www.richmondfed.org/publications/research/economic_review/1985/pdf/er71020.pdf

Kaboub, Fadhel. 2010. IS-LM Model. In *21st Century Economics. A Reference Handbook*, edited by Rhona C. Free, 341–347. Thousand Oaks, CA: Sage.

Keynes, John M. 1920. *The Economic Consequences of the Peace*. New York: Harcourt, Brace and Howe.

Keynes, John M. 1936. *The General Theory of Employment, Interest and Money*. London: Macmillan.

Klein, Lawrence R. 1966. *The Keynesian Revolution*. New York: Macmillan.

Klein, Lawrence R., and Arthur Goldberger. 1955. *An Econometric Model of the United States, 1929–1952*. Amsterdam: North Holland.

Kriesler, Peter, and John Nevile. 2002. IS-LM and Macroeconomics after Keynes. In *Money, Macroeconomics and Keynes. Essays in Honour of Victoria Chick, Volume 1*, edited by Philip Arestis, Meghnad Desai, and Sheila Dow, 103–114. London: Routledge.

Laidler, David E. 1999. *Fabricating the Keynesian Revolution, Studies of the Interwar Literature on Money, the Cycle, and Unemployment*. New York: Cambridge University Press.

Latour, Bruno. 1986. Visualization and Cognition: Thinking with Eyes and Hands. *Knowledge and Society: Studies in the Sociology of Culture Past and Present* 6: 1–40.

Leijonhufvud, Axel. 1968. *On Keynesian Economics and the Economics of Keynes. A Study in Monetary Theory*. New York: Oxford University Press.

Lucas, Robert E., and Thomas J. Sargent. 1997. After Keynesian macroeconomics. In *A Macroeconomics Reader*, edited by Brian Snowdon and Howard R. Vane, 270–294. London: Routledge.

MacKenzie, Donald. 2006. *An Engine, Not a Camera: How Financial Models Shape Markets*. Cambridge, MA: MIT Press.

MacKenzie, D. 2007. Is Economics Performative? Option Theory and the Construction of Derivatives Markets. In *Do Economists Make Markets? On the Performativity of Economics*, edited by D. MacKenzie, F. Muniesa, and L. Siu, 54–86. Princeton, NJ: Princeton University Press.

Mäki, Uskali. 2013. Performativity: Saving Austin from MacKenzie. In *Perspectives and Foundational Problems in Philosophy of Science, The European Philosophy of Science Association Proceedings*, edited by Vassilios Karakostas and Dennis Dieks, 443–453. Berlin: Springer.

Mariano, Roberto S. 2008. Klein, Lawrence R. (born 1920). In *The New Palgrave Dictionary of Economics*, edited by Steven N. Durlauf and Lawrence E. Blume, 2nd ed. Hampshire: Palgrave Macmillan.
Mehrling, Perry. 1998. The Money Muddle: The Transformation of American Monetary Thought, 1920–1970. *History of Political Economy* 30(Suppl.): 293–396.
Mehrling, Perry. 2006. The Evolution of Macroeconomics: The Origins of Post Walrasian Macroeconomics. In *Beyond Microfoundation: Post Walrasian Macroeconomics*, edited by David C. Colander, 71–86. New York: Cambridge University Press.
Michaelis, Jochen. 2013. Und Dann Werfen Wir den Computer An—Anmerkungen Zur Methodik der DSGE-Modelle. *MAGKS Joint Discussion Paper Series in Economics*, 23-2013. Accessed November 1, 2015. http://www.uni-marburg.de/fb02/makro/forschung/magkspapers/23-2013_michaelis.pdf
Miller, Daniel. 2002. Turning Callon the Right Way Up. *Economy and Society* 31(2): 218–233.
Minsky, Hyman P. 1975. *John Maynard Keynes*. New York: Columbia University Press.
Mirowski, Philip, and Edward Nik-Khah. 2008. Command Performance: Exploring What STS Thinks It Takes to Build a Market. In *Living in a Material World: Economic Sociology Meets Science and Technology Studies*, edited by Trevor Pinch and Richard Swedberg, 89–128. Cambridge, MA: MIT Press.
Mirowski, Philip. 2013. "Facebook Teaches You How To Be a Neoliberal Agent." An interview with Philip Mirowski (by Tomas Undurraga). https://estudiosdelaeconomia.wordpress.com/2013/07/22/facebook-teaches-you-how-to-be-a-neoliberal-agent-an-interview-with-philip-mirowski/.
Modigliani, Franco. 1944. Liquidity Preference and the Theory of Interest and Money. *Econometrica* 12(1): 45–88.
Morgan, Mary S., and Malcolm Rutherford. 1998. *From Interwar Pluralism to Postwar Neoclassicism*. Durham, NC: Duke University Press.
Mundell, Robert A. 1963. Capital Mobility and Stabilization Policy under Fixed and Flexible Exchange Rates. *The Canadian Journal of Economics and Political Science* 29(4): 475–485.
Nik-Khah, Edward. 2006. What the FCC Auctions Can Tell Us About the Performativity Thesis. *Economic Sociology European Electronic Newsletter* 7(2): 15–21.
Nützenadel, Alexander. 2005. *Stunde der Ökonomen. Wissenschaft, Politik und Expertenkultur in der Bundesrepublik 1949–1974*. Göttingen: Vandenhoeck & Ruprecht.
Pernecky, Mark. 1992. The Keynesian Revolution from a Philosophy of Science Perspective: Revolutionary or Evolutionary? *Methodus* June: 126–134.
Phillips, Alban William Housego. 1958. The Relationship between Unemployment and the Rate of Change of Money Wages in the United Kingdom 1861–1957. *Economica* 25(100): 283–299.

Richter, Rudolf. 1998. Zur Entwicklung der Makroökonomik in den vergangenen 50 Jahren (1947 – 1997). *RWI-Mitteilungen.* 49 (1/2): 1–37.

Richter, Rudolf. 1999. *Deutsche Geldpolitik 1948–1998.* Tübingen: Mohr Siebeck.

Robinson, Joan. 1975. What has Become of the Keynesian Revolution? In *Essays on John Maynard Keynes*, edited by Milo Keynes, 123–131. Cambridge: Cambridge University Press.

Sachverständigenrat zur Begutachtung der gesamtwirtschaftlichen Entwicklung. 1967. Sondergutachten März 1967: Zur Konjunkturlage im Frühjahr 1967. http://econstor.eu/bitstream/10419/75392/1/749940727.pdf

Sachverständigenrat zur Begutachtung der gesamtwirtschaftlichen Entwicklung. 1968. Sondergutachten vom Juli 1968. dem Herrn Bundeskanzler am 3. Juli 1968 mündlich vorgetragen. http://www.sachverstaendigenrat-wirtschaft.de/fileadmin/dateiablage/download/sondergutachten/sg7-1968.pdf

Samuelson, Paul A., and Robert M. Solow. 1960. Analytical Aspects of Anti-Inflation Policy. *The American Economic Review* 50(2): 177–194.

Santos, Ana C., and João Rodrigues. 2009. Economics as Social Engineering? Questioning the Performativity Thesis. *Cambridge Journal of Economics* 33(5): 985–1000.

Schneider, Erich. 1959. Fortschritte der ökonomischen Theorie in unserer Zeit. *Ekonomisk Tidskrift* 61 (4): 201–212.

Sievert, Olaf. 2003. Vom Keynesianismus zur Angebotspolitik. In *Vierzig Jahre Sachverständigenrat 1963–2003*, edited by Sachverständigenrat zur Begutachtung der gesamtwirtschaftlichen Entwicklung, 34–46. Wiesbaden: Statistisches Bundesamt.

Slater, Don. 2002. From Calculation to Alienation: Disentangling Economic Abstractions. *Economy and Society* 31(2): 234–249.

Snowdon, Brian, and Howard R. Vane. 2005. *Modern Macroeconomics. Its Origins, Development and Current State.* Cheltenham, UK; Northhampton, MA: Edward Elgar.

Solow, Robert M. 1965. Economic Growth and Residential Housing. In *Readings in Financial Institutions*, edited by Marshall E. Ketchum und Leon T. Kendall, 142–164. Boston: Houghton Mifflin Company.

Solow, Robert M. 1984. Mr. Hicks and the Classics. *Oxford Economic Papers* 36(2): 13–25.

Speich, Daniel. 2011. The Use of Global Abstractions: National Income Accounting in the Period of Imperial Decline. *Journal of Global History* 6(1): 7–28.

Takami, Norikazu. 2014. Models and Mathematics: How Pigou Came to Adopt the IS-LM-Model Reasoning. *Journal of the History of Economic Thought* 36(2): 169–186.

Tesfatsion, Leigh. 2006. Agent-Based Computational Modeling and Macroeconomics. In *Post Walrasian Macroeconomics. Beyond the Dynamic Stochastic*

General Equilibrium Model, edited by David C. Colander, 175–202. New York: Cambridge University Press.
Tily, Geoff. 2010. *Keynes Betrayed. The General Theory, the Rate of Interest and 'Keynesian Economics'*. Basingstoke: Palgrave Macmillan.
Tomlinson, Jim. 1981. Why Was There Never a 'Keynesian Revolution' in Economic Policy? *Economy and Society* 10(1): 72–87.
Turgeon, Lynn. 1996. *Bastard Keynesianism. The Evolution of Economic Thinking and Policymaking Since World War II*. Westport: Greenwood Press.
Vercelli, Alessandro. 1999. The Evolution of IS-LM Models: Empirical Evidence and Theoretical Presuppositions. *Working Paper UniversitàdegliStudi di Siena*, 246. http://www.econ-pol.unisi.it/quaderni/246.pdf
Vroey, Michel de, and Hoover, Kevin D. 2004. Introduction: Seven Decades of the IS-LM Model. *History of Political Economy* 36 (Annual Supplement): 1–11.
Vroey, Michel de, and Pierre Malgrange. 2010. From the Keynesian Revolution to the Klein-Goldberger Model: Klein and the Dynamization of Keynesian Theory (Institut de Recherches Économiques et Sociales de l'Université catholique de Louvain Discussion Paper, 2010-19). http://sites.uclouvain.be/econ/DP/IRES/2010019.pdf.
Walker, Donald A. (ed.). 2006. *William Jaffé's Essays on Walras*. New York: Cambridge University Press.
Wansleben, Leon. 2013. *Cultures of Expertise in Global Currency Markets*. London: Routledge.
Wattel, Harold L. 1985. *The Policy Consequences of John Maynard Keynes*. Basingstoke: Macmillan.
Woolgar, Steve. 1993. Science. *The Very Idea*. London: Routledge.
Yonay, Yuval P. 1998. *The Struggle Over the Soul of Economics. Institutionalist and Neoclassical Economists in America between the Wars*. Princeton, NJ: Princeton University Press.
Young, Warren. 1987. *Interpreting Mr Keynes: The IS-LM Enigma*. Oxford: Polity-Blackwell.

CHAPTER 8

Performativity and Emergence of Institutions

Ekaterina Svetlova

8.1 Introduction

Is it not amazing that—after 60 years—our fascination with the idea of performativity has still not subsided? My feeling is that this fascination relates to the 'wonder of creation' that is implicit in the performativity debate. Performativity seeks to explain how social reality (social facts such as money, marriages, and prices) comes into being. Indeed, is it not thrilling to have a glimpse into the nature of a generative, world-producing power which allows to create something that was not here before? Though there has been a lot of skepticism concerning this 'demiurgic tendency' of the performativity concept (Krämer 2014, 226), still, the debate has been very lively. Many disciplines—linguistics, organization studies, philosophy, and so on—consider performativity to be a useful framework that sheds new light on their subject matter. But somehow not economics. Cochoy et al. (2010, 140) suggest that 'the world of the economy' is 'seen as a system of things where language is of secondary importance': This might explain the sheer ignorance of performativity by economic science.

Furthermore, the insufficient perception of performativity in economics can be also ascribed to the general confusion that was characteristic for

---

E. Svetlova
School of Management, University of Leicester, Leicester, UK

© The Editor(s) (if applicable) and The Author(s) 2016
I.A. Boldyrev, E. Svetlova (eds.), *Enacting Dismal Science*,
DOI 10.1057/978-1-137-48876-3_8

the initial attempts to relate performativity to economic issues. For example, the discussion of the strongest case of performativity in the work of Donald MacKenzie, who co-initiated the performativity debate in economic and financial sociology, is quite unprecise. Originally, MacKenzie (2004) referred to 'Austinian performativity' which implies that a new phenomenon (a social fact like marriage) is created in the process of speaking. Later, he switched to Barnesian performativity, referring to Barnes' essay (1983) on bootstrapped induction. However, MacKenzie's reading of Barnes is ambiguous. For instance, applying the Barnesian concept to the Black–Scholes option pricing model, MacKenzie (2007, 66, my emphasis) states that 'its [model's] use *brought about a state of affairs* of which it was a good empirical description'; thus, this interpretation suggests *constitution*. Still, on the same page of the same article, MacKenzie formulates: 'I use the term "Barnesian" simply as a label for a particular subset of the performativity of economics: the subset in which an aspect of economics is used in economic practice, its use *has effects*, and amongst those effects is to *alter* economic processes so as to make them more like their depiction by economics' (my emphasis); this reading is rather about *having influence*. So what is it now: creation of new social facts or merely influence or change?

This confusion offered grounds for critiques of the concept and hindered its wide application in economics. Famously, Mäki (2013) interpreted the shift from Austinian to Barnesian performativity as a shift from *constitution* to *causal influence* and subsequently blamed MacKenzie for abandoning the performativity concept in its actual (original) sense. Some other critics interpreted Barnesian performativity to be *more* than just (a particularly strong) influence, struggling however to find out what this 'more', this mystic creative, productive element could be (e.g., Didier 2007; Guala 2007, 153; Callon 2007, 316).

Consequently, the existing critiques point to a key issue: If performativity is just about influencing social reality by any kind of theories or models, then we either do not need this term which 'portrays a rather classical process in an unnecessarily complex fashion' (Didier 2007, 280) or have to search for its special added value.

In this article, I aim, first, to resolve this confusion about 'genuine' performativity and, second, to show that there is a particular added value of the performativity concept for economics.

I agree with Muniesa (2014, 28) who argued that performativity can enhance 'studies *in the constitution* of economic things'. The explanation of constitution of economic phenomena (how they come into being) has been notoriously a weak point of economic science. Emergent processes such as formation of beliefs and expectations of market participants or emergence and dissemination of new products or new formal models represent the fields where economics traditionally struggles to provide a sound account.

In this paper, I argue that particularly our understanding of the nature of economic institutions can be deepened through the application of the performativity concept. Here, I do not mean 'philosophical interpretations of economic institutions' à la Foucault (Muniesa 2014, 29). Rather, I will use the performativity concept to address the question of the origin of institutions and the *problem of priming*: 'How is the system [an institution] "primed" or set in motion?' (Bloor (2000, 163) with reference to Barnes (1983)). I will show how the performativity concept can contribute to solving the problem of how institutions emerge endogenously, without reliance on the pre-existing institutions and rules. Discussing the emergence of institutions in light of the performativity debate, I seek to shed light on the mystic productive mechanism, on the 'more' of performativity.

Instead of contrasting *constitution* and *causal influence*, I refer to a particular interpretation of performativity, namely the interpretation that focuses on perlocutionary effects of a speech act. I follow Butler (2010) who explicitly proposed to re-focus from illocution (as a traditional perception of the Austin's performativity, initiated by Searle) to perlocution. Both illocution and perlocution are considered in the article as *modes of producing social facts*. While illocution refers to the production of reality by means of *conventional* speech, perlocution draws attention to processes of beliefs' formation by means of theatrical persuasion and conviction (performance). Perlocution contributes to our understanding of institutional reality by focusing on processes of acceptance and *making believe*.

Surely, performativity and dramaturgical aspects of language have been discussed with regard to various issues, for example, rules' change and shifts of meaning (Derrida 1988), performance of gender (Butler 1990), impression management (Goffman 1959), and organizations as scenes of dramaturgical action (Clark 2008; Biehl-Missal 2011). Still, all those discussions focused on the incremental institutional change (the processes of rules' undermining from within) or on individual (idiosyncratic) management of social uncertainties by means of dramaturgical acting.

They have not explicitly touched upon the role of performatives in social coordination, formation of beliefs, and origin of economic institutions. The purpose of the chapter is to show how performativity concept can be applied to clarify those crucial economic issues.

Furthermore, the discussion in this article contributes to the emerging debate within economics and economic sociology about the role of fictions in economic life (Priddat 2015; Ortmann 2004; Esposito 2007; Beckert 2013, also Urpelainen 2011 with reference to institutions). This debate particularly draws on the aesthetic theories that deal with the real consequences of 'the fictive' and 'the imaginary' (Iser 1991; Walton 1990). Primarily, it aims to provide an alternative to the purely rational discourse of the traditional economic science.

8.2 The Problem of Priming and Institutional Regress

In his seminal paper 'What is an institution?', John Searle (2005, 22) wrote: 'I see the theory of institutions as still in its childhood' inter alia because there is no satisfactory explanation for the question as to how institutions emerge. Sánchez-Pagés and Staub (2010) also point to the same issue: 'All [existing] works describe institutional arrangements already in place, but very little has been said on the factors that lead to the emergence of these institutions in the first place'. Barnes (1983) and Bloor (2000) discussed this issue as *a problem of priming*. Derrida (1990) spoke about the 'mystical foundation of authority'.

Obviously, there is one major difficulty: In order to conceptualize institutions, we have to deal with rules that are established through speaking and acting which those rules actually regulate. Those self-stabilizing and self-validating circular processes are the crux of the explanation of institutions. 'On the one hand, individual decisions are the drivers of social action, including the emergence of institutions (e.g., in social contract theories). On the other hand, institutions are constraints on individual decisions (e.g., in North 1990 approach). This ambivalence is also reflected in different game-theoretic conceptualizations of institutions, where institutions can be both emergent states of equilibrium in games and also the rules of the game' (Herrmann-Pillath 2012, 25). These feedback loops bring together the exogenous and endogenous views on institutions as, for example, Aoki (2007, 27) suggests: 'Institutions generated endogenously at one point in time become exogenous constraints and/or enabling facilitators for further institutional dynamics ... There are *spiral moments* for the newly born to eventually become the established, on which basis further institutional evolution can be molded ad infinitum'.

The question remains, however, where and how to start analyzing those 'spiral moments'. There are two possibilities: one is to focus on endogenous generation of institutions 'at one point in time'; the other is to build on the situation where some rules already exist and, consequently, to concentrate on the explanation of rule-following and rules' change.

Institutional theories applied in economics usually follow the second pattern. Kingston and Caballero (2009) demonstrate that focusing on rules and rule-following is the approach taken, first, by 'collective-choice theories' that explore 'contracting', 'property rights', and 'conventions' and, second, by evolutionary theories of institutions.

For example, the contract theories conceptualize institutions as the aggregate of rational individual decisions. If agents *decide* to cooperate and to follow rules (because this behavior is efficient and maximizes their utilities), institutions emerge as a stable pattern of rule-following. To 'ensure' rule-following, however, the contract theories introduce the decision-making environment that to some extent 'guarantees' that actors indeed *decide* to follow rules. Those theories usually refer to the already existing institutions such as legal systems, markets, organizations, and social norms. All those mechanisms introduce *incentives* for rule-following as well as *sanctions* to punish the rule violation. The central postulate is that if the environment is created in which rule-following is efficient (e.g., it contributes to utility maximization through the reduction of transaction costs (Williamson 1985)), particular institutions come into being and will be stabilized.

Another example provides the institutional theory of conventions. Conventions form a basis for interpretations and activation of rules, that is, institutions (Diaz-Bone 2012). Conventions allow actors to agree on the kind of situations and contexts they find themselves in, so that the coordination of actions becomes possible. Guala (this volume) illustrates this concept using an example of the 'hawk-dove', or 'chicken', coordination game. The theory of conventions offers a solution for a problem of how two tribes divide and use a piece of land (i.e., establish property rights) by introducing particular coordination devices. For example, if two tribes historically agree on using precedence as a conventional correlation device, an institution of property will emerge based on this agreement. *Common history* or *shared culture* help to identify the correlation devices and the focal points that allow for the arrangement of new rules (Lewis 1969; Sugden 1986, 1989).

Hence, a kind of meta-rules (conventions) is introduced to explain the emergence of institutions. This is a strong requirement that does not apply to situations where people are strangers and do not rely on shared history or rules. Moreover, the theory of conventions suggests a solution for a very specific type of problem. It does not cover the non-coordination games where agents make decisions independently. For example, in case of Prisoner's dilemma, conventions are too weak a mechanism to secure the compliance with a pre-agreed arrangement (e.g., precedence). Mutual defection would be an equilibrium but not an institution (Hindriks and Guala 2015). Thus, a stronger enforcement mechanism than a convention must be available (Urpelainen 2011, 222), for example, the state or the law. Only then, informal rules as elements of the cultural background become operative and formal.

The examples demonstrate that conceptualization of institutions as deliberate or spontaneous *rule-following* is prone to institutional regress. This approach presupposes the existence of particular stabilization mechanisms that absorb uncertainty and contingency of the social. Those mechanisms usually are other institutions (e.g., law, state, and conventions). If we exclude them from explanation, there seems to be no common ground that 'bears' the institutional reality.

This insight is highly problematic for analysis of many social situations where institutions are involved. Let us discuss trust as an example. Beckert (2005) shows that trust usually is explained by referring to tradition, identity, power, norms, institutions, or calculations. But all those approaches presuppose the already existing, firm common ground for agents' actions, eliminating the uncertainty and making the very concept of trust obsolete. What we have to explain, Beckert points out, is *the production of willingness to trust* without assuming the mechanisms that eliminate all possible contingencies. To do this, Simmel (1990, 179) argues, a 'further element' that 'stands outside the rational categories of knowledge and ignorance' is necessary. Simmel names this further element *quasi-religious faith*, and Möllering (2001) characterizes this faith as a suspension 'of the unknown, unknowable and unresolved', as a kind of jump from nothing to something important and real, from the unknown into the known and reliable. This *suspension of disbelief* refers to the situation when rules just *start* to *become* established and applicable, when actors begin to produce and to share the common ground for actions. In similar vein, Derrida (1990) discusses justice as something that is never present and still to come. These debates draw attention to the beginning of Aoki's 'spiral' of institutionalization, namely the endogenous emergence of institutions through actors' behavior.

To avoid the problem of institutional regress, the 'equilibrium view' on institutions has been developed (Kingston and Caballero 2009). Within this approach, the focus was shifted 'from the rules governing behavior to the behavior itself' (170): Institutions were conceptualized as endogenous entities and defined as 'shared behavioral beliefs' (Aoki 2007, 26). In this view, the emergence of institutions is related to creating and changing actors' expectations and beliefs that govern behavior (also North 2005).

However, exactly the issue of 'how the players acquire shared behavioural beliefs' (Aoki 2007, 20), also known as *puzzle of common knowledge*, could not be sufficiently solved in the economic theory of institutions so far. At the same time, this unsolved problem provides an entry point for the performativity concept.

The performativity-based conceptualizations of institutions (Searle 2005; Barnes 1983; Bloor 2000, 2013) stress the importance of collectively shared beliefs, processes of acceptance and recognition. Institutions exist as long as people *believe* them to exist and as long as they act *as if* they believe. Institutional reality is based on the shared 'human agreement' (Searle 2005), at the beginning of which we find 'making believe', persuasion, and acceptance. Aoki (2007, 8) clearly relates his concept of endogenous institutions to Searle: He writes that Searle's '"collective linguistic and symbolic acceptance" may be thought of as being the essential element of institutions'. The same idea is stressed by Bloor (1997, 33): An institution is 'a collective pattern of self-referring activity' exactly in the sense in which the power of a gang leader is based on beliefs of the gang's members in his power: Power (institutions) and beliefs are *mutually constitutive*. Still, the crucial question remains of how those common, mutually constitutive and self-validating beliefs come into being. This is where the performativity theory can make its contribution.

8.3 Performativity as Illocution: Stuck in Institutional Regress

However, the claim that performativity theory can support our understanding of how social beliefs and expectations are formed might come as a surprise at the first glance. One might argue that we do not learn much about creation of common beliefs from the performativity theory in its traditional understanding: performativity as illocution. This is the reading of Austin (1962) by Searle (1969) and Mäki (2013), for example: the relationship between language and reality is constitutive; the production of reality happens in the very moment of *conventional* speaking.

Indeed, in case of Austin's illocutionary speech acts, the belief system is already given and stabilized. Institutional facts cannot be created without pre-existing institutions and conventions. In case of marriage, for example, such necessary institutions are the church, the institute of witnesses, and the wedding ceremony. The very existence of 'an accepted procedure', that is, of pre-existing shared rules and conventions, is considered by Austin (1962) to be the central condition of felicity of a performative utterance. For him, as Krämer (2014, 223, my emphasis) formulates, the power to constitute institutional facts 'is not rooted in the linguistic and grammatical form of an utterance, but in its *institutional embeddedness*, in the practice of society'. In other words, Austin's concept is involved in the institutional regress which was discussed above.

Similarly, Searle's social ontology heavily relies on pre-existing institutions and conventions. Famously, Searle is concerned with production of institutional facts (e.g., money and marriage) based on the system of constitutive rules: X *counts as* Y *in context* C. This scheme explains how a piece of paper becomes—or is constituted as—money in a particular context. Namely, it happens while we collectively and intentionally assign a status function (money) to a particular physical object (a piece of paper), that is, start to share the belief 'this is money', start to accept this paper as such and to act accordingly. Still, Searle clearly states that one needs institutional concepts (e.g., barter) to produce—and to explain—other institutional concepts (money) (Boehm 2002, 7). More specifically, his scheme X *counts as* Y *in context* C depends on the pre-existing common understanding and acceptance of the status function Y. Guala (this volume) draws a clear parallel between the status function Y and conventions: Y is 'a set of roles, duties, rights that are assigned *conventionally*'. Thus, the speech act in its illocutionary dimension serves as a coordination device similar to precedence, or any other conventions. This analogy has been also discussed by the representatives of economics of conventions (e.g., Diaz-Bone 2012; Bessy 2002). But if this analogy is valid, the explanation of institutions is, once again, shifted to the level of meta-rules (conventions and rituals) and remains entangled in the institutional regress.

This interpretation of the performativity argument in relation to institutions gave rise to the major reproach against it as formulated, for example, by Wettersten (1998, 139, my emphasis): 'Searle offers no social theories which explain the formation of *new* social or institutional facts, of the building of a consensus, for example, or the invention and spread of a new institutional fact'. In this respect, the performativity theory seems not to bring us any further in our search for the endogenous concept of institutions.

8.4 Performativity as Perlocution: Production of Beliefs

However, the focus on illocution as the 'genuine', or 'authentic', form of performativity is just one possible reading of Austin's text. The other possibility would be to give greater consideration to perlocution as proposed, for example, by Butler (2010). Importantly, she claimed that 'most of what is interesting in economic and financial performativity belongs to the latter [namely perlocution]' (153). Guala also argues in this volume that 'the essential aspect of performative statement is the perlocutionary or causal one, while the illocutionary is secondary, even dispensable'.

The perlocutionary dimension of a speech act deserves closer attention because its role in creation of institutional reality is crucial. If in order to understand institutionalization we strive to explain how shared recognition, acceptance, beliefs, and expectations come about, perlocutionary effects should be our focus. Perlocution—as production of consequential effects—relates to social coordination through speech, to affecting beliefs and expectations of a speaker and the audience, and thus to 'making certain things happen' (Butler 2010, 153). Every utterance has a perlocutionary (rhetoric) dimension: If somebody asserts that it is raining, he or she seeks to convince us to share his or her belief. Thus, *production of beliefs* is a typically performative—perlocutionary—act. Guala (this volume) argues in the same line:

> [P]erformative speech acts 'create' things (institutions, promises, etc.) by *manipulating beliefs, and in particular the systems of mutual beliefs* that are crucial for coordination and cooperation in complex societies.

Both perlocution and illocution are *modes of producing social facts*. The distinction between the two 'is tricky, and not always stable' (Butler 1997, 44). Still, there is a difference: 'It matters whether we think we are *building a reality* or *making certain things happen*. The former is the conceit of illocutionary performatives; the latter belongs to the realm of the perlocutionary' (Butler 2010, 153, my emphasis). But what is the exact difference between 'building a reality' and 'making things happen'?

I think that both illocution and perlocution contribute to the production of social facts. The difference between them lies in the fact that illocution is based on the existing *conventions*, while perlocution is a broader concept: Persuasion, conviction, and so on, can be nonconventional, even nonlinguistic (achieved by 'non-locutionary means', as Austin (1962, 117) formulates). Illocution contributes to understanding of production of 'standardized' social facts which are already accepted in the society. Perlocution explains the very process of acceptance as *making believe*.

Furthermore, the time horizon is different: While illocution brings about its effects immediately, at the very moment of speech, perlocutionary consequences occur time-delayed: Persuasion, the formation of beliefs, the processes of *becoming accepted* take time.

In light of this discussion, the strict priority of *constitution* of social facts (as usually associated with illocution) over *causal relationship* (perlocution) should be questioned. As Guala (this volume)—referring to Millikan—convincingly demonstrates, constitution has an aspect of causal relation which might be considered as more important than the semantic one. Thus, Guala argues, 'the idea that the relation between performative speech acts and institutional facts is one of constitution is probably a grammatical illusion'. Crucial is the idea that performatives—in their perlocutionary dimension—trigger, or bring about, a set of beliefs or expectations, and those are causal relations that create and govern institutional reality.

Furthermore, I would not subscribe to the 'mechanistic' view that in case of perlocution 'words are instrumental to the accomplishment of actions' (Butler 1997, 44). The power of perlocution is rooted in *the specific theatricality of language*. While the illocutionary view of performativity relates theatricality to iterability of a sign, perlocution makes things happen by means of theatrical persuasion, convincing staging, and, thus, *making believe*. Hence, in the next section, I will question the common understanding of perlocution as a mode in which words are always distinct from the things they do—*words* can be *actions* also if there is a time lag between them.

8.5 Performativity and Performance: On the Theatricality of Language

The re-focusing on perlocution makes the implicit *theatricality of language*—performance—to the crux of understanding of how institutional reality evolves in *mutually constitutive, self-referring*, and *self-validating* processes of beliefs' creation. Thus, this re-focusing delivers ideas for the solution of the problem of priming.

If we take up the endogenous view on institutions, particularly the self-referential model as suggested by Barnes and Bloor, we will agree that institutional 'realities [are] created by references to these realities... [they are] composed of the corresponding acting, knowing, believing, assuming, thinking and supposing engaged in by everyone else... all the referring, thinking and orienting is part of a practice which is constituted by these very acts of referring, thinking and orienting' (Bloor 2000, 160f.). Here, we discover clear similarities to *make believe* of Walton (1990) and *the act of feigning* (Akt des Fingierens) of Iser (1991): Fictions in form of stories (e.g., a novel or the spoken component of a theatrical play) are developed as common references and gain their own reality while the spectators or readers slip into the story and change their beliefs. However, it is crucial that they also start to behave as if the fictions were true and to refer to them as true. It is exactly what the perlocutionary dimension of a speech act describes: (Fictional) utterances can become real if they are staged and produced by means of the theatrical performance, if they are told and re-told as plausible (*mimesis* of Walton 1990). The perlocutionary theatrical element of language contributes to bringing about the shared (collective) beliefs and expectations while those beliefs and expectations are *staged as existing* and actors act *as-if 'the staged reality' is real.*

We can find references to this performative production of institutional reality, for example, also in Searle. Though, as discussed above, he usually refers to a conventional assignment of the status function, he acknowledges at some points that his formula *'counts as'* requires *make believe* by means of fictional staging of the status function. This is exactly what Searle (2001, 37) meant when he wrote:

> One way to create institutional reality often is to act as if it already existed. This is how the United States was created. There was no way that a group of people could get together in Philadelphia, all of them subjects of the British Crown Colony, and declare themselves to an independent nation. There was no institutional structure to enable them to do that. Well, they just did it. They did it and they got away with it... You can create an institutional reality just by acting as if it already existed.

Only when people *act as if* there is a new state, this new political entity will become—and will continue to function as (to *count as*)—a state.

Similarly, describing how trust can be explained, Beckert (2005) refers to the ideas of *a dramaturgical act* (Goffman 1959) and *a parasocial interaction* (Wenzel 2001). He demonstrates that trust cannot be satisfactorily conceptualized as based on the individual calculus of trust-givers (their advance concession can always be exploited) or on meta-rules (as leading into institutional regress). To understand the *suspension of disbelief* necessary for trust, one has to conceive how a common ground of shared beliefs and expectations is created in situ of physical or virtual actors' encounters. Both sides—trust-givers and trust-takers—participate in this process, whereas a dramaturgical act of self-representation of trust-takers assumes particular importance. The trust-taker *stages* trustworthiness using various devices and strategies, for example, certificates, personal appearance, and voice. Importantly, by doing so, she *does not provide the audience with any (rational) reasons* to belief (in the game of trust, by definition, there can be no reasons) but *makes them believe*.

> Self-presentations ... not only have the function of producing the impression of trustworthiness, but also offer *a common definition of the situation* that prejudices the trust-giver's action. That is, the opening of the trust game leads to the moves of a gambit 'into which those involved gradually draw each other, making the joint project irreversibly successful' (Beckert 2005, 20, quoting Wenzel 2001)

In other words, while agents stage, or fake, the successful game of trust and act *as-if* they trust, the gap between 'no trust' and 'trust' is closed. The 'willingness to trust' is produced in the process of theatrical persuasion: the trust-givers willingly slip into the role of believers—they behave as if they believe in the trust-taker's story that the latter is trustworthy. Beckert (2005, 21) calls the self-representation of the trust-taker *performative commitment* clearly relating staging and 'performance' to 'performativity' of markets.

The more general account of dramaturgical perlocutionary consequences of a speech act can be found in the work of Žižek (1993, 2001). Famously, he describes the *seduction gambit* which is not a part of illocutionary point but has clear perlocutionary consequences. Making a promise of marriage, Don Giovanni performs a seduction: He 'must have believed that the victim believed in the symbolic efficacy (i.e., binding character) of his promise' (Boucher 2014). But because there is no given symbolic authority to rely on in the situation, Don Giovanni has

PERFORMATIVITY AND EMERGENCE OF INSTITUTIONS   195

to convincingly stage it: by swearing to God (using this reference as a replacement for the lacking authority), but also by looking into eyes, holding hands, modulating his voice, and so on.

Here, the focus is on *production of perception*. Krämer (2014, 230, my emphases) explains:

> While 'performance' and 'performativity' were originally understood as attributes of linguistic and communicative actions, the emphasis has here shifted from *communicating* to *perceiving*. This is not a disjunction—'saying' and 'showing' do not exclude, but rather include each other. *Saying, however, is derivative of showing.*

This switch draws attention to the show-like origin of social institutions. The *para-social gambit* as a *seduction gambit*, the necessity of *making believe* are rooted in 'a *making-perceptible* by someone for someone' (ibid., my emphases), not in the correct communication or interpretation of signs.

Perlocution as performance suspends the usual theatrical *as-if pact*. Normally, what happens on the stage in a theater is not supposed to become reality; both parties—the actors and the spectators—believe that they are dealing with fiction and act accordingly. In the case of trust production discussed above, exactly the opposite should happen (Wenzel and Beckert stress this point particularly), namely what is faked in the dramaturgical act of self-representation—trustworthiness—should become part of reality and only then can the performance be considered successful. To achieve this, all concerned parties act as if trust were already there, as if it were reality, and by doing so they enact and effectively produce trust (Weick 1995). Only in this way can the emergence of beliefs and mutual expectations at the beginning of the institutionalization process be explained: Actors fake, perform, make a show and, by doing so, they experience and interpret the performance as real, they develop and confirm the joint definition of the situation—as a new state, as situation of trust, and so on. Thus, there is a theatrically constructed fiction at the beginning of every institution, which continues its existence as a real institution. Indeed, we find fictions at the core of our understanding of socially shared beliefs. Because there is no reason to believe or to expect that the other person will not cheat or break a rule, actors fake those reasons in the process of persuasive theatrical performance: 'In absence of rational reasons, there is no choice but to fake the reasons. Here, we deal with performative processes' (Priddat 2015, 110f., my translation).

Importantly, the *performance* is more than just a theatrical *staging*. While routines in a theater are usually strongly predetermined in terms of process, rules, protocols, and so on, the performance is put forth by the spontaneous interplay of actions of all participants—in the sense of the performance theater (Fischer-Lichte 2012). It is the collective 'fiction-making' when the 'imaginary' takes the form of the 'fictive' and—in process of staging—becomes real (cf. Sutrop (1996, 86) on the Iser's triad of the fictive, the real, and the imaginary).

Austin's ritual marriage is also staged but in a different sense: It has to be performed in particular scenery in front of an audience that already accepts and believes into the procedure (illocution). Performance—in the perlocutionary sense of the joint bringing about beliefs and expectations— evades planning and control and, thus, remains evasive and unforeseeable: „Performance contains the experience of powerlessness" (Krämer 2014, 229 quoting Brock). Hence, focusing on performance and perlocution, we do not exclude the unpredictability and contingency of the social; on the contrary, we make them a part of the concept: Because there is no guarantee for the meaning of an utterance, the concept of perlocution as performance helps to explain how this guarantee is faked—and might become real (however, there is no automatism in the process).

This is exactly the point made by Butler (2010, 153) when she wrote: 'My worry is that the cultural constructivist position thinks performativity works and that it imputes a certain sovereign agency to the operation of performativity that foregrounds the illocutionary over the perlocutionary. If the theory presumes efficacy, then it fails to see that breakdown is constitutive of performativity (performativity never fully achieves its effect, and so in this sense "fails" all the time)'. Indeed, in the concept that emphasizes perlocution and performance, there is no mechanism that radically reduces uncertainty. Performative events are unique and unrepeatable—and thus unpredictable, surprising, and uncontrollable. Every participant remains powerless and empowered at the same time.

This preoccupation of perlocution with failure is more profound than the Austin's theory of misfires of performative utterances. In Austin's example of marriage, there is still a kind of automatism implied: If all mechanisms of uncertainty absorption function perfectly, there is no obstacle for production of a 'new' marriage. In case of perlocution and performance, there are no circumstances under which the performative *always* succeeds. Thus, the focus on perlocution dissociates from the 'demiurgical tendency' of the performative that was traditionally so heavily criticized.

8.6 Conclusion

The article argues that performativity theory can shed light on the process of emergence of institutions. This process is not strictly constitutive: Institutions such as, for example, a new state, a new political party, or a firm do not appear at the very moment when somebody declares them as existent. There is always a time lag between the words (declaration) and an emergence of a social fact. In between, the causal processes of persuasion, becoming accepted, that is, processes of formation of common beliefs and expectations, take place. Those processes refer to the perlocutionary aspects of speech acts and are theatrical in nature. In the first step, new social fictions are developed and performed as existent—this step opens the para-social gambit, or seduction gambit, in which the reasons to believe, to trust are dramaturgically faked. At the origin of every institution is a performative commitment which is based on *making believe* and *making perceptible*. Those processes are very insecure (prone to fail); there is no guarantee (in form of pre-existing institutions) that the seductive gambit succeeds.

Those considerations demonstrate how performativity enhances the studies into the very constitution of economic issues. They pave the ways in which the ignorance of the dismal science of economics toward findings of the performativity studies can be overcome. At the heart of performativity is not the question of how economists form economy but the question of how economic phenomena come into being. This is my take on the 'genuine' performativity and its contribution to economics.

Acknowledgments This paper was first presented at the European Society for the History of Economic Thoughts (ESHET) conference in St. Petersburg in 2012. I thank all participants for the very productive discussion. I also am grateful to Ivan Boldyrev and Birger Priddat for valuable comments and helpful references.

References

Aoki, Masahiko. 2007. Endogenizing Institutions and Institutional Changes. *Journal of Institutional Economics* 3(1): 1–31.
Austin, John. 1962. *How to Do Things with Words. The William James Lectures Delivered at Harvard University in 1955.* Oxford: Oxford University Press.
Barnes, Barry. 1983. Social Life as Bootstrapped Induction. *Sociology* 17(4): 524–545.

Beckert, Jens. 2005. Trust and the Performative Construction of Markets. *MPIfG Discussion Paper*, 05/8. Accessed September 22, 2015. http://www.mpifg.de/pu/mpifg_dp/dp05-8.pdf
Beckert, Jens. 2013. Imagined Futures: Fictional Expectations in the Economy. *Theory and Society* 42(3): 219–240.
Bessy, Christian. 2002. Représentation, Convention et Institution. Des repères pour l'Économie des conventions. Document de travail 20. Paris: CNRS/CEE.
Biehl-Missal, Briggite. 2011. Business is Show Business: Management Presentations as Performance. *Journal of Management Studies* 48(3): 619–645.
Bloor, David. 1997. *Wittgenstein, Rules and Institutions*. London: Routledge.
Bloor, David. 2000. Collective Representations as Social Institutions. In *Durkheim and Representations*, edited by W. Pickering London, 157–166. New York: Routledge.
Bloor, David. 2013. PerformativeTheory of Institutions. In *Encyclopedia of Philosophy and the Social Sciences 16*, edited by Byron Kaldis, 706–709. Thousand Oaks: Sage Publications.
Boehm, Stephan. 2002. The Ramifications of John Searle's Social Philosophy in Economics. *Journal of Economic Methodology* 9(1): 1–10.
Boucher, Geoff. 2014. The Lacanian Performative: Austin after Žižek. In *Žižek and Performance*, edited by Broderick Chow and Alex Mangold, 13–32. Basingstoke: Palgrave Macmillan.
Butler, Judith. 1990. *Gender Trouble: Feminism and the Subversion of Identity*. New York: Routledge.
Butler, Judith. 1997. *Excitable Speech*. Abingdon: Routledge.
Butler, Judith. 2010. Performative Agency. *Journal of Cultural Economy* 3(2): 147–161.
Callon, Michel. 2007. What Does It Mean to Say that Economics is Performative? In *Do Economists Make Markets? On the Performativity of Economics*, edited by Donald MacKenzie, Fabian Muniesa, and Lucia Siu, 311–357. Princeton, NJ: Princeton University Press.
Clark, Tymothy. 2008. Performing the Organisation: Organisation Theatre and Imaginative Life as Physical Presence. In *The SAGE Handbook of New Approaches in Management and Organization*, edited by Daved Barry and Hans Hansen, 401–411. London: Sage.
Cochoy, Franck, Martin Giraudeau, and Liz McFall. 2010. Performativity, Economics and Politics. *Journal of Cultural Economy* 3(2): 139–146.
Derrida, Jacques. 1990. Force de Loi: Le 'Fondement Mystique de l'Autorité/Force of Law: The 'Mystical Foundation of Authority'. *Cardozo Law Review* 11: 919–1045.
Derrida, Jacques. 1988. *Limited Inc*. Evanston, IL: Northwestern University Press.

Diaz-Bone, Reiner. 2012. Elaborating the Conceptual Difference between Conventions and Institutions. *Historical Social Research/Historische Sozialforschung* 37(4): 64–75.
Didier, Emmanuel. 2007. Do Statistics Perform the Economy? In *Do Economists Make Markets? On the Performativity of Economics*, edited by Donald Mackenzie, Fabian Muniesa, and Lucia Siu, 276–310. Princeton, NJ: Princeton University Press.
Esposito, Elena. 2007. *Die Fiktion der Wahrscheinlichen Realität.* Suhrkamp: Frankfurt am Main.
Fischer-Lichte, Erika. 2012. *Performativität: Eine Einführung.* Bielefeld: Transcript.
Goffman, Erving. 1959. *The Presentation of Self in Everyday Life.* London: Penguin Books.
Guala, Francesco. 2007. How to Do Things with Experimental Economics. In *Do Economists Make Markets? On the Performativity of Economics*, edited by Donald MacKenzie, Fabian Muniesa, and Lucia Siu, 128–162. Princeton, NJ: Princeton University Press.
Herrmann-Pillath, Carsten. 2012. Institutions, Distributed Cognition and Agency: Rule-Following as Performative Action. *Journal of Economic Methodology* 19(1): 21–42.
Hindriks, Frank, and Francesco Guala. 2015. Institutions, Rules, and Equilibria: A Unified Theory. *Journal of Institutional Economics* 11(3): 459–480.
Iser, Wolfgang. 1991. *Das Fiktive und das Imaginäre. Perspektiven literarischer Anthropologie.* Frankfurt am Main: Suhrkamp.
Kingston, Christopher, and Gonzalo Caballero. 2009. Comparing Theories of Institutional Change. *Journal of Institutional Economics* 5(2): 151–180.
Krämer, Sybille. 2014. Connecting Performance and Performativity: Does It Work? In *Encounters in Performance Philosophy*, edited by Laura Cull and Alice Lagaay, 223–237. New Hampshire: Palgrave Macmillan.
Lewis, David. 1969. *Convention: A Philosophical Study.* Harvard: Harvard University Press.
MacKenzie, Donald. 2004. The Big, Bad Wolf and the Rational Market: Portfolio Insurance, the 1987 Crash and the Performativity of Economics. *Economy and Society* 33(3): 303–334.
MacKenzie, D. 2007. Is Economics Performative? Option Theory and the Construction of Derivatives Markets. In *Do Economists Make Markets? On the Performativity of Economics*, edited by D. MacKenzie, F. Muniesa, and L. Siu, 54–86. Princeton, NJ: Princeton University Press.
Mäki, Uskali. 2013. Performativity: Saving Austin from MacKenzie. In *Perspectives and Foundational Problems in Philosophy of Science, The European Philosophy of Science Association Proceedings*, edited by Vassilios Karakostas and Dennis Dieks, 443–453. Berlin: Springer.
Möllering, Guido. 2001. The Nature of Trust: From Georg Simmel to a Theory of Expectation, Interpretation and Suspension. *Sociology* 35(2): 403–420.

Muniesa, Fabian. 2014. *The Provoked Economy: Economic Reality and the Performative Turn*. Abingdon: Routledge.
North, Douglass. 1990. *Institutions, Institutional Change and Economic Performance*. New York: Cambridge University Press.
North, Douglass. 2005. *Understanding the Process of Economic Change*. Princeton, NJ: Princeton University Press.
Ortmann, Günther. 2004. *Als Ob: Fiktionen und Organisationen*. Wiesbaden: VS Verlag.
Priddat, Birger. 2015. *Economics of Persuasion: Ökonomie zwischen Markt, Kommunikation und Überzeugung*. Marburg: Metropolis.
Sánchez-Pagés, Santiago, and Stéphane Straub. 2010. The Emergence of Institutions. *The B.E. Journal of Economic Analysis & Policy* 10(1): 84.
Searle, John R. 1969. *Speech Acts: An Essay in the Philosophy of Language*. New York: Cambridge University Press.
Searle, John R. 2001. Social Ontology and the Philosophy of Society. In *On the Nature of Social and Institutional Reality*, edited by Eerik Lagerspetz, Heikki Ikäheimo, and Jussi Kotkavirta, 15–38. Jyväskylä: SoPhi.
Searle, John R. 2005. What is an Institution? *Journal of Institutional Economics* 1(1): 1–22.
Simmel, Georg. 1990. *The Philosophy of Money*. London: Routledge.
Sugden, Robert. 1986. *The Economics of Rights, Co-operation and Welfare*. Oxford: Blackwell.
Sugden, Robert. 1989. Spontaneous Order. *Journal of Economic Perspectives* 3(4): 85–97.
Sutrop, Margit. 1996. The Anthropological Turn in the Theory of Fiction: Wolfgang Iser and Kendall Walton. *REAL Yearbook of Research in English and American Literature* 12: 81–95.
Urpelainen, Johannes. 2011. The Origins of Social Institutions. *Journal of Theoretical Politics* 23(2): 215–240.
Walton, Kendall L. 1990. *Mimesis as Make-Believe: On the Foundations of the Representational Arts*. Cambridge, MA: Harvard University Press.
Weick, Karl. 1995. *Sensemaking in Organisations*. Thousand Oaks, CA: Sage.
Wettersten, John. 1998. The Analytical Study of Social Ontology: Breakthrough or Cul-de-Sac? *Philosophy of the Social Sciences* 28(1): 132–151.
Wenzel, Harald. 2001. *Die Abenteuer der Kommunikation. Echtzeitmedien und der Handlungsraum der Hochmoderne*. Vellbrück: Weilerwist.
Williamson, Oliver E. 1985. *The Economic Institutions of Capitalism: Firms, Markets, Relational Contracting*. New York: The Free Press.
Žižek, Slavoj. 1993. *Tarrying with the Negative: Kant, Hegel and the Critique of Ideology*. London: Verso.
Žižek, Slavoj. 2001. *On Belief*. London: Verso.

Index

A
accounting, 6, 10, 81n9, 85n29, 111, 118,
 national, 13, 161, 174n12
actor
 rational, 88, 89, 91, 97, 103–6
 situated, 90–1
actor-network theory (ANT), 5, 6, 17, 26n8, 27n1, 82n12, 111, 112, 128n2
aesthetics, 186
agencements, 5, 42, 144, 145, 147
agent/agency, 5, 9, 14, 75, 82n12, 86n33, 90, 103, 120, 132, 140, 144, 145, 172n3, 196
 distributed, 9, 140
analogism, 128n6, 129n20
anthropology, 11, 12, 112, 113, 116, 120, 127n1, 131, 132, 135, 172n2
Aoki, Masahiko, 71, 72, 85n28, 85n30, 85n32, 186, 188–9
Austin, John, 4, 6, 9, 11, 12, 15, 16, 29–32, 36, 43, 48, 49, 52n9, 133, 134, 138–40, 146, 147, 185, 189–92, 196

B
Barnes, Barry, 5, 26n3, 184–6, 189, 193
beliefs, 8, 11, 14, 31, 36, 37, 39, 42, 43, 47, 48, 52n8, 52n9, 61–3, 68, 114, 185, 186, 189–97
Black–Scholes model, 31, 38–43, 48, 52n10, 153, 167, 184
Bloor, David, 5, 185, 186, 189, 193
Bourdieu, Pierre, 5, 29, 129n12
Butler, Judith, 4–6, 12, 14, 15, 29, 134, 137, 140, 141, 143, 146, 147, 185, 191, 192, 196

C
Callon, Michel, 5, 6, 8, 9, 11, 12, 16, 17, 26n6, 29, 31, 42, 53, 81n9, 82n12, 82n15, 88, 93, 104, 106, 111, 112, 120–2, 127n1, 128n2, 129n15, 129n18, 129n20, 132, 133, 141, 143, 144, 147, 153, 154, 168, 170, 172n2, 172n3, 184
capitalism, 71, 121, 156

causality/causation, 17, 64, 81n11, 152, 167, 192
  vs. constitution, 31, 43–8, 184, 185
  semiotic, 12, 56–61, 64, 66–70, *See also* causal mechanism
causal powers, 80n5, 81n8
ceteris paribus, 54, 55, 60–1, 79n1
choice, 3, 55, 64, 66, 68, 80n3, 89–91, 93, 94, 106
  policy, 161
collective, theory of, 187
collective intentionality, 81n9
constructivism, 87, 112, 117–8
contingent/contingency, 9, 117, 128n6, 171, 188, 196
convention, 8, 9, 11, 15, 30, 32–6, 41, 44, 45, 48, 51n6, 81n10, 116, 139, 140, 185, 187, 188, 190, 192, 193
counter performativity, 16, 52n12, 86n32, 168

D
derivatives, 37–9, 41, 137–8
Derrida, Jacques, 4, 6, 15, 29, 185, 186, 188
Descola, Philippe, 12, 112, 127n1, 128n6, 129n20
description, 2, 4, 6–8, 12, 13, 31, 45, 119, 121, 131–47, 151, 171, 172, 184
devices, 8, 11, 17, 42, 84n22, 121, 163, 166, 167, 172, 194
  calculative, 6
  coordination/correlation, 11, 30, 31, 35, 36, 39, 41, 43, 49, 52n8, 48, 187, 190
  equilibrium selection, 34, 40
  judgment, 15
  market, 9, 82n12
  material, 145, 153
  policy, 13
dis-entanglement, 10

E
economic policy, 3, 8, 13, 16, 26n2, 54, 119, 133,152, 155, 157–67, 171, 173n11, 174n15, 174n16
economic reason, 12, 109, 110, 113–15, 117, 120–3
economization, 5, 10, 13, 122, 153
empathy, 63, 83n19
epistemology, 3
equilibrium, 15, 30, 33–6, 39, 40, 51n6, 55, 73, 118, 156–61, 163, 166, 169, 171, 172, 173n7, 175n20, 186, 188, 189
  Nash equilibrium, 33, 34
ethics, 11, 132, 133, 144
ethnomethodology/ethnomethods, 11, 12, 87–91, 103, 105, 106, 110
expectations, 2, 3, 43, 46–9, 52n9, 88, 90, 95, 96, 139, 173n8, 185, 189, 191–7
  rational, 111, 165, 171, 174n15
experiments
  breaching, 90, 110, 123
  breaching thought, 109–123, 128n7, 128n9, 128n10, 129n13, 129n15, 129n20
  economic, 3, 12, 17, 61–2, 64, 74, 80n3, 82–3n16, 83n17, 83n19, 83n20, 84n21, 84n22, 84n24, 87–106, 141, 145
  policy, 158, 168
  thought, 142, 145
explanation, 55, 58, 59, 61, 63, 74, 75, 155, 156, 186
  constitutive, 53–7, 74, 185
  covering law, 54, 55, 57, 60, 61, 64, 74, 79n1, 82n16
  mechanistic, 57, 80n4, 82n14

F

fact/value dichotomy, 13, 133
felicity, 31
  conditions of, 15, 16, 18, 30, 138, 139, 190
financialization, 71
focal point, 34, 35, 39–40, 187
Foucault, Michel, 5, 119, 162, 171, 185
frames/framing, 10, 12, 17, 64, 65, 68, 84n24, 94–5, 104, 106, 132, 143, 145–7, 152, 161
Friedman, Milton, 10

G

Galilei, Galileo, 113
game
  coordination, 30, 31, 33–4, 187
  hawk-dove, 34, 35, 187
  ultimatum, 60–2, 64, 82n16,
  See also language game
game theory, 11, 60–1, 82n15, 118, 129n18, 186
Garfinkel, Harold, 87, 89, 90, 105, 110
governance, 1, 5, 13, 155, 168
  corporate, 11, 54, 57, 69–74, 85n32
Grounded theory, 91
Guala, Francesco, 3, 9, 11, 15, 29–49, 83n17, 86n33, 92, 95, 106, 123, 128n3, 129n18, 170–1, 184, 187, 188, 190–2

H

Hegel, Georg Wilhelm Friedrich, 17, 27n12
hermeneutics, 14, 81n7, 134, 141, 143, 144, 146

Hicks, John, 152, 156, 157, 159, 166, 174n17, 175n21
Holm, Petter, 3, 127n1, 129n14, 129n16, 135

I

incentives, 3, 9, 11, 12, 53, 54, 57, 60–9, 71–5, 84n21–3, 85n25, 85n30, 93–4, 96, 97, 104, 105, 169, 187
Induced value theory, 93
illocution/illocutionary, 12–13, 15, 30, 36, 43, 44, 46–8, 133, 138–41, 144, 185, 189–92, 194, 196
institutions
  emergence of, 13, 183–97
  endogeneous view, 186, 193
  exogeneous view, 186
  institutional regress, 186–90, 194
  interpretation, 12, 56–8, 61, 66–8, 81n7, 82n16, 91, 92, 95, 106, 187, 195
IS-LM model, 13, 152, 155–61, 165–7, 169–172, 173n6, 173n8–11, 174n13

K

Kahneman, Daniel, 3, 94
Kant, Immanuel, 144
Keynes, John M., 152, 155–9, 161, 162, 166, 168–72, 173n5, 173n6, 173n8, 174n17, 174n19
Knorr-Cetina, Karin, 5, 87
knowledge, 3–5, 7, 8, 11, 15–18, 26n2, 39, 61, 63, 71, 72, 87, 95, 97, 99, 103, 115, 135–7, 142, 144, 146, 151–4, 158, 161, 170, 188
  overemphasis on, 15

L

language, 1, 3–4, 9–11, 14, 15, 18, 29, 35, 81n10, 115, 122, 136, 140, 147, 161, 183, 185, 190, 192–6
  game, 90, 95, 102, 103, 105
Latour, Bruno, 5, 6, 17, 26n8, 82n12, 87, 111, 113, 127n1, 128n5, 132, 141, 165
Lewis, David, 30, 33, 34, 39, 40, 51n6, 48, 52n6, 187
Lyotard, Jean-François, 6

M

MacKenzie, Donald, 2, 3, 5, 6, 8, 11, 13, 15, 16, 26n3, 29, 31, 36–40, 43, 51n1, 52n13, 53, 81n9, 86n32, 109, 111, 127n1, 129n15, 129n21, 132, 133, 137–9, 153, 166–8, 172n2, 184
macroeconomics, 1, 3, 11, 13, 151–75
Mäki, Uskali, 11, 26n3, 29–31, 36, 43–4, 46–8, 138, 154, 184, 189
make believe, 193
market, 1, 3, 5–9, 12, 15–17, 27n11, 29, 30, 37–9, 41–3, 48, 52n13, 71, 72, 85n32, 86n33, 111, 117–21, 131–5, 137, 139, 140, 144, 146, 147, 152–4, 156–8, 160, 163, 168–72, 172n3, 175n18, 187, 194
marketing, 6, 7, 9, 16, 111
marketization, 3, 132
Marx, Karl, 4–5
mechanism, 3, 8, 9, 14, 15, 38, 40–2, 53–75, 80n2, 80n3, 80n6, 81n7, 81n8, 82n13–16, 83n19, 85n31, 119, 141, 185, 187, 188, 196
  causal, 12, 13, 54–6, 61, 136; in mechanism design, 15, 55, 60–1, 80n3, 172; in neurosciences, 55–7, 63, 74, 80n6; performative, 11, 12, 53–75
Merton, Robert K., 62, 83n18
Miller, Daniel, 15, 112, 120, 129n16, 172n2
Millikan, Ruth G., 44, 45, 49, 192
Mirowski, Philip, 3, 15, 17, 27n11, 112, 116, 117, 120, 121, 129n17, 129n18, 131, 154, 170
models, 6–8, 15–16, 31, 42, 43, 48, 52n12, 55, 57, 61, 69, 70, 74, 80n3, 82n15, 82–3n16, 89–91, 104–5, 118–20, 135, 139–42, 146
  Black-Scholes-Merton model, 31, 37–42, 48, 52n11
  financial models, 8, 11, 140
  IS-LM model, 13, 151–75
money, 33, 58, 62, 73, 84n22, 84n24, 114, 117–18, 157, 158, 165, 169, 173n7, 183, 190
moral, 13, 115, 131–47
  moral consequences of performativity, 13, 18
Muniesa, Fabian, 3, 6–8, 10–12, 27n11, 82n15, 88, 93, 104, 109–23, 128n2, 129n18, 133, 137, 138, 143, 146, 185

N

naturalism, 10, 12, 58, 81n7, 81n8, 109–23, 128n6, 129n20
neoliberal/neoliberalism, 3, 5, 119, 120, 129n14
Nik-Khah, Edward, 3, 15, 17, 112, 120, 129n17, 129n18, 131, 154, 170–1
novelty, 4, 12–15, 56

O

observer-independent facts, 56, 80n5
observer-relative facts, 12, 56, 58, 60, 62, 80n5
ontology, 8, 9, 12, 18, 26n6, 30, 44, 46, 48, 51n4, 58, 60, 63, 70, 74, 75, 80n5, 81n8, 85n31, 133, 136, 137, 143, 190
   naturalistic, 58
order
   situational, 91, 95, 97, 99, 103, 105–6
   social, 89, 91
organizations, 8, 10, 54, 68–9, 174n12, 185, 187
overflow, 10, 12, 106, 132, 143, 146

P

Parsons, Talcott, 90
Peirce, Charles S., 81n11
performance, 1, 5, 12, 14, 15, 43, 52n12, 61, 66, 69–72, 74, 83n16, 85n27, 99, 135, 138, 141, 185, 192–6
performative practice, 2, 4, 7, 8, 12, 18, 87–106
performativity
   as convention, 15
   Barnesian, 13, 16, 81n9, 133, 137, 153, 167, 184; effective, 13, 153, 166, 174n16; effective, 13, 153, 166, 174n16: generic, 13, 153, 166; effective, 13, 153, 166, 174n16: politics of, 10, 13, 18
perlocution/perlocutionary, 11, 13, 15, 30, 36, 43, 44, 46–8, 138–40, 147, 185, 191–7
Polanyi, Karl, 5, 10, 132
pragmatism, 4, 5, 7, 12, 31, 121, 128n2, 137
preferences, 3, 12, 53–4, 57, 62–8, 73, 111, 114, 145
   social, 62–5, 73
prices, 10, 37–41, 52n13, 65, 101, 111, 143, 153, 158, 161–5, 169–71, 173n7, 183
priming, in experiments, 73, 84n24, 186–9, 193
   institutional, 185–9, 193
principal-agent model, 69, 72

R

rationality, 3, 8, 15–16, 64, 73, 90–1, 128n3, 132, 140, 141
   bounded, 80n3, 90
reality, 2, 4, 5, 7–14, 16, 37, 89, 110, 118–23, 129n21, 134, 135, 137, 141, 142, 153, 154, 167, 183–5, 188–93, 195
reason, 12, 109, 110, 112–15, 117, 120–3, 127n1, 162
reciprocity, 27n9, 68
relativism, 117, 118, 122
rhetoric, 11, 12, 26n2, 147, 191
risk, 3, 37, 41, 90, 102, 111, 138, 139
routines, 8, 14, 15, 80n2, 153, 196
rules, 3, 9, 12, 15, 17, 30, 32, 33, 35, 36, 44–9, 51n3, 52n7, 55, 81n10, 92–5, 97–106, 117, 141, 143, 144, 147, 185–90, 194–6

S

Sahlins, Marshall, 128n4
Schelling, Thomas, 33, 34, 39, 40, 48
science and technology studies (STS), 5, 6, 9, 15, 26n6, 82n12, 110–12, 114, 117, 128n2, 132
Searle, John R., 4, 9, 15, 29, 30, 32, 33, 44, 49, 52n9, 56, 80n5, 81n9, 81n10, 185, 186, 189–90, 193
seduction gambit, 194, 195, 197

self-fulfilling prophecy, 42–3, 62, 83n18
semiosis, 58–60, 62, 68
sign, 9, 12, 56–62, 64, 66, 82n13, 84n22, 192, 195
Simon, Herbert A., 90
Smith, Vernon L., 93
status function, 33, 190, 193

T
technology, 5, 9, 41, 59, 72, 85n32, 128n2
theatricality, 13–14, 192–6
totemism, 128n6
transaction costs, 69, 111, 154, 187
trust, 90, 188, 194, 195, 197
truth, 31, 62, 111, 112, 121, 132, 140, 171
Tversky, Amos, 3, 94

U
utterance, 15, 31, 32, 36, 43, 56, 133, 138–40, 147, 190, 191, 193, 196

V
valuation, 68, 71, 103, 143, 144

W
Weber, Max, 5, 81n7
Wittgenstein, Ludwig, 9, 81n7, 90

Z
Žižek, Slavoj, 194

The manufacturer's authorised representative in the EU is Springer Nature Customer Service Centre GmbH, Europaplatz 3, 69115 Heidelberg, Germany. If you have any concerns regarding our products, please contact ProductSafety@springernature.com

Printed and bound by CPI Group (UK) Ltd, Croydon, CR0 4YY

23/03/2026

02076662-0002